Glider Infantryman

I0808050

Number 136:
Williams-Ford Texas A&M University Military History Series

TEXAS A&M UNIVERSITY
Williams
Ford
MILITARY HISTORY SERIES

Glider Infantryman

Behind Enemy Lines in World War II

Don Rich and Kevin Brooks

Texas A&M University Press | College Station

Third printing, 2014
This paper meets the requirements of ANSI / NISO Z39.48-1992 (Permanence of Paper). Binding materials have been chosen for durability.

Library of Congress Cataloging-in-Publication Data

Rich, Don (Donald J.)
Glider infantryman : behind enemy lines in World War II / Don Rich and Kevin Brooks. — 1st ed.
p. cm. — (Williams-Ford Texas A&M University military history series ; no. 136)
Includes bibliographical references and index.
ISBN-13: 978-1-60344-424-8 (cloth : alk. paper)
ISBN-10: 1-60344-424-6 (cloth : alk. paper)
ISBN-13: 978-1-60344-529-0 (e-book)
ISBN-10: 1-60344-529-3 (e-book)
1. Rich, Don (Donald J.) 2. Soldiers, American—Biography. 3. United States. Army. Glider Infantry Regiment, 327th—Biography. 4. United States. Army. Glider Infantry Regiment, 327th—History. 5. World War, 1939–1945—Regimental histories—United States. 6. World War, 1939–1945—Campaigns—Western Front—Personal narratives, American. I. Brooks, Kevin (Kevin W.) II. Title. III. Series: Williams-Ford Texas A&M University military history series ; no. 136.
D769.31327th .R53 2011
940.54'81092—dc23

2011018190

Contents

Illustrations

Drawings

Maps

Acknowledgments

To Betsy Brooks, my wife, and David Brooks, my son: thanks for the countless hours spent working on *Glider Infantryman* and for your support and help while tirelessly poring over mistakes and unclear words. Also, thanks to David for constructing the index.

To Michael Brooks, my son: thanks for your work on the maps.

To Mary Rich, Don's wife, thanks for helping Don with the computer and listening to him recount the memories—many times.

To John "Lefty" Wilson, who drew the eight cartoons in this book. Airborne soldiers lived each day under stress, and cartoons depicting the circumstances of everyday soldiers were comforting to many of the men.

Screaming Eagles Heroes

Thanks for your help in putting together the memories, and for your valiant service to our country:

Roy Neff, 401st Glider Infantry Regiment
Lloyd Gross, 327th Glider Infantry Regiment, Company G
Manuel Hildalgo, 327th Glider Infantry Regiment, Company G
George Koskimaki, 101st Airborne Infantry Division, Headquarters
Denis Parsons, 327th Glider Infantry Regiment, Company G
Jack Sherman, 327th Glider Infantry Regiment, Company G

European Historian Helpers

Dennis Digger
Reg Jans
Erwin Janssen
Laurent Olivier
Tom Peeters
Robert Remackle

US Historian Helpers

Mark Bando
Charles Day
Ken McAuliffe
Rich Riley
Mark Sheldon
Mark Stephenson

Soldiers' Wives

Audrey Borzymowski
Erma Parsons
Phyllis Sherman

Soldiers' Families

Lloyd Gross family
Manuel Hidalgo family
Tom Niland family
Michael Panic family
Henry Proppe family
Louis Simpson family

Our Agent

Gayle Wurst
Princeton International Agency for the Arts, LLC
626 Brickhouse Road
Princeton, NJ 08540

Glider Infantryman

Prologue

Memorial Day 2007

"Went pretty well today," Don says to himself, referring to the Memorial Day ceremonies put on by the local American Legion. For sixty-one years he has joined in honoring those who served in the US armed forces and are no longer living.

Getting into his car, he backs out of the driveway and heads to Central Park to pick up the flags decorating the memorial markers. These markers are special. The soldiers whose names are on them died while serving their country.

At the park, Don bends over and picks up a flag from a World War II marker dated 1945, Eddie Mathieu's. Eddie was older than Don, tall, stocky, well built, with brown hair, a marine who died on a Pacific island. Don recalls his dad telling him about the time Eddie stopped by to visit when Don was in training. Eddie was a little cocky but very friendly. "We jump out of airplanes and don't bother to use parachutes!" Eddie remarked as a gung-ho marine, trying to show how tough marines were. "Dad got a good chuckle out of that one."

Next in line are the markers for Thomas Buodewns, Benne Ricks, and Walter Manning. "Can't remember much about these guys. Knew who they were, but can't picture them. I'm slipping, I guess," the eighty-four-year-old murmurs.

"Harold Allred, . . . I knew him. Died on Luzon, in the Philippines. Cause of his death was never said."

"Orlon Wyse, . . . Mennonite, . . . four or so years older than me. Made quite a ruckus flying over town in his B-17 bomber. Last anyone ever heard from him. Tall, lanky, dark brown hair, . . . handsome and winsome. Didn't even have to go, due to his religious beliefs. Parents objected, too. Family didn't even put up a grave marker."

Don stares at the markers for a few seconds. "So many . . . so many. . . ."

Don looks at his watch. He wants to get all the flags put away before dark. Six cemeteries need flags picked up. He pulls into the Sugar Creek

Mennonite Church cemetery. A gloomy, empty feeling of depression fills him as he navigates the gravel path.

"Get out!" Don hears a voice. "Get out!" He hears it again. "Get out and pray. . . ."

Don is confused. "Must be my meds," he thinks as he gets back into his truck and drives home.

Don has been suffering from depressionlike symptoms for decades. Post-traumatic stress disorder from the war is what doctors call it. The Veterans Administration doesn't even recognize it for World War II vets. He tells his wife Mary what happened, then turns and goes out the door and back to the cemetery. He can't get the words out of his mind.

At the cemetery, with tears running down his face, he gets out of the truck, takes a few steps, goes down to his knees, then lies face down on the ground. He is sobbing quietly. Half praying, half in anger, he repeats over and over, "So many . . . so many . . . !"

Don loses track of time. It's getting quite dark. As he lies prostrate, his mind focuses back six decades ago to a young soldier who lies out in front of a fallen tree that is protecting Don and others in the squad from German bullets. No one can get to him. The defeated enemy is getting revenge by letting the young soldier die in agony, slowly.

"Rich, stay put! That's an order!"

Don can't stand it anymore. "Medic! Medic!"

Coming over to Don, the sergeant speaks. "Can't risk a medic. We don't have enough if they kill him."

The young soldier's agony continues for hours. Through the evening he gasps for breath. The gasps turn to gurgling sounds. The sounds get softer and softer until there is silence before nightfall.

"If only some of them would have at least volunteered for medic duty!" Don agonizes with God. He has been holding a grudge against those who did not serve in the war. He looks around and realizes the truth, as if for the first time he is seeing the names on the markers. Those who didn't have to serve, because of their beliefs, but did anyway: Elmer Wagler, Eddie Ebner, Dan Good, Robert Reschly. . . .

Don thinks back to his high school teacher, Mr. Gingerich, who argued with him about being a conscientious objector. Don remembers that Mr. Gingerich was a fine man. Don has taken another step on the road to emotional recovery from war.

37664459

November 1945 (about six months after the end of the war in Europe)

My name is Donald J. Rich, private first class (PFC) of the US Army. I left my family and home two years and eight months ago. Maybe you've heard of the 101st Airborne Division, which I've been a part of. Most of the guys I left with on a ship bound for England didn't come back to the United States with me. Some left early to go back home, having suffered injuries during the war. Many others are still over there in Europe. Some eventually will make it home. Others are in military cemeteries near where they were killed.

When I left home, I was an ordinary young man, really a boy, a farm kid. Since leaving home I've seen and done a lot of things, some of which I'm quite proud of. Then there are other things that I'm not sure about. I guess I just need more time to figure everything out. I've been shot at, wounded, and blown out of a building. I've seen many young men my age killed and maimed. I've taken out a machine gun at the cost of a human life and lost a battle with a giant metal monster. My assistant bazooka man, with whom I'd spent many days, I never saw again. Now I'm almost back home.

"Hello, Mom?" I feel excited and nervous at the same time as my mom answers the phone.

"Donald? Is that you, Donald? Where are you?"

"I'm at Uncle Nick's. I got here about midnight last night."

"Why didn't you call? You should have called. We were so worried." Mom continues to chew me out for not calling.

"Sorry, Mom, I should have called," I tell her. Mom starts crying. Through the tears she says they'll be coming right away to pick me up.

Within the hour, Mom, Dad, and my brother, Albert, are at Uncle Nick's front door. I am excited to see them, but, as with the phone call to my mom, I also feel a little nervous. I greet them on the front porch and give my mom a big hug as I lift her off the ground.

After I put her down, Mom, remembering that I had been shot in the leg during the war, asks, "How's your leg?"

"My leg's fine, Mom."

"You should have called last night." Mom starts crying again.

"I saw that German car you captured in Germany at the state fair," Dad remarks rather proudly.

"Helped capture, Dad. I didn't do it all myself."

"I sold your car," Dad continues.

"What?"

"A guy offered three hundred for that old '29 Chevy. I couldn't pass that up," Dad explains. I am upset, but three hundred is quite a bit for that old car, and I realize my parents probably needed the cash.

Albert comes up to me for a hug. He is really glad to see me. He's grown a lot in the two years, three months, and fifteen days since I've seen him last. We stay at Uncle Nick's for about another hour. On the way home we talk about our family. Looking out the car window, I scan the surroundings for signs of danger.

"Grandma and grandpa are doing fine," Mom adds, jolting me back into the present. A peculiar feeling comes over me. I am emotionally numb, not really wanting to talk about the war. I'm happy to be home, but I don't feel quite right. The car stops. As I get out, again I look around for signs of danger, then quickly move into the house.

Bruno, my dog, remembers me: jumping up onto me, he barks and wags his tail eagerly. Mom begins preparing Thanksgiving dinner. The war is over, and in November 1945 I am finally home.

✪ ✪ ✪

Leaving home for the army wasn't my choice, although I had thought seriously about joining the army voluntarily. The official notice that I had been drafted into the US Army came courtesy of the US Post Office on what otherwise would have been an ordinary day in February 1943. Even before I opened the light brown envelope with the Great Seal of the United States printed in black, I knew exactly what the letter inside would say. I tore open the envelope and glanced for several seconds at the enclosed letter addressed to me, Donald Rich, of Wayland, Iowa. I wasn't horribly nervous, but my heart pounded a bit. I had known for a long time that this letter would one day find me. In a sense I was relieved finally to get the letter.

As I unfolded the letter, Mom was standing in the corner of the kitchen. Her facial expression could be read easily: she was quietly upset by the words she knew were in the message. Dad was still at work. Lots of thoughts raced through my nineteen-year-old mind. I thought I was ready to go, because I believed in the cause, but I didn't want to kill anyone. However, I knew I needed to defend my country.

Looking back, I realize that my thoughts were really quite naïve, although not at all unusual for a young man who had barely seen anything outside of Henry County, Iowa, a place that bore distinct similarities to rural Midwestern stereotypes of simple life in a small town. Now I would be going to a faraway land to help people in need, fighting the enemy thousands of miles away from my home. Not knowing what lay ahead of me for the next two years and eight months, I reflected quietly about the opportunity the US Army had put before me. I hoped that I would be able to prove that I was finally a man. If only I had known how much my life was about to change, quickly and dramatically, forever.

The war was on everyone's mind almost every day in eastern Iowa, with most of our news coming from the local movie theater. Before each show, newsreels, usually about the war in Europe and Asia, were shown. The theater seats were just hard, uncomfortable wooden benches. Vivid images of the Ethiopian army on horseback fighting massive Italian tanks were permanently etched into my mind. It saddened me that the Ethiopian people were getting their freedom stolen by the Italians under the leadership of dictator Benito Mussolini.

In 1940 Germany invaded France, and much of western Europe was soon under Nazi control. War news glued everyone to the movie screen: we all wanted to catch every word so that we could better understand the confusing situation. The newsreels brought the war into our daily lives.

Hollywood made political statements about the war. In 1940 the famous silent movie actor Charlie Chaplin made his sound screen debut in *The Great Dictator,* which helped us look at the horrors of a world at war and gone crazy in a funny yet very serious way. Following Pearl Harbor, everyone in town went to see the musical *Yankee Doodle Dandy.* This movie raised most viewers' feelings of pride in the United States because of its patriotic music. My buddies and I felt like marching out of the theater and into the US Army right then and there the night we saw that movie.[1]

In Wayland, Iowa, which had a distinct German heritage, people discussed the war in detail. Some of the older people in town spoke English with a heavy German accent, and it was not uncommon for some families still to speak German at home. Many of these people thought the United States should stay completely out of the war. A few of them openly supported their German cousins, but not necessarily Hitler and his Nazi thugs.

Others in Wayland openly supported helping our British friends, stressing that Hitler's armies needed to be stopped. Local Mennonites, also of German descent, maintained that they were neutral. "War is not for believers," they would say. Despite their religious objections to war, some of their children would serve and even die in defense of the United States.

After December 1941 brought the Japanese attack on the US naval base at Pearl Harbor, life certainly didn't seem secure anymore. I wondered how this could be happening and what it would mean for me and my family. My folks didn't say much about the war after the Pearl Harbor attack. The US government had been drafting young men for the military since 1940.

By early 1942 the war efforts weren't going particularly well for the Allies. In my own personal world, my last high school baseball game and then my high school graduation came and went. I had started the year pitching and had won five games before my elbow got sore. I was one of the few pitchers who used a curve ball, and other teams couldn't hit it. At a game against Olds, the umpire was Mr. Pritchard, our school's music teacher. As an umpire, he wouldn't call anything a strike that didn't cross the plate from the front. Mine crossed from the side, meaning that all of my pitches were called balls. Part of his reasoning was that my coach, Mr. Gingerich, who was also a science teacher, had explained to him that a curveball was only an illusion, so if the ball didn't cross the plate from the front, then it wasn't a strike. At this game I offered to put some poles out on the diamond to prove that the ball would curve around them, but they wouldn't listen. I then brazenly told the coach to take me out of the game because Mr. Pritchard wouldn't call strikes. I wasn't afraid to confront people in leadership, a trait I would continue in the army. The coach took me out, somewhat to my surprise.

Later in 1942, the tide of war began to look more positive for the Allies. In April, Col. James Doolittle led sixteen B-25 bombers in a surprise air raid on Japanese industrial cities. The attack caused very little damage in Japan but raised U.S. morale. British leader Churchill rallied his troops at El Alamein in North Africa, where the British army finally had its first major victory over the enemy. Shortly after El Alamein, the United States launched an invasion against the Nazi-controlled North African countries of Morocco and Algeria.[2]

In the battles of the Coral Sea and Midway Island the US Navy slowed the Imperial Japanese Navy's advances in the Pacific.[3] Newsreels at the theater showing dead US soldiers at Guadalcanal brought the war closer to home. We had never before seen such sights involving US soldiers. We were shocked.

Mom and Dad still didn't say much about the war. Maybe my high school graduation in May made them nervous about what could happen to me if I were drafted or joined the army. Still, almost everyone, including Mom and Dad, knew the cause itself was important and the consequences of letting dictator thugs go unchecked would not be good for the United States and the rest of the world.

For national security reasons the US government began a forced evacuation of 110,000 Americans of Japanese heritage into camps that were like prisons.[4] These camps made for interesting discussions on race in the country. There was talk in the news of black Americans not being allowed into combat alongside white soldiers in the US Army. In rural Iowa we didn't think about that too much. I rarely saw a nonwhite person at all, except when my family traveled to Saint Louis. Racial segregation didn't seem right to me, but for the most part I didn't pay attention to it because it didn't seem to affect my life.

Hungering to make sense of a world at war, I asked a lot of questions, probably driving many adults crazy. The truth was that adults didn't have the answers. If adults didn't have the answers, who could help me figure things out? I thought often about why God allowed these things to happen, or whether He even exists.

As high school graduation neared, my questions were becoming more personal as I began to think about my responsibility in the world.

"Should I join the army?"

"What can I do to help?"

Boys who graduated from Wayland High School in the grades ahead of me were drafted or joined as volunteers. One young Mennonite volunteer, Orlon Wyse, joined the US Army Air Corps despite the objections of his family. On a summer day in 1942 he made the war a bit more real for us when he buzzed Wayland several times with a B-17 bomber he was piloting. On his way to the Pacific war theater, the young officer had received permission to break off his flight group to fly over his hometown. Barely above the treetops, Wyse made several passes over unsuspecting residents. Houses shook and cupboards rattled as people ran outside to see what was going on. The roar of the engines startled all. Several months later we heard that Wyse was missing in action in the Pacific. He was never heard from again. A plaque honoring his name is in Wayland's Central Park. His family never placed a cemetery marker for him because of their objection to his military service.

News reports began to talk of Hitler's efforts to wipe out the Jewish people. These reports seemed quite hard to believe, and there wasn't much information about it.

As for me, Donald J. Rich, the US Army finally answered some of my questions in February of 1943. Soon, with my draft notice in hand, I would be on my way to report for duty at Camp Dodge, near Des Moines, Iowa. I packed the few things I thought I'd need in a bag the night before I left. Little did I know that the army would soon be making just about every decision for me.

The day I was to leave for the army arrived much too quickly. The night before, I was a little nervous and lost a bit of sleep, but not too much. The morning was cold and gray, the kind of day that makes you want to stay in your warm bed. I woke early, and Mom fixed a nice breakfast. My parents were very quiet. Picking up my belongings, our small family headed out the back door, shuffled down the steps, and got into the car. Dad drove while Mom rode in the front passenger seat. My eleven-year-old brother, Albert, was in the back seat with me.

My cousin Marvin Rich and a cousin by marriage, Jay Hill, were also drafted and leaving. Uncle Nick and Aunt Oleta of Mount Pleasant met us at the bus station along with Marvin. Jay and his parents arrived a little later. For a while the three families stayed together and chatted, and then we broke off into our own family groups as the time for leaving drew closer. We had time for a bit of small talk. Nothing big was discussed in our conversations. Everything seemed unreal to me, and I thought to myself, "Could I really be leaving?"

Standing inside the station, I could hear a couple of buses drive up. I was surprised at the number of drafted young men there. The large group inside headed for the door and mixed with the crowd already outside. I was separated from Marvin and Jay. Tears were flowing among the women, and Mom's eyes were getting moist, but there were no tears falling. Just before I boarded the bus, my dad began to cry. This surprised me; saying goodbye was hard on me, but seeing Dad this way really choked me up. I tried hard to fight back my tears but was not successful. My dad had never shed a tear in front of me before. I expected Mom to cry, and she did, eventually, but I didn't expect to see this from my dad. None of us said much more after that—some quiet goodbyes, a few hugs, and that was about it. I felt nauseated as I turned and walked toward the bus. My arms and legs felt a little weak. Marvin and Jay were on another bus.

Boarding, I noticed the aisle was narrow. I stumbled down it as my bags banged against the seats. As I walked, I looked at the faces of the people who would be joining me on the ride. Most were expressionless. I wondered if others on the bus were heading to Camp Dodge as well. Looking around for a place to sit, I continued to stumble toward a worn-out seat in the back, hoping that I could find enough privacy to sort out my feelings. The bus lurched forward, dumping me awkwardly into the seat as my bags whirled out from under me. This was kind of embarrassing and not a good way to impress the men around me. My head swirled with emotions. Now was the time for me to grow up. Mom and Dad couldn't help me with that now.

The gears of the bus ground into action, and through the window I saw my mom's outline as the bus pulled away. Wiping condensation off the window, I felt nausea grow more intense. I stared back at Mom and Dad, wondering when I would see them again, and the images of my teary parents shrank and disappeared. My concerns were more for their well-being and safety than my own. I had never been far from home and family before and would now be training to fight in a foreign land. The army doesn't care much about homesickness. I would learn this soon enough.

The bus bounced along, heading west on US Highway 34 toward Fairfield and the next stop. The old fifty-passenger bus wasn't very comfortable as it jerked and jumped down the road. US 34 was not paved all the way to Ottumwa, and the state roads weren't very good, either. There wasn't a lot of traffic, but getting through the bigger towns seemed to take forever. Seeing new sights and people helped break the monotony. Gradually we made our way northwest toward the big city of Des Moines.

✪ ✪ ✪

My emotionally exhausted mind is numb. "Boy, am I tired," I think. I doze off from time to time. Just as I am about to get a wink of sleep, I am jostled awake, either from the bumps in the road or the jerking caused whenever the driver shifts gears. I don't feel much like talking to anyone.

I decide to take a closer look at the other guys on the bus. They all seem to have the same blank expression. These guys are all new to me, and I can't tell what they are thinking, but if their thoughts are anything close to mine, they are trying to act confident and tough. This is how I want to look, hiding any feelings of being scared.

Late in the afternoon the bus finally rolls into the station in Des Moines. I get off just as I got on, slowly and awkwardly, banging my way up the aisle. When I finally step off, I head toward where the schedules are, although some of the guys apparently know where we are supposed to go. After a quick trip to the restroom, I find the bus that is heading to Camp Dodge. The other draftees are slowly heading out the door to the loading area where the bus is parked. Some of us engage in small talk.

"Where you from?" I quickly find out that there are boys from all over the state: Bettendorf, Iowa City, Mount Vernon, and some places I haven't even heard of.

"What's your favorite baseball team?"

Talking about major-league baseball was easy for me. I had imagined myself being a famous baseball player back when I played on the Wayland High School team. Among the new recruits there are fans of the Cubs, White Sox, Cardinals, and Saint Louis Browns.

"Have you seen the latest movie?"

Most of us are more willing to admit seeing the drama *Casablanca,* a love story set in war-torn Africa, than the animated *Bambi,* although *Bambi* does make me think a lot about the possibility that I might have to kill somebody using a gun.

After about a half-hour ride, we arrive at Camp Dodge, northwest of Des Moines. Through the window I can see that the place is busy. Men in uniform are moving crisply and confidently. Those of us still in civilian clothes don't have the same gait. As we get off the bus we are quickly told what to do and where to go. Being ordered around will take some getting used to.

A burly guy in his mid-twenties and dressed in a plain uniform marches over to us. The stripes on his shoulder indicate some rank of importance, but I don't know yet what it is. He has a very short haircut, not much more than stubble.

"Attention!" he barks. Most of us just look at him; his eyes glare with fire. His face is locked in place as if he expects someone to punch him in the jaw and he isn't going to flinch.

"Fall in, *now!*" he orders.

Almost in unison we look at each other and then head toward him. The guy looks like he is going to blow a cork. We form a straggling line, the guy in charge grumbles a few words, and we follow him rather hesitantly into a building for check-in.

"At ease," the man in charge barks, but in a little less threatening tone. Life is sure changing in a hurry.

After standing in line for about twenty minutes, I get my turn. The soldier behind the desk mumbles some words to me and asks me to sign some papers before providing me with some new Class A clothes, consisting of a jacket, wool sweater, pants, and a few other things. Then I am on my way to a barracks where bunks are assigned.

After I haphazardly dump my stuff onto a bunk, several of us chat. One guy does a funny impression of the gruff officer, who we later learn is a sergeant. Soon another sergeant barks instructions at us. I fall in line with the other guys trying to march, not knowing how (or caring much, for that matter).

After marching right outside and down the street a short distance, our straggly line comes to another building, recently constructed. Judging by its rough appearance, the builder must have been in a hurry to get the project done. Once inside, we stand in line, waiting again for instructions. We engage in small talk again, and it becomes clear that many of us are farm boys or from small towns.

"Where you from?" is asked repeatedly. Soon we are like old buddies, and it seems like we have known each other since grade school.

In some ways I feel like a kid in school again, being constantly told to do this, go there. Although I feel insecure because I have no idea what the next few years will bring, being bossed around gives me a good feeling; at least someone is looking after me.

First up is a haircut, if it could be called that. The army barber is a wiry man with a balding head and muscular arms. With no mirrors on the wall, I can't see what he is doing, but I can feel. That barber shaves my hair right off.

"I look like a skinned onion!" I speak out loud to myself as I look into a mirror after getting back to the barracks. I wonder if it will ever grow back, and I feel as if I weigh a lot less. A couple of guys chuckle until they see themselves in the mirror.

A while later an army doctor gives me a physical.

"He's alive and will do as a soldier," the doctor says.

"Of course, I'm alive," I think, and then wonder, "Will I really do as a soldier? Will I be up to the task?"

Next I am issued my army fatigues, which are a drab green color. My new uniform is so big. I don't think my body could ever fill it out.

"How am I supposed to fit in these?" I ask.

My thoughts are quickly interrupted by the sight of a needle coming at me, carried by a stern-looking man in white.

"Ouch!" Vaccinations are a necessary pain, I suppose.

My head is swimming with concern, excitement, and wonder. A few of the guys are already going back home, having failed to pass the physical exam. I think that it must be embarrassing to get sent home like that.

On the second day at Camp Dodge not much happens in the way of activity. Officers order us to the main hall, where we swear an oath of allegiance to the United States. After this we head back to the barracks, where we have some time to chat more with our new friends.

"Hey, Don!" Behind me I hear a couple of voices I recognize. Cousins Marvin and Jay have found me. Both are taller than me, maybe six feet tall or more, and they each have at least forty pounds on me. Jay takes nothing from anybody. Marvin is pretty tough as well, but not as scrappy. A friend of Marvin's from Mount Pleasant named Smith is also at the camp.

Some guys pull a few boyish pranks. Others talk as if they are about to win the war all by themselves. Hitler doesn't stand a chance. Most of us don't really know how to act in a uniform, at least not yet. Swearing, which I am not much used to at all, becomes a part of everyday language.

The time at Camp Dodge goes by quickly. On the third day we awake bright and early after a night of sound sleep and are herded onto a train heading to California, where we will undergo basic infantry training. This is my first train trip ever. Jay and Marvin are on the same train, but I never get to see them.

The train rolls through the countryside as soft flurries begin to turn the dreary hues of winter a bright white. The seats aren't very comfortable—they are hard, just like those on the bus—and the constant stopping and jerking means getting sleep will be difficult. We stop on a railroad siding, settle in for a while, and then, just when sleep comes again, clank, bang, we are moving again. Loud sounds echo when the train stops along a long row of buildings.

Across Nebraska and into Colorado the plains are flat as can be. Later in Colorado the snow-covered mountains are unbelievably beautiful and bigger than I have imagined from pictures I've seen. How I wish to get off the train for a while to enjoy the magnificent beauty longer. Like the scenery, my life is hurriedly changing. The mountain views take my mind off of war for a while, and then a jolt brings me back to its reality. Now I am but a number, 37664459, being told where to go. I had to memorize my serial number back at Camp Dodge. This number is a call to duty, and I am answering the call.

The train from Camp Dodge to Camp Roberts in California is a long troop train. A modern diesel engine is at the front, followed by passenger cars and then a boxcar, where cooking is done. Steam engines are still prevalent, and some of the guys look at the diesel engine with interest because of its novelty. The trip takes four days in all. I rarely get much sleep.

Sometimes at night the troop train pulls onto a siding track. Things get quiet, and then the rumble of an approaching freight train begins to sound. As the freight train gets closer, the sharp click clack of the steel wheels on the track becomes quite loud. Some of the guys sleep right through the noise, but I can't. The night is slowly illuminated as the headlight of the freighter comes near.

Occasionally, we pick up additional passenger cars, leading to more lurching and banging. Crumpf! Crumpf! Bang! Bang! The noises echo.

The air becomes stale-smelling, as the cars' closed windows prevent proper ventilation. Refueling and picking up new soldiers are the main reasons for stopping. The food isn't much to get excited about, but the cooks provide plenty.

At station stops new soldiers make their way into my car. Most of the recruits have the same wide-eyed look. A friendly hello coupled with a concerned look tells a lot. Just like back in Iowa, a few act outgoing and tough, but it doesn't appear natural. A few others seem truly scared and intimidated.

Night and day, the young men chatter. Guys are playing cards and telling stories, crowing about their athletic accomplishments. Others brag about their girls back home and enjoy showing off their pictures. Most of these guys are from places I've never heard of before.

Change is hard. Homesickness begins to set in. As the miles flash by, my mind again drifts back to home, Mom, Dad, friends, and even my brother. I already miss them horribly. I miss the farm to the southwest of Wayland that my dad worked when I was little. My dad, Forest Milo Rich, had rented eighty acres, from which he supported our family for a time. Memories of me and my brother playing cowboys and Indians in the barnyard or hayloft come back to me. My family was relatively poor, but it didn't matter much, as most other families were in about the same situation during those Depression years. Mom and Dad did what they could to get us by. Dad was often awfully short on cash for supplies, but we never went hungry.

Men, usually uncles and neighbors without much to do because work was hard to come by, would stop and visit while dad was working. My mom, Lillie, was sensitive to the bad habits I picked up from those men. Swearing and other improper language were easy for a young boy to pick up and copy. At first Mom tried to whip the swearing out of me. I wasn't being rebellious, just imitating. Finally, Mom decided to focus on changing the men's behavior.

"You men are a poor example to Donald," Mom chided them. "You'll have somewhere else to go tell your stories if you don't clean up your language!" This helped tone down their obscenities, I think.

A large bump in the track jolts me back to the present. I am in the US Army and not at all sure what the future holds. I feel homesick, excited, proud, scared, and brave, all at the same time. The wheels clicking on the track go on and on.

Soldiering Basics

In the midafternoon after four days of travel, the troop train pulls into the destination station, somewhere in California. After sitting so long, my legs don't really work right, and the weight of my bag makes me walk off balance. I struggle to negotiate a sharp turn near the exit and end up banging into the train's bathroom door. I've never had any alcohol to drink in my life, but I am pretty sure that the feeling is similar to that of being drunk. Awkwardly, I step back and negotiate my way onto solid ground. I wobble a bit standing on the walkway next to the train.

"This way soldiers," says a strong voice that immediately grabs our attention. We are herded like cattle onto buses.

"Fill the back rows first!" the driver screams at the top of his lungs, trying to make his voice heard over the rumbling of the engine. My heavy bags again make it hard to go down the aisle without banging into seats. The air in the bus is hot and filled with dust, making it hard to breathe, and the smell of body odor turns my stomach. I long for fresh air and wonder if California will always be like this. Soon the old bus is underway.

I am excited about being in California. "Am I really in America?" I ask myself, almost feeling like I am in a different country. The landscape looks so different from Iowa. The ground looks like it needs a soaking rain.

Before long the bus makes a turn into Camp Roberts. New barracks have been built to house all the new soldiers heading to war. Sergeants motion this way and that, prodding us like cattle into lines for sorting at the slaughterhouse. Idle chitchat breaks the busy sounds, and I make many new acquaintances. After we have all been sorted out, we are again told where to go. I am really getting tired of being told exactly what to do. I miss the bit of freedom I had on the train, where at least I could get up and walk down the aisle whenever I wanted to.

Someone asks me where I am from. "Southeastern Iowa," I answer. The guy looks confused. "Near Iowa City," I add. That response brings an even more puzzled expression.

"Is Iowa next to Ohio?" the young soldier asks. I ignore the question. He goes on, "Got a girl back home?" I want to say yes but can't bring myself to lie and instead give a vague nod.

I am hearing accents that I have never heard before in my life. Some guys are obviously from the South, and they tend to stick together. Others are from the East Coast, and they can be annoying at times, because they talk nonstop whether or not anyone is listening. Some of the guys seem to have known each other for a long time, even though they have only recently met each other. Friendships are easy to form at this point. Except for how they talk, my fellow soldiers don't seem much different from the guys at home.

The rest of my first day in California is a blur. Cousin Marvin is in the same training company but not the same barracks. I haven't seen Jay, though. Chow is served, but it isn't very appetizing. I get barked at by officers and then we are ordered back to our barracks. After a bit of conversation, lights are out and it is time for sleep, even though I don't feel sleepy.

Sleeping in the barracks with lots of other men is going to take some more getting used to. Some of the guys snore unbelievably loud. Do I snore? I've never really thought about that before. Sleep must come at some point. A bugle blare, which I'll soon grow to hate, breaks out through the darkness, startling me out of bed as the lights pop on. A fresh-looking sergeant with a stern face and flashes of anger in his voice and eyes charges aggressively into the room. He must be related to the sergeant back at Camp Dodge. We are being barked at again. I make my bed and get ready for inspection. A couple of guys are singled out for doing a despicable job of making their beds, but I can't see how their beds differ much from anyone else's, including mine. I am sure glad I didn't get made an example. After we all have perfectly made our beds, we are given an opportunity to use the latrine, which is strange to me. Modesty was very important back home, but now I am sharing a bathroom with hundreds of other young men.

Next it is time for breakfast, something I am desperately looking forward to, because I am starving. I am anxious to get into line, but once I see what we are supposed to eat, I'm not so hungry. A number of guys make wisecracks about the food, but I don't find their banter very funny, because food is serious business. This army chow isn't at all like my mom's food back home.

The army doesn't waste any time getting us started on our path to becoming soldiers. Just after breakfast we do calisthenics. Some of the guys don't know how to do jumping jacks very well, which surprises me. Soon I learn to crawl on my belly, which makes me feel like a snake baking in the hot sun as I slither along. I don't want to act like a snake, but my survival might depend on my ability to do so. Keeping my head low is of utmost importance and is easy for me to learn, because some drill sergeants fire live ammunition just over our heads during training. I can hear the bullets pierce the air with a zinging sound just a few inches from my ears. This is unnerving at first. Staying down is not natural, but after a while of fighting the urge to stand up and run, a person gets used to it. Well, almost used to it, anyway. Having bullets fly close overhead is about as natural as watching a swarm of bees crawling up your arm without swatting at them. The guy in front of me is shot in the foot because his left leg sticks up too far as he crawls up and over a log instead of going around it. He sure does holler. I want to help but can't without risking my life. In some ways the drills don't seem real. Maybe they are a dream. At night I ask God to just help me survive training.

Day after day the air is dusty and hot. At times, when crawling on our bellies during a live-fire drill, the dust chokes me so badly that I can't breathe. I think I just have to get up to get a good breath, but I fight off the urge and stay down. During one live-fire exercise a fellow soldier comes upon a live snake, and boy, does he panic. The guy is terrified of snakes. He immediately bolts up from the ground, either forgetting about the bullets being fired over him or deciding that he is more scared of snakes than of being shot. Attentive officers are able to stop firing, but I think the chewing he gets from the furious officers may be worse than getting shot. Everyone learns from his lesson.

March, march, march. We march a lot at Camp Roberts. March, march, march, and then march again. The temperature sometimes climbs as high as 115 Fahrenheit, and sometimes I think I'll pass out under all the army gear. We don't get many breaks to recuperate. Drinking lots of water is very important. One can't drink too much, and it seems I can't get enough. But at least the air is dry, not at all like Iowa's summer humidity. By the end of each day I am so tired that sleeping through all the snoring is no longer a problem.

After we crawl on our stomachs for several weeks, the army thinks enough of us to teach us to fire virtually all of the infantry weapons: rifles (including the Browning automatic rifle, or BAR), machine guns, mortars, and the rifle grenade. The rifle grenade is basically a grenade mounted on the end of a 1903 Springfield rifle, making the rifle unbalanced and thus hard to aim. I wonder if I could hit a big barn with the grenade, much less a German or Japanese tank.

The officer in charge lines up three of us to fire the grenades. I feel pretty good about being chosen. We carefully fix the grenade in place at the end of the old Springfield rifle. We are to fire in unison at a target flag out in the field in front of us.

"Ready! Aim! Fire!" Instantly the three of us are on our butts. My shoulder hurts.

"First thing to learn about rifle grenades: you never fire standing up. If you'd been leaning back on something, your shoulder would be busted!" the officer barks.

I don't get to see if I hit anything from my current position. The officer proceeds to show us how to plant the rifle butt on the ground and aim the barrel into the air.

Thirteen weeks of basic training go by quickly. I am often tired, but in a good sort of way. Blisters on my feet and hands are being replaced by hard calluses. Putting up with army discipline is not so bad after experiencing it for a couple of weeks. Teamwork is essential; when one person goofs up, everyone suffers. One day, as a team we spend the whole day scrubbing the floor with toothbrushes because one man had dust under his bed. Teammates need to look out for one another in order to avoid this type of punishment. We are becoming tight-knit.

During basic training I get off the base only twice. Once I go to visit a nearby city to see the sights. I really want to go see the ocean but never get the chance. The other time I visit my dad's brother Rex, who moved to California from Iowa during the early days of the Great Depression, before I was old enough to remember much about him. Visiting with someone who looks so much like my dad seems kind of odd, but it is nice to spend time with someone that seems to be glad to see me. His wife, Mary Jo, and his five children are really kind, even though I've never met them before. My cousin Marvin is with me on the visit. "My, you two look handsome in uniform," Aunt Mary Jo says, going on and on as the kids gawk at us with pride.

From the start of basic training we have been ordered to shave every day. This seems kind of silly, since many of us really don't need to. Shaving so much makes my face feel raw, so some mornings I make it look like I am shaving even though I don't have a blade in my razor. I am carefully deceptive, because I certainly don't want other team members to pay for my behavior. Maybe others are doing likewise, but some things can't be shared, so nothing is said about it.

The hard work we are putting in during training is transforming us young men into tough soldiers. At nineteen, though still a youth, I am quickly becoming a man. I wonder if my mom and dad will notice the difference if I ever get the chance to see them again. The carefree days of my childhood are becoming a distant memory. Training is precise; I need to pay close attention to every detail. Leaving dust under a bed is embarrassing enough. Accidentally killing someone is unthinkable. There is no place for youthful or childish ways here.

I am in a strange environment. We don't have much free time to ourselves, and I spend the little free time I have thinking about home life. My family moved for a short time to Mount Pleasant, and I hated giving up my school friends, but there hadn't been any other option for me, kind of like now in the army. On my first day at the Mount Pleasant public school, I saw kids having a grand old time on a slide. So up to the slide I went, waiting for my turn. When I got to the top, I looked at the school and then down at the ground, far below. I didn't know anyone, and I was scared. All I wanted to do was go home. As I looked behind me, I could see two African American kids standing partway up the ladder, apparently brother and sister. They startled me, because I had never seen anyone of a different race before and felt a little scared of them. "Are you going down or not?" someone grumbled. Gathering my wits about me, down the slide I went.

Being in the army is a lot like that experience; new and different things are scary and yet interesting and exciting at the same time. For me the biggest differences are that Mom, Dad, and Albert aren't around.

Before moving back, Dad secured a spot for me on an International Harvester tractor in the county fair parade, which was a really big deal. My being in the parade made me feel like a very important person. Marching with my fellow soldiers during drills reminds me of that parade and once again gives me the feeling that I am important.

Just as in Iowa, my mailing address is about to change. We complete training, and friends that I have quickly made at boot camp are being lost just as quickly when they are shipped out to different places around the country—and the world. The quick changes make missing my school friends and familiar surroundings even harder. The sense of anticipation brought on by this rapid change makes life more interesting, but can't I go home for a while? The desire to see a familiar face is beginning to become a craving.

Basic training is over, and I find myself getting ready to get on another troop train, which will take me to even more training. We leave on July 20.

"Goodbye Camp Roberts," I wave, but this good-bye is easy, except for saying goodbye to cousin Marvin.

Just before departing Camp Roberts, one of the officers asks me which type of combat unit I'd like to be in. I think this question seems a bit odd; the army has never asked my preferences before. I remember overhearing some fellows talking about a type of fighting unit called the airborne. It seems the army is looking for volunteers to jump out of airplanes into combat. After hearing about them, I daydreamed about becoming one someday. The thought is intriguing. There would be extra pay, and the airborne is considered to be elite. Yeah, the idea sounds pretty good, but after thinking about it awhile I look down at my skinny feet and ankles. Growing up, I'd often had ankle sprains and sore feet.

"Sir, I'd love be in the airborne. Trouble is, sir, I don't think my feet could handle it. I had trouble a lot as a kid. Sir, I'm not sure these feet could handle the parachute landing. I don't think I'd make a good airborne trooper, sir," I answer the officer with a good deal of honest disappointment.

"Okay, Rich. You'll make a good foot soldier in the infantry instead," the officer replies.

I'd seen a brochure that talked about airborne soldiers who ride into battle in motorless gliders. "Could I volunteer for the gliders?" I ask.

"You can't volunteer for gliders. The army assigns who gets to go to the gliders. Only thing you could volunteer for is to be a paratrooper."

"My feet will probably hold up to riding in a glider," I think out loud as I make my way back to the barracks. I am consoled with the thought that I'll at least have my feet with skinny ankles on the ground even if this means that I'll have to do lots of marching when I go into battle.

We soldiers don't always know where we are going, but in some ways this adds to the excitement of what is becoming a painfully slow trip. Cousin Jay is going to the same place I am, but again he is on a different part of the train, which is often sidelined to wait as other trains, also loaded with troops, pass by. Loud and boisterous young men keep the noise at a low roar. I'm thankful that on this trip there is no picking up more passengers or adding cars.

In the early stages of the seven-day trip we are allowed to get off the train to stretch our legs. This is a luxury, and as a result my legs stay in better shape than they did on the trip to California. Soldiers smoke cigarettes and play blackjack for all of the seven days, often forgetting about sleep. The July weather is stifling, and there is no air conditioning. Cigarette smoke hangs heavy in the air of the passenger rail cars, and breathing is hard at times.

Being young, we walk back to the boxcar often for food. The menu contains a very limited selection and isn't very good. But because I am hungry much of the time, the food quality really doesn't matter much. Food is food, and we eat it. With all the hungry young men on the train, if you don't eat right away, someone else will.

As the train moves from California into Arizona, I become hot and restless. The train stops in the middle of the desert, and we are ordered out to do calisthenics in the intense heat. When we reboard, hotter and sweatier, some of the restlessness is gone.

In spite of the card games and lack of sleep, there still is a serious atmosphere to this trip. We have been ordered not to call home at stops along the way and absolutely not to let relatives know where we are and how we are traveling. This is to keep information about troop movements from the enemy. I wonder if there are any spies on the train. All we can tell is we are heading east, which means we are heading toward Europe and away from Japan.

This secrecy is also to prevent sabotage. Not everyone in our country supports the war effort. After all, many US citizens emigrated from other countries. For some, loyalty to their home country runs deep. Because of this, fear exists that Americans still loyal to a home country such as Germany or Japan might try to blow up the train if they know we are coming.

At the first stop the train makes in Texas, a soldier from that state disobeys orders and calls home, giving away our whereabouts and where we will be traveling. He is forcibly removed from the train and arrested by military police. I'm not sure how the army found this out, but his being led away in handcuffs makes a big impression on all of us. After that, we are not allowed to get out of the train car at all.

The terrain becomes greener as the train makes its way across the Great Plains, the American South, and on into Fort Bragg, North Carolina.

When I get off the train, my legs again are wobbly. The day is July 27, 1943.

"Rich, looks like you got your wish!" one of the guys blurts. There is a big sign at the station that says, "Welcome to Fort Bragg, Home of the 101st Airborne." I don't understand why I am here.

By the time we have everyone unloaded from the train, the sun is going down. We are ordered into barracks, curious about what we are doing here. I am tired and fall asleep right away.

The next morning, the up and at it whistle sounds, and we are greeted by a sergeant. "Welcome, soldiers. You're in the airborne, boys," he informs us with a grin.

I'm surprised but happy and proud to be a member of what is considered to be an elite group. The concept of troops brought into battle by air is a relatively new one. While some of the troops are to be trained specifically for parachute jumps, I have been assigned to a glider regiment, which means I will ride in a motorless aircraft into combat. The glider will be towed by a powered aircraft to a position close to where we will land and then released to glide to a landing, controlled by a pilot. The enemy will probably be nearby, and if we survive the landing, we'll get out and fight. Bets are made that the 101st is heading to Europe, since we were now in the East—although we still don't know for sure.

I am placed in Company G of the 327th Glider Infantry Regiment. Soon I find out that Company G has been together since 1942, so many of the men in it already know each other, but we new guys seem to fit in pretty well. The older troops have already been on glider flights. Nothing to it at all, some of them say. Others are silent about the subject and just grin.

Officers at Fort Bragg are even more serious than those in California. Training is tough. Bayonet and hand-to-hand combat practices are terribly exhausting. Soldiers grumble whenever they think they are beyond the hearing range of officers. The weather is hot, the food is lousy, and rain falls every afternoon. The conditions don't make for much fun. Maybe the training will one day help keep us alive, but I hope never to have to use this hand-to-hand stuff. I don't want to kill anyone.

In spite of the grumbling, the abundance of hard work is making real soldiers out of us and getting us into amazing shape. During my first ten days at Fort Bragg, I lose ten pounds while at the same time bulking up in my arms and legs. Cousin Jay is also in the 101st, but as a truck driver, not a foot soldier. I guess the army thinks his feet are too bad for fighting. This seems crazy to me, as Jay is so tough. I only see Jay occasionally.

We each receive a couple of passes off base while at Fort Bragg. Wanting to see Southern culture, I venture into Fayetteville, located near the base. At local bars a lot of fights break out between glider troops and paratroopers. The paratroopers are a pretty cocky bunch and are rude toward us glidermen. The paratroopers are generally younger than the glidermen as well. Someone says the average glider guy is almost twenty-eight years old, while most of the paratroopers are around my age, nineteen. Not wanting to get involved in the fighting, I roam the streets to see the sights.

Jay gets into fights, though. If someone says something insulting about being a truck driver, he lets his temper go. His fights are impressive—round and round they go. Sometimes Jay will be on the bottom with several on top of him, but no one stops the brawl at that point, as he can always fight his way out. Most often he will be on top and pounding the guy pretty hard. Then someone breaks up the fight before his opponent gets hurt. I sure wish Jay could be in my squad—I'd feel safer.

There are lots more trees here than at home. The hills are beautiful and the people seem very nice and courteous to me. My uniform seems to garner a bit of respect, in spite of my youth. However, I also notice some very disturbing sights. I am utterly shocked to see black people step out of the way when a white person, including myself, approaches. The African Americans seem too intimidated to even look at me. The whole concept that I am considered "superior" because of my race seems ridiculous to me. In the African American section of town, there are shacks being lived in that farmers back home wouldn't even put chickens in. Wayland seemed poor during the Depression, but nothing like this. The living conditions are so appalling that I have a hard time processing what I see and just can't get the poverty and the treatment of black people out of my mind. I quit walking around town and just stay on base.

Training at Fort Bragg continues in earnest. We primarily spend the days marching from one place to another, but we also step up our physical conditioning and undergo intense weaponry training. A bazooka is placed in my hands by a sergeant, and suddenly I find that I am a bazooka gunner. And on top of it all, my company begins receiving its first training in Waco gliders. At first I am excited to get an opportunity to fly. However, as the day approaches for my first flight, I begin to realize that I am about to fly in a flimsy, motorless flying contraption that looks like it is about to fall apart at any moment, and this dampens my enthusiasm.

Rumors go around the camp that the wings can come off the gliders in flight. Apparently, the city that made the gliders had a big festival commemorating the first one ever made by the company. The mayor, other government officials, and managers of the company all went up for the first ride, and a wing really did come off, killing all on board, or so we are told.

The time for my first flight arrives. Getting into the glider is awkward, as I am loaded with equipment and someone gives me a shove from behind as I try to climb up through the door. As I board, I am surprised at how flimsy the glider looks. The floor is made of plywood and the sides are canvas. Not much protection, I think. The flooring of thin plywood won't stop many bullets

Don in uniform, 1943

from coming through. The sides, of canvas over a frame of metal pipe, are even worse. If we crash there won't be much left to hold the flying contraption together. The nylon rope that connects the glider to the towplane doesn't seem strong enough. I'm not too sure about the glider pilots, either. After I listen to some of them talk, I get the impression that they don't really know what they are doing. Certainly they have had more training at piloting than we have had at being soldiers . . . right? Towplanes and gliders are lined up along the runway.

Taking off in a Waco is an ordeal. The towplane pilot runs the engine throttle wide open until it seems that the towplane will shake the glider and us apart. Then, just before disintegration, the pilot releases the towplane's brakes, and it lumbers down the runway as the rope, which has been laid out in a continuous S pattern, unwinds like a slithering snake. The rope goes straight, stretching out like a three-quarters-inch-thick but very long rubber band. Getting tighter, the rope stretches even more until, with a strong tug, acceleration pulls my head toward my shoulder, and we are airborne in a matter of seconds. The glider becomes airborne first, shooting above and behind the towplane. Looking out the front of the glider is like viewing through a big picture window, and ahead and slightly below us we can see the towplane as it pulls us through the air. The conjoined aircraft seem to move ever so slowly, with the lead craft finally leaving the ground.

Wrapped around the tow rope is a wire that allows communication between the pilot of the towplane and the glider pilot; I do not ever see them speak. The noise is loud and becomes almost unbearable when the glider passes through the prop wash of the towplane. Everything moves in slow motion. Getting out is not an option at this point.

Higher and higher the pair of manmade birds climbs, the glider mimicking turns of the towplane. Ahead of us are other gliders and tows. Most of the time, the glider stays above the towplane. Finally, it is time for the glider to be released. With a quick jolt, the glider is on its own. Men begin to vomit into their helmets, and soon, I lose my lunch as well, splashing it into my helmet. The guy in the back pours the helmet contents into a bucket.

As soon as we unhook from the towplane, it feels like we are suddenly braking. I have a helpless feeling, because I have no control over the circumstances. It is quieter now that we can't hear the towplane, but the air moving around and against the glider still makes quite a bit of noise. Our glider seems to be dropping rather than flying as we make our descent toward an open field. I am thankful when, with a hard bounce, we make a successful landing. I am relieved to be on the ground.

Troops inside a glider. Courtesy Denis Parsons collection, 101st Airborne Division Belgian Friendly Association.

A towplane and glider take off.

As time goes on and our training advances, we are becoming more comfortable with each other and beginning to bond. We are becoming comrades. But our conversations reveal how naïve we are. I frequently hear my buddies talk about how they are going to "easily whip those Germans," and some even worry that the war will be over before they get a chance to fight.

Before long, more arguments break out between the glider troops and the parachute troops. Some of the paratroopers are arrogant, thinking they are superior because they jump out of an airplane. They even get better pay than glidermen do. I thought we were all a team, fighting together against a common enemy, but not everyone is acting like it. Several of the cocky paratroopers volunteer to go up in a glider just so they can tell us how easy

A glider in flight

A glider landing. Landings could be bumpy because of turbulent air near the ground as well as the rough ground itself.

we have it. During the flight they start throwing up and are scared to death. Afterwards, they tell us they would rather parachute out of an airplane than crash land in a glider. Some justice is served after all.

We bazooka gunners get more training at Fort Bragg. When the sergeant first put the weapon in my hands, I guess I was volunteered for the job without my knowing it. It seems I am getting volunteered to do things a lot without my knowledge. Bazookas are fascinating, though, and it is exciting to fire one—except that when I launch a rocket, fragments in its exhaust cut my face and hands, causing them to bleed. The rocket launcher is big and cumbersome. The barrel is fifty-four inches long, and it weighs twelve pounds, while the caliber of the rocket is over two inches. The weapon's maximum range is four hundred yards, but hitting something at that range would take quite a bit of skill and a whole lot of luck.

The bazookas are needed to counter heavily armored German tanks. The lighter American Sherman tanks alone are no match against the bigger and faster German armor. The bazooka's main punch is achieved by using a hollow-core warhead that can penetrate thick metal. Weapons experts on both sides of the war know the effect this type of weapon can have on armor plating. The bazooka is capable of penetrating six inches of armor plate, and under the right circumstances the tank's fuel supply and ammunition will blow up.

Being a bazooka gunner is very serious business. We are warned that bazooka men will be targets. A bazooka team has to take about thirty seconds to load and take aim, and in such close proximity to the enemy this doesn't leave much time to keep from getting shot at. Rifle and machine gun fire is the most serious danger that bazooka men like me face, because it takes so long to fire the weapon effectively.

My skills at firing the bazooka are high, and I am called on to demonstrate the weapon. In one exercise we aim at railroad rails that have been buried upright in the ground with about six feet of rail exposed. I fire from fifty yards away, and apparently the rocket continues past the target and into the hillside. But when the group looks closely at the target, we see that in my rail is a hole about the width of a pencil right through the middle. Still, I wonder how it will be possible to avoid enemy bullets while trying to aim this thing.

For rifle training I am using an M1 Garand, a huge improvement over the Springfield. Both have about the same power and are about the same size, but the Springfield requires that I pull the bolt back on each of the eight shots in the clip, whereas the Garand allows me to get eight off as fast as I can pull the trigger.

Later, while I am still at Fort Bragg, the army gives out fourteen-day furloughs. Longing to see my folks, I eagerly look forward to going home for a visit. I travel again by train, this time pulled by a new steam engine. The seats in the passenger car are wooden, because metal is a vital war material and is being rationed. They are not at all comfortable. The train itself is much quieter than the troop trains I have become used to on my previous trips. Although soldiers on furlough make up a sizable portion of the passengers, most of the people on board are civilians. The train goes from Fort Bragg to New York and then on to Chicago. My last stop is Mount Pleasant, Iowa, where I arrive after three days. I wonder if my parents will be proud of me, but my thoughts are primarily on what lies ahead of me in the coming months.

Finally, seeing Mom and Dad when they pick me at the Mount Pleasant station, I am overcome with emotion. My parents' faces show me they are proud and surprised when they see me in uniform for the first time. Smiles, hugs, and tears happen all at once. Words immediately fly from my mouth: "How have you been? Is Albert breaking my things? Mom, Dad, it's so good to see you," and so on.

Mom and Dad also ask a lot of questions, but I can't answer all of them, because of military intelligence rules. I certainly don't want to have military police come to Wayland to take me away. Questions concerning private military secrets, such as where we will be heading and when we will be leaving, simply can't be discussed. Besides, I really don't know where I will be going or when I am to be deployed, but I don't want to say that, either.

I try to avoid topics that will make Mom upset, so I don't tell her that during my training bullets flew above my head, and I certainly do not tell her about the guy who got shot in the foot. Instead, discussions center on my newfound buddies from around the country. I also avoid discussing some of my buddies' bad behaviors, knowing Mother would find them objectionable.

My few short days in Wayland blow by way too quickly. Over the course of my furlough, I meet up with a few school friends who haven't been drafted yet. Walking around town in my uniform makes me feel proud, but I am not exactly sure how to act or talk. Eyes are on me. Out of the corner of my eye, I can see people pointing and talking. This gives me some feeling of importance and maturity.

One day in Wayland, near Central Park, in front of the grocery store I see my friend Bill's brother Charlie Brooks, a captain, looking good in uniform. Beside him is Private Andy Tschantz, on leave after completing basic training. Charlie is about twenty-five years old, while Andy's got to be pushing forty, the oldest-looking enlisted man I've seen in the army. Andy is quiet, but Charlie is carrying on, a real chatterbug. The women around him seem to enjoy his presence. Finally, Andy speaks up awkwardly: "Look at you, Charlie! You're a officer! I can remember when you were born!" Andy seems even more nervous. After Charlie leaves and the crowd disperses, Andy looks at me and says, "Hell, I didn't know whether to salute him or what to do; he's so much younger. So I didn't do anything."

Just before I leave to return to Fort Bragg, Dad takes a picture of me in front of the Wayland Methodist Church. I can tell from his facial expression that he is proud of me. All too soon, the two weeks are up and I am packing my things. Mom bakes some goodies and packs lots of food for the trip back.

"I wish I had a longer stay," I say to Mom.

"I don't imagine the army would miss you a bit," Mom jokes back. Our eyes meet; Mom is about to cry.

"I'll be back before you know it, Mom. I'll bet Hitler's about to give up already. Sure do miss your cookin', Mom. Maybe the army needs some more cooks. Want to come along?" I am trying my best to comfort her by making a difficult departure lighthearted.

Joking aside, I have mixed emotions. There is no telling when or even whether I will ever see my family or friends again. The thought is a little depressing. On the other hand, I am extremely excited about what lies ahead. I am about to embark on new adventures, see parts of the world I thought I would only read about, and, I hope, find out who I am deep inside. Quietly I pack my belongings in the car. My family and I engage in some small talk as we motor down the road to Mount Pleasant. I am hoping to avoid a display of emotion. I know it won't be long before I will be going to Europe or Asia to become involved in the real war. And this time there will be no looking back.

The train comes steaming into the station. After a tearful goodbye, I confidently walk up the ramp and into the passenger car. This time a grown man is leaving home.

The train station disappears quickly, but my feelings aren't the same as when I left home the first time. I now have a mission to accomplish, and I am committed to the cause, scary as it is. I will do my best. The trip back to Fort Bragg seems like a blur. Soon, the familiar landscape that surrounds the base rolls into view, and before I know it I am doing more training. Shortly after getting back, we receive word that all off-base passes are being canceled. This probably means the 101st is about to be shipped out on assignment.

Within a few weeks of my return to Fort Bragg, we receive orders to move to New York's Camp Shanks, just north of New York City, where we undergo further processing and immunizations.[1] Camp Shanks has row after row of twenty- by one-hundred-foot buildings with three rows of bunks in each one, making it very cramped.

Officers push us even harder while at Camp Shanks, in not so obvious ways. To motivate us, our company commander, Capt. Charles Zimmer, tells us, "Men, work hard and train well, and you all can have passes out of camp to see the big city." He has a big smirk on his face as he says it, which should have warned me that he might not be serious. But the idea of seeing New York sounds pretty good to me. I really want to see the tall buildings and the Statue of Liberty. I like Zimmer. The guys say he's a lot more tolerable than Lieutenant Evans, who was leading the company prior to my arrival in North Carolina.

We are divided into platoons and squads. I get to know most of the guys by their last names, and a few I know by their first names, such as Walter Burton from the mortar section, a friendly guy from Oregon. Everyone works hard and performs well, hoping for a chance to see the sights. But in spite of our efforts, the next thing we know we are restricted to camp and not allowed to leave.

Camp Shanks is my home for only about a week and my company's last stop in the United States before we ship out to Europe, which we have just learned is our destination. Visiting Europe is something I've dreamed about but never thought would happen. Towards the end of my stay at Camp Shanks, my squad is given another challenge by Captain Zimmer: "I don't want anyone in my company that can't sneak out of camp. If you're not man enough to get out, you ain't man enough to be in my company."

I look at the other guys, who look around at everyone else. Most of us want to see New York really badly. Sergeant Hanlon looks indifferent. My newfound buddy Walter Burton seems to want to get right at it, as I can detect a smirk on his face. I am still upset that we were denied passes to visit New York City, and the chance to see the city makes the idea of sneaking out very tempting. Anyone caught would be in some serious trouble, but a lot of my new buddies decide to sneak out anyway. Some of them get out, or should I say escape, right away, but others wait. Not sure of what to do about the challenge, I bounce different escape plans through my head. After several days of thinking things over, I finally decide that it is worth the risk. After all, this might be the only chance I will ever have to see New York City. All that I need now is a plan and the nerve to carry it out.

Later that day I see another unit marching out the front gate. When no one is looking, I step right into line with them and make it out and then step out of formation when I know no officer is looking at me. I'm sure some of the privates must have noticed, but no one says anything.

The sights and sounds and the people of New York are eye-opening to a small-town boy. Men wearing business suits race into tall buildings, and women dressed in fancy clothes are everywhere. Everyone talks fast with funny accents.

The smell of car and truck exhaust fills the air. Nobody seems to pay attention to anyone else, although occasionally a girl will smile at me, probably because I am in uniform. I have a little bit of money from my army pay, so I eat at an Italian restaurant where they are speaking Italian, or at least I think they are. I wonder if they are talking about the war. I don't stray very far into the city, because I don't want to get lost far away from camp. After walking around for a while, I go to see a movie at a fancy theater that is so big that all of Wayland could probably fit into it.

My day in New York City is delightful, but I now face a very serious problem: I have not worked out a plan to sneak back into camp. The sun is going down, and if I don't return soon, people will realize I am missing. Thoughts race through my mind as I try to come up with a plan. I make my way back toward the base just as the sun is setting, although the sunset is blocked by all the tall buildings. Unfortunately, I cannot think of a plan that seems good enough to work. Waiting until just after dark, I walk up to the guard on duty, hoping that he might be sympathetic.

"Halt!" the guard bellows, "What's your business?"

"Just need to get in," I respond politely.

"This base is restricted. No one gets in without clearance. I can't let just anyone in."

I am getting concerned. We talk for a while. Apparently he is a Red Sox fan.

"The Red Sox are a great team. Who's your favorite player?" I ask, trying to butter him up.

The guard still won't budge, so I do the only thing a proud young soldier can think of: I beg. "Can you please let me back in? I snuck out earlier on order from my captain. Please let me in."

The guard thinks about it for what seems like a long time. "Okay, private, but you better not leak a word of this to anyone or you won't be the only one in trouble. You understand?"

"Yes, sir! Thank you, sir!" I answer quickly. Sweat is running down my forehead and onto my brow.

My heart skips as I stroll through the gate. I feel as if a big load has been lifted off of me, and I also feel ten feet tall. When I get back to my barracks, I realize that a lot of the guys I live with snuck out that day as well, and most of them had not made reentry plans, either. Most of them get back in underneath a fence, and as a result their faces are covered with scratches, and their uniforms are a mess. I did it the easy way.

England

The last few days in Camp Shanks before we ship out to war are quiet. Any soldier lucky enough to have received a pass out of camp is promptly forbidden to leave base. No contact is to be made with family or friends. Soon the 101st Airborne will be leaving for England by ship. Stories of German submarines patrolling the waters off New York and England swirl among the guys.

German spies are known to be operating within the United States, so it is feared that they might learn the time of our scheduled departure and notify German submarines, which could then sink our ships, killing us before we even get into battle. German spies are said to have been caught within the United States and executed.[1] Naturally, this information is concerning to a lot of us. Being on an oceangoing vessel, like many things I have done while in the army, is an exciting first for me. The thought of a German U-boat firing a torpedo at my ship crosses my mind, but I try not to think about it too much as I busy myself getting ready to ship out. Packing isn't difficult, because I don't have much to take.

When the order to depart comes, we are loaded into army trucks and taken to the harbor. Ferries then take us out to the troopship. It is September 4, 1943.[2]

The *Samaria,* an old British cruise ship that has previously been used to carry passengers between Europe and the United States, is to be my home for the next week and a half. The ship is big, but not as big as some of the other troopships I see in the harbor. I can see soldiers walking up the gangway. Because the ship is going to be carrying many more soldiers than it was designed for, I know there will be very little privacy. In fact, we are packed in like sardines. Shortly after nine in the evening we leave New York with all lights out. My squad is assigned below the top deck; we are below the waterline. All on board are given strict orders to keep the portholes closed to hide light. German submarines have been spotted in the area, so secrecy is of utmost importance.

Back in 1921, when the 600-foot-long *Samaria* was built as a cruise ship, it could carry twenty-five hundred passengers and crew members.[3] Now the big boat is carrying four thousand troops and crew. Naturally, we troops find it concerning to be so overcrowded, but I don't think the army cares much at all. Hammocks are available to sleep on, but their constant swaying makes for seasickness. When I can, I try to sleep on a table, which isn't much better. Lots of men packed into such crowded space create odors that don't help my stomach, either. I need fresh air. I think about how awful it would be to be trapped in a sinking ship.

In the morning, when I go on deck, all I can see is the big expanse of the Atlantic Ocean and a long line of ships. Seeing all of the US Navy destroyers escorting us is both comforting and unsettling, because they provide a constant reminder that we are beyond the safety of the United States and are now in a war zone. I hear from a shipmate that we are part of the largest naval convoy of the war. We are already so far away from New York that no land is visible.

Early on in the voyage, I get massively hungry and decide I can wait no longer for food. I open up the mess kit provided just before leaving Camp Shanks. Looking into the can of fruit, I see little worms, so I don't eat. Later, kidney stew is prepared for us and I eat.

Troops are allowed only two meals a day while on board. Typically, for breakfast the crew serves stewed tomatoes and fish. The afternoon or evening meal consists of boiled potatoes. The food isn't very tasty, but we are hungry, so we eat. What keeps us from starving is the fresh bread the British cooks bake each day. When we are done eating, our plates are rinsed in the same can we use for garbage. After a while this practice changes when someone realizes that it is a good way to make us all sick.

Some guys in my company are awfully seasick the entire time it takes us to cross the ocean. When possible, some of us go above deck for fresh air, which helps lessen the seasickness, but frequent rainstorms force us back below, limiting the amount of time we can spend on deck. On the third day of our voyage, I ask my buddy Burton to join me in a card game. I am already bored out of my mind. Burton promptly throws up, indicating that the card game isn't going to happen. The smell of the vomit makes all of us sick to our stomachs, and several others soon follow Burton's lead.

The general dirty feeling that goes with the stink in the air is not helped by the fact that we are allowed only two saltwater baths per week. They don't make us feel very clean. The soap won't even make suds.

I spend a lot of time on deck, watching the destroyers. One day a siren goes off on a destroyer and it turns and heads away from us. In the distance it drops explosive depth charges. No one says much of anything about it.

After twelve days at sea—the day is September 16—we are all struck with excitement by our approach to the coast of England. I can't wait to be on land. Seeing the rolling green hills of the English countryside is even more exciting than seeing the mountains of Colorado for the first time, but I wish that I were seeing England under different circumstances.[4]

I stagger under the weight of all my bags as I step off the ramp and onto firm ground, which feels strange to walk on. I stumble a couple of times, anticipating the land to rock back and forth. I am surprised again by how different the people speak from those in Wayland. Some speak proper English, while others, mostly dockworkers, are very hard to understand because of their accents.

Marching the two miles to the train station is difficult on wobbly legs caused by the ocean voyage. It's a good thing we don't have to fight right away. Most of the guys around me are quiet; they are probably thinking and reflecting on what we've been through and what lies ahead.

Finally, we make it to the train station and board a train that will take us to our new base, Camp Ranikhet, near Reading, about forty miles from London. On the way, the train stops about ten miles out of London, where I witness my first bombing raid. It is nighttime, and everything is dark; all lights are off to keep German bombers from zeroing in on their targets. The only lights are the big floodlights that scan the sky and explosions. The muffled blasts and flashes of light seem surreal. I am glad the Germans can't see our train, but I feel bad for the people in the area that is being bombed. Occasionally, a British fighter flies overhead, hurting my ears with the deafening roar of its Merlin engine. A few German bombers are shot down, and some of them make loud screaming sounds as they spiral down. Others fly silently, trailing a long line of smoke. Momentarily, I think that maybe we should go home.

Early on in my stay in England I become close friends with Hank Proppe and Al "Boz" Borzymowski, both of Polish descent. Boz, from Milwaukee, is a very likeable little guy, all 120 pounds of him; he can't be more than five foot three and has blond hair. Although he is the youngest in the squad, born on September 1924, and has some sort of chest injury or birth defect, he is as tough as anyone and a very good soldier. We call him Boz, as no one can really pronounce Borzymowski. He likes to drink, but not too much. He quit school early to join the army. His dad has a grocery store that he talks about often—so much so that I remember the store address: 313th and Euclid in Milwaukee.[5]

Back home, Boz has a close friend from high school named Audrey. She isn't Boz's girlfriend, as she already has a boyfriend. She writes letters to Boz, Proppe, and me. The letters are fun to read, and she writes on and on as if we are old friends.

Proppe, from Fulton, New York, is about six feet tall, 175 pounds, handsome and winsome. He often has a smile on his face. He has his serious moments, but just like Boz, Proppe likes to have fun and tease. Proppe enlisted while working in a chocolate factory. While in England, from time to time he disappears for several days to work with and learn about the British. "Rich, it's pretty funny," he says, smiling. "I walk into a room as a private, and the Brits all stand at attention, like I'm famous or something."

The three of us are inseparable. Hank and Boz are a lot different from me, but we get along well. Boz bunks right beside me in the barracks, and Proppe is not much further away. Talk, talk, talk, boy they can talk, although Boz sometimes has a quiet side about him. The Polish duo never miss Catholic Mass on Sunday, which the army offers before the Protestant service. When they come back from Mass, they make sure I am up and on my way to the Protestant service. "Okay, Rich, up and at it. Sunday is for church," they chide, prodding me incessantly.

"Let me be," I grumble, rolling over in my bunk.

"We've already been to church. Now it's your turn." They are persistent.

"Come on, leave me alone!" I say, somewhat annoyed.

"No, it's time to get up, get going," they insist in their heavy accents.

Boz and Proppe will pull and shake me as they try to get me out of my bunk. If I still refuse to wake up, they will usually just pull me right out of my bed. This Sunday ritual becomes a game with us, and the three of us soon become very close.

Soon after meeting Proppe and Boz, I meet another person who quickly develops into a close friend and has a big impact on my life: Chaplain Gordon Cosby. On September 20, 1943, he talks with me about what it means to have a personal relationship with God. I don't really understand what such a relationship might be, but I know I will need God's help to cope with whatever lies ahead in the coming months.

Chaplain Cosby is one of the finest men I have ever met. He can converse at length on just about any subject. With Cosby, there is no doubt about his commitment to God. He also is very persuasive; his charismatic

Henry Proppe. Courtesy Joe Proppe collection.

personality and message win the hearts of many soldiers, a pretty tough group to win over. A Baptist by training, he makes faith in God relevant to anyone, regardless of denomination or background.

The company medic, Henry Scherrer, is also serious about his faith. Scherrer has an English girlfriend whom he adores. He doesn't participate in the carousing with other soldiers. He wears his faith quietly. The medic has to be the nicest guy in the whole company.

Chaplain Cosby holding a service. From *The Epic of the 101st Airborne: A Pictorial Biography of the United States 101st Airborne Division,* courtesy Weider History Group, 2006.

Life quickly settles into a routine in England. Training consists mostly of war game after war game. The basic stuff is over. Our days are filled with fifteen-mile hikes and mock battles. The army tries to make things as much like real war as they possibly can, but there are stringent rules to the games—lots of rules that both help and hurt in the effort to make things real.

I have more opportunities to learn to fire the bazooka. Launching the rocket is exciting, but I also hate it, because the army still hasn't solved the problem with the hot exhaust, which burns my arms and face, much like welding without protective clothing. Captain Zimmer watches our live firing and afterwards says, referring to the skin damage done by the rocket, "You guys are a mess. You look awful! We'll get something done about it." The bazooka training also requires me to identify US, British, and German tanks quickly, so I have to study a lot of pictures.

Louis Simpson and I become pretty good friends, but we are complete opposites. He loves writing and spends a lot of his free time writing letters or poems about his thoughts. He is dark and handsome, with a winning smile that makes him very popular with the British girls, who love his poetry. He is also a British citizen, as his father is Scottish. His mother is Russian, and he grew up in Jamaica. Louis is a good soldier and someone I can trust. He seems smarter than anyone in the army and knows it, but he's not arrogant about it.

When we aren't training we have good times as buddies. To pass my free time, I play a lot of basketball, although I'm not particularly good at it. After one pick-up game, Tom Niland, a lieutenant from battalion headquarters whom I think is a pretty good guy, comes up to me.

"Rich, I'd like to talk to you," he says.

"Yes, sir!"

"I've been watching you play ball. I'm putting together a team from 2nd Battalion for the divisional basketball tournament. I'd like you to play for us."

"There are plenty of good basketball players for sure better than me," I protest.

"I've been watching you for a while," he goes on. "You're a team player. That's what I'm looking for."

With that I am on the basketball team, and we go on to win the whole tournament. I quickly find out that the short and stocky but fast Niland is a heck of a ball player. No one can stop him. He says he learned to play with his numerous brothers and cousins in Tonawanda, New York.

Niland and I strike up as good a friendship as an officer and a regular soldier can have without getting into trouble. He is three or so years older, but we like doing the same things, except he is much better than I am at sports. We probably shouldn't have become friends, but since he isn't directly my superior, he doesn't seem to care. Niland is involved in intelligence and trains me in several things involving intelligence gathering, such as sighting azimuth (using calculations of artillery trajectories to determine the distance of enemy gun locations), looking for signs of enemy activity, and enemy interrogation techniques.

Once, Niland involves my squad in a mock battle. Our objective is to take out a fake antitank gun in a concrete pillbox. The target is surrounded by a moat about eight feet wide and about eight feet deep. There is a footbridge we might have used to cross the moat, but the referee says it is "blown," meaning that we have to find another way to the other side. I try to ford the moat with seventy-five pounds of equipment on my back, but I am not confident in my ability to swim, never having been taught, and I soon find that I swim like a rock. Quickly the water is over my head. At

Lt. Tom Niland and his brother Joe. Courtesy Thomas Niland collection.

Lt. Tom Niland at his desk. Courtesy Thomas Niland collection.

first I panic, thinking I am going to drown. My lungs burn as I try to hold my breath. I try to stay calm, knowing that panicking almost certainly will result in death. I crawl on the bottom of the moat, trying to keep a cool head. "I have not gone through all my training back in the States to die at the bottom of an English moat," I think to myself. Finally, I feel the moat bottom begin to angle upward. Figuring I must be close to shore, I try to stand up again, which is hard to do with heavy equipment on, especially since the struggle has been so exhausting. Thankfully, I soon find my head above water, and I reach the shore, utterly spent and gasping for air, my heart pounding. I soon notice that I am on the same side of the moat that I started on; I must have gotten turned around while on the bottom. I decide then and there that there is no chance I am going to risk drowning again by reattempting to cross the moat, so I stand up, sway around a bit, and then proceed to slosh my way toward the "blown" bridge, which seems perfectly good to me.

"Hey, you can't do that, soldier." The war judge is laughing hard at me for crossing a blown bridge. "Hey private, you can't do that! You're violating the rules!"

"What difference does it make? I've already drowned," I smart back.

Still out of breath from my near-death experience, I trudge on across the "blown" bridge, water trailing from my clothes and gear with each step. The judge is still laughing. This makes me angry, but I bite my lip and continue on as a "drowned" soldier.

Mail from home brings delight to the troops, including myself. Mom writes to me about once a week. I try to keep up on my writing using the half sheet of mail paper the army provides us each week.

"Why haven't you written?" Mom writes in a scolding letter after receiving no letter from me in over two weeks. I have been too busy to write. I wonder why she is so upset, because I have not received anything from home in some time, either. After doing some checking, I discover that my mail is being sent to another Pvt. Donald Rich. I hope he has enjoyed the letters. Not all guys get mail from home; I am one of the lucky ones. Current news from the States is even harder to come by.

I first meet a local Englishman, Bill Hollingsworth, at a pub near the camp. Playing darts is a favorite activity at the pub for young soldiers wanting to stay out of trouble while passing the time, and somehow or other I get locked into a dart game with Bill. I'm not very good at it; Bill makes us young guys look pretty silly. I probably should stay away from the pub—I'm sure Mom would not approve—but I am on my own now, and I am old

The Hollingsworth family

enough to be served alcohol in England. Occasionally I have a bitter, which is basically warm beer. I think the bitter definitely lives up to its name, and I really don't care for the taste. Refrigerators are nowhere to be found in England, so naturally everything is served warm.

Boz, Proppe, and I are soon invited to Bill's home, where we meet his family. Their thatch-roofed brick house is in Reading, just a few blocks from the pub. Gas heaters in the fireplaces generate heat to keep the family warm, because it is winter. To get heat, a coin is put in the machine, just like a pop machine; the gas company collects the coins periodically.

Within a few weeks of our first visit, Proppe, Boz, and I adopt the Hollingsworths—or I guess I could just as easily say that the Hollingsworths adopt us. We visit Bill, his wife, Josephine, and their two children as often as we can. Their twelve-year-old son, Jimmy, and ten-year-old daughter, Josie, are delights. We immensely enjoy the family's company, which helps ease our homesickness.

The Hollingsworths don't have much in the way of material things. Fresh food of any kind is a rare luxury for anyone in England because of war rationing. Occasionally I get an orange from the mess hall and give it to the kids, who really enjoy the fruit. Like most English kids, they are always bumming gum from American soldiers. My K ration biscuits aren't much to eat, so I feed the biscuits to their chickens, and in return the family gives me an egg.

Bill once was a soldier in the British army, having served in India, and retired a corporal. He wants to fight for his country now, but in his upper fifties he is considered too old for service and is instead serving in the home guard. He also works odd jobs for a little bit of pay, but Josephine does not work outside the home. These are uncertain days for all of Britain and of course for families. Unlike the situation in United States, so distant from the war, the war is very real to British families. Air raids and intense rationing regularly disrupt life. Bill smokes to help relieve the anxiety caused by the uncertainties of the war. Neither he nor Josephine smokes heavily, but the habit is probably limited by the lack of money. As a nonsmoker, I give my ration of cigarettes to them.

Josephine, who is much younger than her husband, is somewhat plain, but her friendly personality makes her attractive. Her heavy accent is difficult for me to understand at times. She cleans and presses our uniforms with a rag. On occasion I can get her to take some money for the work, but Bill doesn't approve of that. The family travels about either by bicycle or bus.

Jimmy, Josie, and some other kids come to camp at chow time to get a bite to eat. For us soldiers it is like taking care of younger siblings, and this time is enjoyed by kids and soldiers alike. The group of children coming to eat at camp grows. Most of them probably haven't had fresh fruit in more than four years. After a while, though, the army brass finds out about the chow sharing and puts a stop to it, but for a while the innocence of the kids has made life away from home more meaningful.

After I am in England for several months, I am lucky enough to obtain a weekend pass. Even though I am excited to get the pass, there is only one, which means that I can't do anything with my buddies. The thought crosses my mind to spend the time seeing London with the Hollingsworth family. I approach Bill enthusiastically, although I think he will decline the offer.

"Hey Bill, you and the family, come with me to London. You can show me around."

"We're pretty tired, Don," Josephine responds. "We just got back home from being away last weekend."

"Bill, come to the kitchen, I have something to show you," I say. In the kitchen I pull out some pound notes—enough to pay for the weekend. "Can we go now?" I ask.

"I don't think so, we're awfully tired," Bill answers, but I see the reluctant interest in his face, so I hold the money out in the open and wait, using an old sales technique I picked up somewhere. After a few interesting facial expressions, Bill finally agrees, "Okay, that will get us there and back, I guess. I need to visit my sister, anyway."

Early in the morning the Hollingsworths and I board the train for London. First, we go to his sister's house, located in a heavily bombed section of the city. Bomb damage to the buildings makes it difficult to guess how wealthy the neighborhood was before, but I think most people are lower middle class.

Bill's sister's home has been damaged. One upstairs wall is pulled away from the flooring. Outside, two big wooden poles are propped against the front of the house in an attempt to keep the wall from falling down. Surveying the damage, I come to the conclusion that a fairly small German bomb would probably bring the structure tumbling down.

Inside, I meet the family, who are all very polite. Then a pretty young woman enters the room. Like many British women, she is dressed very plainly, but her physical appearance is anything but plain. She stands about five feet, five inches tall and has dark hair. She is introduced to me as Betty.

Later, when I am with Bill in a room away from the others, I chide him: "You didn't tell me about her!"

"About whom?" he gives it back to me.

"Betty," I answer. "Why didn't you say anything about Betty?"

"Oh, Betty," Bill says, adding, "Hold on Don, she's already taken."

"'Already taken,' what do you mean?"

"She's engaged," Bill explains.

I ask Bill more about his niece Betty, and he tells me she is engaged to an English soldier serving in Africa. Disappointed, and knowing that a relationship cannot go anywhere, I still think it would be fun to develop a friendship with her.

When the chance comes, I ask Bill's sister if it will be all right to take her daughter to a movie. Betty's mom frowns and glances over at Bill. She and Bill talk it over quietly. Bill must have given me a good endorsement, because I hear the mother say: "I guess there'd be no harm."

Betty and I leave for the theater. She is a little uncomfortable with the situation, but talking with her is easy. She asks about life in America. I don't ask about her boyfriend.

After the movie, we walk about Hyde Park. She seems too innocent to be alone in a park with an American soldier she doesn't know.

When we are ready to head back to Betty's home, the hour is too late to take the bus, so I get a taxi for us. This is my first ride in a taxi. When we get back, the adults are still up. "Goodnight," I say to the group, while looking at Betty. She picks up on the hint and walks with me upstairs to the room I am sleeping in. As we approach the door, Betty looks up at me.

"I don't believe the stories about American soldiers anymore," she says quietly. "You've been a perfect gentleman."

As I start to turn to go into the room, Betty gives me a kiss. It is a sweet kiss, and my head swims from the surprise of it. With that I turn away from her, enter the room, and close the door. I go to sleep hoping her boyfriend makes it back home okay. He is a lucky guy.

The next day, I go to the market and buy Bill's sister's family some grapes. The price seems high, but it is a good way to say thanks for their hospitality. They haven't tasted grapes since 1939. The Hollingsworths and I leave for their home in Reading the next morning.

Proppe, Boz, and I are invited to spend Christmas Day of 1943 with the Hollingsworths. We deliberately come late so that the family would already have eaten their fill of Christmas dinner. We also fill up on our turkey meal at camp so as not to eat too much of the family's food. To us they seem quite poor, and we don't want them to spend so much on us. The three of us have bought candy for the kids at the PX (post exchange).

Homesickness hits me hard during the holidays, even though I am having a great time. I wonder what Mom, Dad, and Albert are doing, and soon I am reminiscing about Christmas when I was a kid. At Christmastime my parents would take me for a car ride so Santa Claus could come to our home while we were gone. Like the Hollingsworths, Mom and Dad didn't have much, but Christmas had been a fun time, leaving lots of good memories.

"Don, are you going to play? Will you play cards with me?" Jimmy Hollingsworth interrupts my thoughts. Jimmy's insistence on playing a card game brings me back to my life in England. The kids really enjoy attention from the soldiers, and Jimmy's smile is hard to resist.

Josephine tries her best to make us feel at home. She even kills one of their chickens for our meal. The three of us feel spoiled when we are also served pork chops. Meat is such a luxury that it will likely be six months or more before the family will be able to eat meat again. Josephine serves a delicious Yorkshire pudding as well, and she brings out a pineapple she has been saving since 1939. She uses it all up: meat, pineapple, and everything else. Completely full, the three of us are very grateful; so much for our not wanting to impose on the Hollingsworths' generosity. To feed three

American soldiers is obviously a financial hardship on the family. Food is scarce and expensive, yet they share with us. I never do hear the Hollingsworths complain about anything that life is dealing them.

I write Mom and Dad about how the Hollingsworths are taking care of me and how it is a hardship because they have so little themselves. My brother tells me later that Mom and Dad send the Hollingsworths care packages to help them make ends meet. That is a nice thing to do, as Mom and Dad also have very little for themselves.

Because we are young and energetic, food and entertainment are important to us soldiers. We are anxious to get off base whenever passes are available. If we have a place to stay for the night, London is our favorite destination. To get an off-base pass, we have to have a place to stay, or we can't go. Unfortunately, the Red Cross is usually the only place that we can stay, and their facilities are often full, so most of the time we are stuck on base. My buddies and I are angered that the army won't let us leave without having somewhere specific to go, but young men with no place to sleep can lead to trouble, so the army won't let us leave.

Boz and another Polish American buddy, Ed Spikula (a member of my squad), have an advantage. They are members of London's Polish Club, which has rooms only for soldiers of Polish descent. I am a Pole for several nights when Ed lets me use his membership. Off I go with Boz to the London Polish Club, where I become Ed Spikula for three days.

I am keenly aware of always being hungry, and off base I have no choice other than eating in the local English restaurants. But with the war going on, there don't seem to be a lot of sanitation standards at the restaurants, and good quality food is hard to find. I desperately want a good meal with meat. I can think of nothing else, although I know meat is hard to come by. After entering several restaurants and pubs, looking for my ideal meal, I finally find one that seems good to me. The place looks clean enough and smells pretty good, too. The hunger pains are growing. As I sit down to read the menu, I hope to find something to satisfy my desperate need, but I soon discover I am not able to order off this outdated menu because of war shortages. I stand up and walk to the counter.

"What do you have?" I ask. "Anything with meat?" The waitress points to a pot on the stove. It smells good.

"What is it?" I ask.

"Rabbit stew," she replies tartly.

"Anything else?" I ask, already knowing the answer.

"No."

I am so hungry I think I could eat a horse. Surely I can handle a little rabbit.

"I'll try some," I say.

I eat one serving. The rabbit stew isn't very good.

The real problem comes several hours later during the night, when I begin to feel sick to my stomach. Soon I feel absolutely horrible. Moaning and groaning, I make it through the night until early morning. Waking up, Boz notices I'm not quite right.

"What's wrong with you?" he asks.

"I need a bathroom, fast!" I say, trying to hold everything in.

Bolting out of bed, I run out of the Polish dormitory. I have a terrible time finding a bathroom. Finally, I storm into the closest one I can find. Boz, trailing behind, knows the place quite well. When I emerge from the bathroom, he is laughing hysterically.

"Glad you found the nice British ladies' bathroom," he blurts, gasping for air because he is laughing so hard.

"Wouldn't have mattered anyway, as any ladies would have had to get out of my way," I respond. I feel dizzy and weak in my legs. Boz gets a good laugh, and I don't try rabbit stew again.

When we get back to the barracks, guys are talking about the bombing in London. They know we've had passes and are glad to see us back. The Red Cross has been hit in a German bombing raid, they say. We don't know if anyone is hurt. I decide it was a good time to be Polish.

After the rabbit incident, I am more inclined to stay on base. Friendships are solidifying in the barrack as we get to know each other better. In my barrack we have two whole platoons, and two of the guys are twin brothers Dominic and Lawrence Gentile, nice-looking guys with dark skin and hair. They are inseparable but always fighting with each other; it seems they can find almost anything to fight over. Sometimes the rest of us think about breaking up their fights, but since we don't know which one has started it or even which is which, anyone who dares to be the mediator likely will have to fight the two of them together. We decide there is no reason to get wounded before we get to the real enemy. They'll either work it out or kill each other.

Sgt. Joe Slish of 2nd Squad, 2nd Platoon bunks across from me in the barrack. Joe is very outgoing and quite polite. Most noticeable about Joe is his physique. He is a body-builder and a real physical specimen, standing over six feet tall. He isn't someone to mess with in the barracks or on the battlefield. It seems he could lick the whole German army by himself. I think staying close to Joe during battle will be a good thing to do.

Denis Parsons, a tall, lanky guy of six three with blond hair and a bit older than me, is also a good buddy. Denis's parents emigrated from England to Ross, California, in the northern San Francisco Bay area. His dad is a fireman, and Denis loves to tell stories of his dad's firefighting. Denis is a high school tennis legend back home. He was working as a manager for Blumenfeld Theatres when he was drafted. Denis's girlfriend, Erma, is also a big part of his conversations.

I also become friends with a couple of the machine gunners, Harry Green and Sgt. Lloyd Gross. Lloyd is a very friendly guy from Little Falls, Minnesota. He is good at both basketball and baseball, and he plays anytime he can. He also carves beautiful things from wood. He joined the army several years before and has been with the regiment since Mississippi. Lloyd treats the men like friends, and they respect him. He is fluent in German and spends time telling us about his sweetheart, Laura, and his nephews. His brother's boys gave him a knife as a going-away present, and he cherishes it.[6]

We have to function as a team to be a formidable enemy to our enemy, and all of us have our position on the team. The level of our platoon's overall teamwork gets better the more we practice, and I figure Hitler doesn't have much of a chance against us. One of the flaws of the team is that Lt. Frank Hibbard can't read a map. Second Platoon's staff sergeant, Manuel Hidalgo, who grew up in Spain and speaks accented English, has no problem reminding him: "You sum bitch don't even understands how to read a damn map."

"Stop talking to me like that!" Hibbard responds.

"You sum bitch, you knows I'm right, dammit!" Hidalgo keeps up the criticism, half serious and half joking. Hidalgo knows his stuff and Hibbard knows it. Hidalgo also seems to know how far he can push it.

I am confident in my soldiering abilities and don't mind showing them off. I'm not intimidated by rank. I must have developed this attitude in high school.

Back in Wayland we had two team sports in which we could participate, basketball and baseball. I wanted to do both, but Mom and Dad made me choose one. At first I decided on basketball, but I found that I, along with a couple of friends, Bill and Dale, made pretty good benchwarmers. My high school basketball coach, Mr. Gingerich, was a small guy, and as teenagers we thought we were smarter than he. Sometimes I think he gave us lower grades in English and religion class because of our challenging attitudes. Bill

Denis Parsons at Camp Roberts. Courtesy Denis Parsons collection, 101st Airborne Division Belgian Friendly Association.

Denis Parsons (kneeling, r.) and Lloyd Gross (far r.), who was fluent in German. Courtesy Denis Parsons collection, 101st Airborne Division Belgian Friendly Association.

A machine gun squad of G Company. Courtesy Denis Parsons collection, 101st Airborne Division Belgian Friendly Association.

and I were often in his face, arguing about grades or something, and sometimes the arguments were about his Mennonite position on not fighting in the army. Coach would only put Bill and me in a basketball game with a minute remaining if the score was pretty much settled. At one game, Bill and I left for the locker room as the clock was winding down so he couldn't put us in late. Still, Coach was a nice guy. Maybe he was too nice. Once I walked in on Bill shaking his finger in Coach Gingerich's face about a grade on an English paper. I felt a little bad about it, but I had a lot of confidence in my ability, so I figured Bill must have been right as well. I was a nice kid but maybe didn't have enough respect for my superiors. Now in the army, I still have a disrespectful attitude toward some officers.

My army pals are becoming good friends, just like the guys back home. Being together at work and play strengthens our friendships and teamwork. The idea of going into battle together is a good thought. The thought that some might not make it out of combat is a momentary worry, but I don't dwell on it.

Our training becomes much more serious toward the end of 1943. The glider riders learn how to attack enemy pillboxes properly, and we have to make numerous fifteen-mile marches loaded with all seventy-five pounds of gear. Tensions within the company grow, and fights occur between soldiers under the influence of alcohol. To break the tension, whenever we have enough time, Proppe, Boz, and I continue to visit the Hollingsworths or go to the local pub to throw darts.

Boz is put up for promotion to sergeant, and he is pretty excited. I stay behind, but he goes out with the guys to a bar. There are African American soldiers in the bar, something that never would have occurred back in the States. One of them says something about how he is going to date a sister of one of the white guys when he gets back to the States. A brawl breaks out between the outnumbered black troops and the white glidermen. The glidermen pick up the mouthy black soldier and drag him up and down the bar, knocking over beer bottles and wine glasses. Boz's promotion never goes through, as he is identified as being involved in the fight. Boz never before or after says or does anything indicating that he doesn't like black soldiers. Like me, he's never been exposed to them much.[7]

Instead of fighting, guys in G Company take to playing football without protective gear. Captain Zimmer joins us. Some of us give him some pretty good hits, and he doesn't seem to care, but you can expect a pretty good shot back from him. His hits really hurt, as he is so muscular, but he still seems like a regular guy. The football games are stopped after a couple of broken legs.

The army schedules a regimental rifle shooting contest for us, with the winner to receive twenty-five dollars. I think I can win, as I'm always the most accurate in my training groups. We compete in groups, and the winner advances on to the next round. An officer counts down, and we have a short amount of time to fire a whole clip of eight rounds at a target moving up and down, three hundred yards away. I win my "battles" round after round, and eventually I'm in the final round against a soldier I do not know.

However, a new officer is in charge, and he doesn't count down as the previous officer did. The other contestant starts shooting, getting off several rounds before I can start, and I lose by one shot.

"Why didn't you count down?" I ask, but I get no reply. I'm not very happy.

As a bazooka man, I am issued an M1 carbine as my personal firearm. It is about a third lighter than the M1 Garand, making my overall load easier to carry. The carbine seems to me to be more like a peashooter than a deadly weapon, but I can fire off shots with it as rapidly as with a Garand. I'm not sure the Germans will be very afraid of it, though.

Training also includes working with explosives, which isn't always a good thing to have in the hands of a bunch of young men. One day we are being trained to remove a tree with explosives. An explosives expert is showing us how to attach a detonator to a two- by two-inch block of plastic explosive. The contraption is to be fastened to a tree, and triggered by a detonator, but for the demonstration the instructor is wiring the device on a table. The squad gathers around close. The "expert" hasn't yet attached the detonator to the explosive, but I don't like the way he is handling the detonator during the demonstration. I back away from the table, sensing danger. Blam! The detonator goes off while the guys are close. Blood and smoke go everywhere. Most, but not me, are bleeding rather profusely, and several are on the ground. I am unhurt except that my ears are ringing.

Captain Zimmer, hearing the commotion, comes over and says, "You guys are a bloody mess. Now I've lost a whole damn squad, and we aren't even fighting Germans yet!" Most of us recover in a few days. For me, the only damage is the ringing in my ears. The "expert," though, having lost an eye, is shipped back home.

Captain Zimmer notices I have a keen sense for properly identifying enemy tank types and volunteers me to be trained to identify German aircraft as well. No one else from the company attends the training.

"What's that?" the captain asks during a flyover. The plane is moving so fast overhead that I really can't see it.

"Spitfire, sir!" I shoot back instantly. I can tell by the engine's roar.

During the spring of 1944 all correspondence home stops. The army is trying to keep things secret because the invasion of Nazi-controlled Europe is right around the corner. The success of the invasion will require surprise, and the army is making sure that no soldier gives hints, even by accident. Even before the mail stoppage, we aren't allowed to give any important information, including anything in the letter that might reveal a home address.

The army goes through everything we write. I'm not exactly sure how the letters make it home, but they usually do. We can't even keep address books of relatives. Letters take four or five days to get home.

In Exercise Beaver, from March 27 to 31 of 1944 the division begins to prepare for the invasion of France.[8] The 327th is practicing an attack on the French coast using British Horsa gliders, which are much bigger than the American Wacos. The army tries to make the training as realistic as possible. I think we are using the Brit gliders to get as many of us trained while using the minimum of aircraft and fuel: two whole squads can fit inside the British gliders. The takeoff isn't much different than in a Waco, but once airborne there is an immediate noticeable difference. The Horsa seems like a giant bathtub being pulled through the air, whereas the Waco is much more responsive to pilot maneuvers, and in it I can feel the turbulence more. The British glider is towed by a thick hemp rope rather than the thin nylon cord the American gliders use.

Before takeoff we all hope the British glider pilots are better than the American pilots seem to be, or so we joke. We really don't know. From what we hear, most of the American glider pilots are officers who didn't pass the Army Air Corps flight school for one reason or another. Still, the American glider pilots we get to know are great guys, and most of them seem like someone you'd want to have with you in combat.

I really try not to dwell on the danger, even though it is right in front of me as I gaze out the front window. Because most of the training is over the English Channel, there aren't a lot of options in case of an emergency.

Being in a glider can be unsettling to one's stomach. During Beaver I make the mistake of eating cheese from a can just before the flight: I really like cheese. Soon the big Horsa is rolling back and forth and back and forth as we fly out over the English Channel. We've been airborne only a few minutes when the vomiting chorus begins. One after another the soldiers in the two squads begin to vomit into their helmets. A few of the guys are really retching horribly. So far, my stomach is doing fairly well compared to the others.' But as the vomiting continues and as the glider continues to roll back and forth, back and forth, back and forth, my head begins to feel funny. Vomit begins to run along the floor, and the whole airplane starts to reek. Then nausea hits me really hard, all of a sudden. Grabbing my helmet, I place it in front of my face, hiding my eyes a bit as I fight off the urge to throw up. Then up it comes, cheese splashing into my helmet, onto me, and onto the floor. The heaving doesn't stop until my stomach is totally clear. My head still feels funny, and even though the temperature in the glider is cool, I sweat profusely. I continue with dry heaves for quite a while, then when done I pass my helmet toward the back for emptying into the glider's bucket.

Leaning back, I try to ignore the terrible smells in the glider's cabin. Someone opens the door to dump a bucket filled with vomit. The fresh air feels good, but the smell is still there. My head is swimming. Soon some of the guys are standing at the open door, relieving themselves.

Hoping the ordeal will be over soon, I glance out the window and see land. The tall cliffs don't look much like those of England. We are close to the French coast and therefore close to the enemy. My head continues to hurt, and some of us are still heaving from time to time without bringing anything up. We are being escorted by an assortment of aircraft, mostly British, judging by the wing insignia. A British bomber with a short wingspan separates itself from the formation ahead of us off to the right. It looks so awkward that I don't understand how it could even be flying.

"Brace yourself, Yanks," the glider pilot yells. "You're in for a bit of a show!"

With that, the tail gunner on the bomber opens up with a machine gun, firing right over our glider. The tracers from the machine gun glow as they scream overhead. This is live-action training. As the gunner in the bomber sprays his bullets too close for comfort, I think to myself how terrible it would be to get killed before I have the chance actually to fight the Germans. A few more guys throw up. After several minutes the firing stops, and we head back to the English coast, rolling back and forth all the way. The landing is pretty smooth. After this training, I am never happier to be back on land in my life.

Bazooka training also takes a more serious tone. A framed bedsheet is towed twenty-five feet behind a truck. We are supposed to hit the sheet from seventy-five yards. I know I can hit it, but I wondered how safe the truck drivers are from some of the other bazooka men. The seriousness of the training makes it clear to us that the time for the real thing is fast approaching, and I begin to think a lot about the meaning of life. I know that very trying days are ahead of me. I am terrified at the thought of real combat.

During the spring of 1944 we pack into an old gymnasium in Reading to listen to Chaplain Cosby speak, and when he invites those who want to accept Jesus as their personal savior to stand, I stand. Attending church as a boy, I had many questions about God but never had gotten them answered. The chaplain seems to know God personally and has answers. I know right then and there that I want the same confidence in God that he has.

I am impressed with Gordon's personality and confidence, and I want the inner peace that he has. I don't understand much about faith, but my heart is ready. In my limited understanding before being introduced to Jesus, I believe that being a Christian is about being good. Do not smoke, do not drink, do not whatever. Now I decide to do my best to live my life for God. No doubt the approaching invasion has an impact on my decision, as I know heaven and hell are real places, and I want to be in heaven if I die in the war. I give my life to Jesus. Others stand as well. Knowing what is ahead, with the real possibility of death, makes the decision easier on a lot of us. I make a promise to God: "Lord, if you help me make it through the war, I'll serve you when I get back home. I'll do whatever it takes to make the world a better place."

Continued visits with the Hollingsworths also help to soothe the loneliness I feel from being so far from home. Some of the questions I ponder the most are: Do Mom and Dad think of me as often as I think of them? Will I survive to have a family? What will the world be like if Hitler succeeds? This last question really hits me, because I realize that this is why we are here in England: we are trying to help shape the world for the better by making sure that the world is rid of Hitler.

The order to assemble passes down through the ranks. Dignitaries are here, big dignitaries. This means the time for the invasion is fast approaching. General Eisenhower and Prime Minister Churchill come to speak to us. We gather to listen to them.

Churchill is quite a sight with his funny hat, cane, and serious face. He is still hoping to join the troops in the attack, something that does not go over very well with the British generals. General Ike is more polished, and it hits me pretty hard when he says that over half of us probably won't make it back to base. As he speaks, I glance at the guy to my right and then the one to my left. As I ponder the general's words, I say to myself, "I guess they're not going to make it, the poor guys, because I know I am." The soldiers are somber and serious. Still, we are quietly pumped up and ready to go.

After speaking, Churchill and Ike make their way toward our position. They stop at the machine gun section, where Churchill speaks to Lloyd Gross: "Son, what is your position of duty with this company?"

Lloyd, not hesitating, answers, "Light machine guns, sir!"

"Very good, young man!" Churchill exclaims and nods. Ike has a slight grin on his face; he is trying to hide it.[9]

Shortly after Eisenhower and Churchill visit camp, we embark on a training mission that at the time seems to be entirely random and pointless.

Exercise Tiger occurs the last week in April.[10] The exercise is very confusing. The army loads us onto boats for a day of training. All we do is sit below deck while the ship goes out into the English Channel. The crew of the ship feeds us while we are out to sea for the day. The motion of the boats makes almost everyone seasick, especially after we eat. All we do is sit. We don't do any mock action, such as disembarking under fire. Maybe this is motion sickness training or something. I wonder what it's about, knowing there must be a reason for it, but all this army training sure makes me sick a lot.

Next up is Exercise Eagle, in which we practice attacking enemy positions.[11] We immediately can tell that this exercise is very serious, as its purpose is to train us to stave off an enemy counterattack on the beach. We will be operating behind enemy lines, trying to keep the German reinforcements from reaching the beaches. Then, abruptly, all the training ends. The time for liberating Europe from Hitler has arrived.

The Screaming Eagles, as the 101st Airborne Division is known, will be led into battle by Brig. Gen. Maxwell Taylor, a small-town boy from northern Missouri. Taylor was promoted to the position after Maj. Gen. William C. Lee suffered a heart attack in March. Taylor is military through and through, a graduate of West Point. Precision and image seem to be very important to him, as are blunt honesty and integrity. We hear that he actually parachuted in full uniform behind enemy lines in Italy to help the Italians prepare for an airborne assault on Rome.

Second in command of the Screaming Eagles is Brig. Gen. Don Pratt. Pratt is an older guy, maybe in his upper fifties. He has a blunt personality and seems to have a desire to jump into just about anything, maybe even head first without a parachute.

Col. George Wear leads the 327th Glider Infantry Regiment. The colonel is an older man. To me, he seems too old and set in his ways, and I have doubts about his ability to lead the regiment in combat. He seems like a stereotypical old soldier who would prefer to die in combat with his boots on, and I don't want to join him in doing so.

Also with us is Col. Joseph "Bud" Harper. Harper is not West Point; he joined through ROTC while attending an agricultural college.[12] I like Harper a lot. He seems fair and analytical, listening to what his men have to say and then making an informed decision. Harper has earned the nickname "Dig-them-deeper Bud" for his penchant for insisting that foxholes be dug deeper to save a man's life.

In the spring, command decides to reinforce the 327th. The 401st Glider Infantry Regiment is divided, and its 1st Battalion becomes our 3rd Battalion, while its 2nd Battalion is transferred to the 82nd Airborne Division. The commander of the 401st, Lt. Col. Ray C. Allen, stays on as commander of the 3rd Battalion.

In the days ahead of the invasion, Capt. Charles Zimmer is replaced as leader of the 327th's G Company when he is transferred to the 82nd Airborne. Regimental leadership thinks he is too close to the common soldiers. I am pretty steamed about it. Zimmer is very popular, and I like him like a friend. It seems the top division brass wants formal leaders like themselves, and Zimmer doesn't fit the mold; he is one of the guys.

First Lt. Hugh Evans is now the leader of the 149 men in G Company.[13] Evans is from Tennessee, and he seems arrogant and overly strict to me. The original guys in the company know him, as he led the company before I came in, and they seem to tolerate him more than like him. He is very military and serious, not friendly, and wants everything to be perfect, especially when higher-ups are around. This makes me and some of the others like him even less. Some of the guys seem to like him, though, especially Southerners and sergeants. I prefer Zimmer. I don't respect Evans and don't want him telling me what to do.

Second in command of G Company is 1st Lt. Frank Hibbard. I am concerned about Hibbard's heavy drinking, but when leadership is needed, he seems more than capable. I like him a lot; he seems to know what he is doing, except he has difficulty finding his way around during maneuvers. I am called up several times to help him figure out where we are.

Company G's first sergeant, Jewell Hayden, is a serious man but quite approachable, and he seems mature beyond his years. Hayden treats men with respect, if they deserve it. I can ask him for advice and expect a reasonable and fair response. I listen to him and do what he wants done.

Second Platoon, my platoon, is led by T.Sgt. Manuel Hidalgo. Hidalgo left Spain during the Spanish Civil War and settled in Beckley, West Virginia.[14] He seems quite capable, very military, and apparently is a very good soldier. We respect him very much, although, we can't understand everything he says because of his heavy Spanish accent. Every other one of his words is profane, and the swear words he pronounces very well. He tells funny stories, made even more so by his accent. He is a nice enough guy, but very tough, and not someone to mess with. I am impressed by the way he chews out the married men in the platoon who flirt with British girls.

One of the stories Hidalgo likes to tell is of Gen. Omar Bradley's mishap during the Louisiana Maneuvers near Camp Claiborne, Louisiana. Hidalgo was in charge of one station, a rope swing across a ditch, during obstacle

TSgt. Manuel Hidalgo. Courtesy Steve Hite collection.

Sergeant Hidalgo with his firearm. Courtesy Steve Hite collection.

course training. The men had to run, grab the rope, and then swing across the ditch. As an added incentive, the ditch was filled with sewage from the nearby latrines. For the most part all went as it should have. But as fate would have it, General Bradley arrived on the scene at Hidalgo's station just as a young soldier balked at making the swing. As Hidalgo berated the young troop to "get his ass across the ditch" or suffer the consequences, General Bradley inquired what the problem was. Hidalgo informed General Bradley that the soldier was afraid of swinging across the ditch. General Bradley, known by some as a soldier's general, talked to the lad and assured him he needed to conquer his fear. As an example, he offered to demonstrate the rope swing, asking the soldier to follow. The general took a quick run as he grabbed the rope, but it slipped through his hands midway across, and he landed closer to the far side of the ditch than the middle, but still in the ditch. Once he had climbed out of the ditch, General Bradley looked at the soldier and said, "Why don't you walk around, son." He then returned to his jeep for the trip to a much needed shower and change of clothes.[15]

Another good soldier in our company is Sgt. Carl Hanlon, leader of 1st Squad, 2nd Platoon, my squad. Not much for conversation, he is an effective leader of our tight-knit group. He is a bit shorter than me, but stocky. Nobody ever says a bad word about him. Hanlon's assistant is Sgt. Joe Slish, the bodybuilder.

Other G Company noncoms, such as Sgts. Edward Grapentine, James Mills, and Lloyd Gross, are good as well. They are approachable and offer good advice. Lts. Stanley Morrison and Tom Niland seem like ordinary guys with lots of personal confidence and calming personalities.

Welcome to France

THE ARMY FEEDS THE TROOPS LOTS OF FOOD; I MEAN *LOTS* OF FOOD. I feel like a hog being fattened for the slaughter. I also feel like I am eating my last meal. Maybe the army doesn't know when we will get another chance to eat well and wants us charged up. Regardless of the reason, we have plenty to eat, and the food isn't too bad, either, for army food.

On May 28, trucks are brought onto Camp Ranikhet to transport troops and smaller equipment to what is called Camp X-10. I think we are near Tottenham, north of London. The exact invasion date is still a secret, known only to the highest military brass. The next day, we move to Camp X-9, where Colonel Wear addresses us. We understand quite well the invasion time is near. On June 1 the company is split up between two camps referred to as X-7 and X-8.[1]

At this point it is apparent a big change in plans is in the works, for on June 2 we are trucked to the harbor at Brixham.[2] Questions and comments are flying.

"It looks to me like we're joining the navy," Boz says. "Wonder what's up?"

Rumors spread that the army doesn't have enough planes in place to get us to France. They have enough gliders, but not enough towplanes.

"The 327th is going in by boat," Hanlon finally reports.

To say the situation is a pretty big emotional letdown would be an understatement. We've trained so much and so hard for the glide into France. However, some of the guys take a different perspective: maybe there is a reason why we trained on the boats for what seemed like no good reason at the time.

"Sounds good to me," squad scout Frank Delarosa observes. "A big metal boat sounds a lot safer than swooping in on plywood and canvas."

"Why didn't the top guys give us some real training when we took our boat ride out in the Channel?" Mel Barton asks.

"What happens if we trip in the water?" I ask, remembering my experience of falling in the moat. I am nervous. There is some validity to my complaint. If an emergency occurs, we'll be loaded down with seventy-five pounds of gear, which will make it hard to swim.

A big sand pile is set up on a table, and officers use a model to show us what will happen. Soldiers will wade ashore after leaving the ship. Next, we will gather on the beach, and shortly after that we'll move inland and await instructions.

We are divided into two groups, based on which camp we are at. One group loads onto LCT 290. My squad spends the next several hours loading onto a smaller ship. Parts of the 4th Infantry Division are loading onto both ships as well. The ship in which we will be crossing the English Channel is called a landing craft, infantry, or LCI for short. "The ship looks like a water bug," Proppe says with a combination of seriousness and humor. LCIs are designed to deliver fighting infantry troops to a beach quickly and then pull back to get more soldiers, and they have a crew of about thirty sailors. To get us close to the beach, the LCI is designed with a flat bottom, which, according to the officers, means we will feel every wave as the ship gets closer to land. To get off the craft and into the water, we have to go down ramps on each side. It looks to me like it will be easy to trip and fall while getting off.[3]

"Keep your pills, you'll need them." I hear Slish suggest, speaking of anti-seasickness pills.

"Not this again!" soldiers moan, remembering our last excursion in a boat.

"Maybe we should go back to gliders!" The banter continues.

Company G's LCI isn't as small as I expected. The landing craft is about 160 feet long and 23 feet wide. We can move about some, but we have no amenities, no windows, no bathrooms (only buckets), and no seats (only hard benches). To me, the soldiers seem like a bunch of sardines being loaded into a can with a lid on top. But as a soldier, you do as you're told.

After finishing the loading of the LCI, we wait and wait for the ship to head out to sea. The air in the cramped vessel is stuffy, and I have some difficulty breathing. I wonder how close we'll get to shore before we are told to jump into the water. My near-drowning experience has strengthened my fear of water, but I can't dwell on that too much. We'll be under way soon. During the wait on board we continue to prepare down to the last detail for our part in the largest seaborne invasion in world history. Most of us are calm. We've trained and trained. Now we'll get the chance to prove ourselves in combat.

Almost the entire 327th is going to France by sea. Only HQ, antitank platoon soldiers, and a few officers are going to go in by glider. I guess this is because the brass do not want to sit in a cramped boat. The second in command of the division, General Pratt, is one of the high- ranking officers going in by glider. In order to ensure his safety, his glider is armored with heavy metal plates in the hope they will protect him from enemy fire.[4]

June 3 and 4 pass with a lot of waiting. After we are geared up and ready to go, Lieutenant Hibbard, who has been topside, comes to us, saying, "Relax, guys. No invasion tomorrow. We're not shipping out, at least not yet. The whole invasion is being postponed. Bad weather across the channel." I don't have strong feelings about the stand-down, although I am a little disappointed. Staying in the cramped boat makes me stir-crazy.

While waiting to leave the port area, most of us can't see what is going on outside, although we occasionally hear airplanes coming and going and ships sounding horns in the harbor. Our squad anxiously waits things out, sitting on a bench and mostly looking down, heavily into our thoughts. Frank Delarosa, who is of Mexican descent and a darned good scout, is packing and repacking his equipment. The little guy also takes the time to write a letter to his wife, who he seems to adore. Art Rutherford, in his upper twenties, looks older than his age. He is distant but occasionally talks to Gilbert Wallach, with whom he has a friendship. Both men are tall and seem especially cramped in the crowded space. Art seems arrogant, and he doesn't like taking orders, either. Gilbert is quiet by nature and doesn't say much back to Art.

Milford "Mel" Barton is of average size with a ruddy complexion, and he looks ready to go, with everything in its place. He has a determined look on his face. Barton is one heck of a soldier. Proppe and Boz joke quietly back and forth with me and Spikula. Spikula and Boz have built a friendship based partly on being Polish and partly on being the smallest guys in the squad. Sergeant Hanlon relaxes quietly, spread out on the floor, not seeming to have a care in the world.

Leonard Green is quietly to himself, although he is usually friendly. Art Price is always an outcast, and I don't think he is treated right by the guys, but I don't offer him friendship, either. He seemed to struggle during training and is physically and emotionally immature. I wonder about his real age. He has a hard time learning the ways of being a soldier and got restricted to KP duty a few times, once for handling weapons dangerously in training. Paul Thayer, a hillbilly who is constantly mixing it up, sometimes in fun and other times not so much in fun, pushes and shoves the guys some, but he isn't getting much of a response, so he stops. Delbert Pierce, a likeable private from headquarters, walks by. I hope he can tell me something about what is going on, but he can't. Different as we all are, we are a team.

The 501st, 502nd, and 506th Parachute Infantry Regiments are going to drop during the night, well behind the beaches, before the main invasion force lands at 0630. Success of the operation depends on securing the beaches so that men and supplies can be delivered to shore, so the paratroopers' goal will be to disrupt the enemy's ability to launch a counterattack on the beaches during the invasion. The role of the 327th will be to provide reserve in order to support the paratroopers as needed. Company G is scheduled to arrive during the day, when it is light out.

June 5, we sail from Brixham Harbor.[5] I've lost track of time below deck. We use buckets to relieve ourselves and then dump their contents overboard. Some more news comes in, but still overall there is very little real information. The invasion begins during the night, with paratroopers jumping into France right after midnight on June 6, 1944. While the paratroopers are dropping into Normandy, we are somewhere in the English Channel. We sleep as we can and talk a bit about home. Soldiers pass the time cleaning weapons, repacking equipment, playing card games, daydreaming, and talking. In the morning we can hear lots of commotion going on outside.

Finally, we are briefed. The only thing we really know so far is that the 101st is finding its mission behind the lines to be very difficult and that casualties have been heavier than expected. Some of the paratroopers accidentally have been dropped far away from the target area.

We are updated: Company G is to go into France late in the afternoon of June 6, in this old tub of a boat. The captain will maneuver the LCI as close to shore as possible and lower the ramps, and then we'll wade to shore carrying at least seventy-five pounds of gear. Am I nervous? By now I am beyond nervous. I am completely convinced I am going to drown. Regardless, the Screaming Eagles are a well-trained machine. We have a job, and we are going to get the job done, even if it is not according to plan. If part of my job means stepping off the boat into deep water loaded down with equipment and drowning, then that is what I am going to do.

Company G, 327th Glider Infantry Regiment, 101st Airborne Division, is now a part of one of the biggest events in history as we join thousands and thousands of Allied troops making our way to France. The battle for the freedom of Western Europe has begun. For some of the unfortunate early invaders, the journey has already ended as Allied casualties pile up on and behind the beaches of Normandy.

The flat-bottomed LCI goes up and down and side to side with each wave or change in current in the rough sea. Soon we are all seasick. Once again, buckets are passed around. For an hour and a half the landing craft heads east, then it takes a heading to the southeast for another couple of hours, maybe more. Ships are lined up like ducks on a pond, one after another, all going in the same direction on their way toward France.

Some guys who make it topside say they have never seen such a sight. The sky is filled with aircraft and balloons, which are supposed to keep German planes from getting too close. Allied fighter and bomber aircraft are making their way to mainland Europe. Other fighter planes are providing air cover for the transports. Surely Hitler knows by now we are coming in full force. The trip from England to our landing in France isn't all that far, maybe eighty miles or so.

Seasickness finally hits me hard about halfway across the English Channel. The sickening stench caused by others who have already lost their suppers is too much for me.

After crossing the channel, we have to wait our turn to head to the beach. Down below deck, I can't see what is going on at all. I never do get topside, and I have a strong desire to get out of this big tub and onto land, but I have little hope, because I know I will be drowning. I think about how hard it will be on my family when they get the news.

After another course adjustment, the ship heads almost due south for not more than an hour. Fresh air and a chance to stretch sounds like a good idea to me. I am feeling stir-crazy. Next comes a turn back to the southwest. Officers walking by tell us to get our gear ready. We really don't know what to expect and have no training for this type of assault. I wonder how close we can get to shore before the ship will hit bottom. Certainly we can't get very close in such a big ship. It is almost 1700 by now. Occasionally we can hear the roar of naval guns as we ready our gear. Shells scream in the distance. Whatever they are aiming at, the target can't be very close: we don't hear any explosions in the distance.

"Get ready, boys!" Slish barks.

"You heard him, get at it!" Sergeant Hanlon yells. With that order, our squad begins loading up. Putting everything in the right place takes a while in the cramped conditions. I keep thinking about the fact that each of us still has over seventy-five pounds of gear.

Sergeant Hanlon groups us together, and we line up for our turn up the stairs and to the topside of the ship. Moving slowly, we go out the door and onto the deck. My squad isn't in the front or the back. Even though the day isn't overly bright, the light outside is blinding, as we have been shielded from the sun for quite some time. In single file we make our way along the slick deck toward the water.

The rocking of the ship makes going down the ramp a little awkward, especially with all the weight on my back. Before I get to the bottom and fully into the water, I can see that the guys in the water are in pretty deep, some up to their necks. The time for my drowning has arrived. I wish I had learned to swim when I was a boy. I hope that I can keep my head above water. If I fall, I know it will be the end of me; no one carrying all that gear can possibly stand back up. And with all that gear it would be impossible to help someone else in trouble. The last steps seem kind of tricky for the guys ahead in the line as they battle the weight of equipment, weakness from seasickness, currents from the water, and the motion of the LCI.

Boz goes in ahead of me, and only part of his face shows above the water. Now it's my turn. No one says much of anything to me except for "watch your step." I glance toward the beach, which seems too far away, and step off into the water. Slosh, I am in, leaning forward, holding my carbine above my head to keep it dry. The force of stepping off and leaning forward propels me. I expected the water to be cold and am surprised that it is lukewarm. I have stepped off cleanly and am able, after a brief moment, to steady my feet on the rocky sand. My heart skips a couple of beats as the anticipation takes away my ability to breathe. My head is above water, but not by a lot. I make sure my first couple of steps are solid so that I do not fall. I also don't want to get pushed from behind by the next guy. Scared, I stumble a little.

Feeling like I am learning to walk all over again, I slowly lean forward. Doing otherwise is hard under all that weight. The seventy-five pounds include my bazooka, which is slung over my shoulder, three bazooka rockets, rifle ammo, hand grenades, and a land mine. Each step is a little wobbly. About a hundred yards and I'll be on shore.

As I slowly walk toward the beach, the water level gradually gets lower on my chest. My arms are getting tired from holding the carbine above my head, and I can hear a new noise. Bullets are whizzing just over our heads. Someone is shooting at us. Still trying to keep myself from falling and drowning, I try not to think about getting shot. Mostly, I just want to stay on my feet. A commotion to my right indicates some guys have been hit. Naval

Troops wading to shore from a landing craft, infantry (LCI). Courtesy US National Archives.

guns roar behind us, but I don't think much about that, either. I am getting tired and want desperately to make it to shore without drowning. I'm beginning to think I might get there. Looking straight ahead toward the beach, now about fifty yards away, I can see tanks, bulldozers, soldiers, jeeps, and supplies. Behind the beach, up a gradual slope, are buildings, some with steep, thatched roofs. I've probably taken almost ten minutes to go about fifty yards in the water.

The closer to shore I get, and the lower the water level, the more awkward the walking, as my gear and clothing feel even heavier. If I fall, I'll still probably drown. I continue to take small, shuffling steps in the hope that I can keep my balance. A few more bullets whiz by, but I am just thankful to be making it closer to land. When I am about twenty yards out, I can tell there is smooth sand under my feet. As the water level lowers, my legs begin to feel as heavy as tree trunks. A wave almost knocks me over, and I stumble. Now my legs seem to be made of rubber. My breathing is labored. "I'm going to make it. I'm not going to drown," I think. Near the water's edge I almost trip over the sandy incline. My waterlogged uniform and equipment must weigh an enormous amount now.

On the beach, I gasp for air. My legs can hardly hold me up, and I wobble around as I walk. I want to lie down. Officers are hollering and pointing like traffic cops. After walking about ten yards or so from the water's edge and making my way toward Boz, I try to gather my wits. I hear a strange noise that is getting louder and louder, almost as if someone is screaming at me. I turn to face whatever is making the screaming noise and see sand flying into the air, heading my way.

"Down, down, down!" Hanlon yells.

From the east, two fighter planes are coming toward us. The guns of the first, a German Messerschmitt Bf 109, are blazing toward us on the beach, throwing sand into the air. The second, a British Spitfire, fire spurting from its guns, is right on the German's tail. Sand flies by me as I fall to the beach with my hands over my head. Lifting my face, I see the Spitfire peel off over the water. The Messerschmitt then banks left and disappears over the hill up from the beach. Dazed, a group of soldiers close to me look around, and one by one they begin to stand.

"Look, here he comes!"

We all look up and see a big, bright, white parachute coming down with the German pilot attached. Guys pull out guns and begin firing up at the enemy pilot who has just tried to kill them. Their shots miss badly. Maybe our training isn't so good, after all. I figure we'll get him when he comes down, and I let the others do the shooting. Proppe, Boz, Spikula, and I just watch. Nobody hits him.

The pilot keeps dropping, waving his arms and frantically yelling something in German. He comes down not more than forty feet from us. He is about thirty years of age, badly burned around his neck and face, and obviously in quite a bit of pain. Members of our platoon, still anxiously waiting to see real action, want to shoot him right then and there. To the west on the beach is a hospital tent with big red crosses on the top and sides, and they believe the German has tried to attack it. At least that is their excuse.

"Shoot him now! Shoot, shoot!" holler some of our troops.

"The Kraut doesn't deserve to live," shouts one. "He was gunning for the hospital."

"Stop, dammit! Stop! It's against the war rules," argue others. Someone, I think Sergeant Hanlon, steps in front of the prisoner to shield him from harm.

Fortunately for the enemy pilot, a German-speaking GI is handy. The pilot emphatically and frantically maintains he hadn't seen the big red crosses on the hospital tent. He goes on and on. His story is plausible, since he was flying only a few hundred feet over the hospital tent and moving at three hundred miles per hour. Some of the guys point their rifles at him and motion toward an area of the beach where German prisoners of war are being processed.

"Hey soldier, welcome to France!" a soldier I don't recognize greets me as he carries supplies by. Quickly we are herded into an open area to regroup before we move again. I am still breathing heavily.

"Sound off!" Sergeant Hanlon goes through the squad list. All are present and accounted for. Several in other units are wounded during the wade to shore, but no one in mine. "There are pockets of Germans scattered around the area," Hanlon tells us. "Tonight we dig in and wait for orders." He directs us to where we should be. Proppe is called to regiment headquarters and leaves. Most of 2nd Battalion and the rest of Company G are still in ships waiting to come ashore.

We head off the beach and up a path to higher ground. It is soft and moist. Every five feet or so Hanlon places a soldier in a foxhole. Company G digs in, creating a defensive perimeter near Beau Guillot. My foxhole doesn't look like much, but it will do for the time being.

Daylight gradually dwindles away. Some of us joke around lightheartedly. I am tired and somewhat overwhelmed by my thoughts. The episode of the Messerschmitt and Spitfire replays over and over in my mind. I have dried quite a bit, but the weather is cool. No fires are allowed because of enemy activity in the area.

Before nightfall I am getting extremely thirsty. I risk getting sick and fill my canteen from the muddy puddle at the bottom of my foxhole. I drop a water sterilizing pill into the canteen and mix it with the canteen water, but still I wonder if I should drink; it looks disgusting. Looking around, I notice others are drinking, so I drink. This quenches my thirst, but my mouth feels dirty.

That first night, we settle in our less than cozy foxholes. The day has been exhausting and emotionally draining, even though we haven't seen any real action, other than a few bullets whizzing over our heads as we got off the landing craft and the Messerschmitt shooting at us. Back behind our camp, trucks, jeeps, and supplies are being unloaded quickly. There is a lot of activity back along the beach area. During the night this section of G Company stays put, waiting for the arrival of the remainder of G, 2nd Battalion, and the machine gunners, but we are on our guard in case of German counterattacks. The foxholes are getting even wetter because of the marshy ground we are dug into. I never can get completely dried out. We don't know what to expect. I look out toward the southeast, wondering who and what is out there. I only manage to sleep a few winks, but before I know it the sun is rising and we need to be up and at it. (This second day is known as D+1.) Boz is ready to roll, up and about early.

"Seen Proppe?" I ask Boz.

"Nope, maybe he couldn't find us in the dark," he responds.

A couple of paratroopers from the 506th come into camp and walk right by my foxhole. They look weary.

"Have a rough day?" I ask them as they walk on by. They don't even look my way.

"Yeah, it was rough," is all one says as they continue toward the beach.

Through the evening and night I think about how pathetic they looked. I am exhausted, but I can't sleep at all again. I wonder if it can really be that bad out there.

We wait further for the remainder of the company. In the late afternoon, June 7, they arrive and are welcomed by German fighter planes. They organize and head to our position.

"Had to wait offshore," Sergeant Gross informs us. "They said it was due to rough seas." The machine gunners are a little wound up, as they have just experienced their own ordeal with a German fighter plane, only this pilot lands in the water before being captured.[6]

We soon find ourselves on a path in the dark. Our orders are to provide support for the 506th. To get to the main road, we advance through several farm fields surrounded by hedgerows: thick, almost impenetrable brush growing along fences and roads. "Bocage" is what the natives call this land of pasture, fields, wooded areas, and hedgerows.

The main body of the 506th is located in and around the ancient, tiny village of Sainte-Marie-du-Mont, about three miles to the south of Utah beach. That's where we are heading. The march isn't bad. After being in the ship for so long, and then spending time in a foxhole, it feels good to get some exercise for a change. The roads aren't anything but big paths, although many are blacktopped. I see a tall church steeple, damaged by shell fire, in the middle of town. We set up camp just to the southwest of the village. To get into the field, we have to crawl through a small opening in the hedge. Then we spend the rest of the night digging foxholes, readying equipment, and preparing for combat. I give up on digging, as I can't get through the hedge brush roots. I'm close enough to the hedge anyway, and it offers some protection. Company strength is currently listed as 149 men.[7]

Our defenses are in a large circle, much like a wagon train in a western movie. There is a blacktop road to our left on the other side of the hedgerow. We have to be careful. Soon it is apparent that the Germans are very close—just on the other side of the southwest end of the field. The hedge barriers are almost impossible to get through, so for a while they leave us alone and we leave them alone—except for the taunting. They are hidden very well in the hedges. When our patrols try to get through the hedge where the Germans are, the Germans shoot at them.

A few more patrols are sent out a short distance to snoop around, checking for enemy soldiers. Every once in a while the enemy launches a mortar at us, but nothing concentrated. I guess they are afraid of what our big naval guns offshore could give them.

The nearby Germans are still taunting us. Lloyd Gross is called up to tell us what they are saying.

"Come and get us! Come and get us!" The enemy soldiers taunt in German.

"You are fighting for the wrong damn side," Gross replies in German.

"No, you are fighting for the wrong damn side." The taunting continues.

The patrols continue, but I am sitting in the dark and cleaning my rifle. Suddenly, boom! an explosion rocks the camp. The shell is on us without any sound before the explosion. My heart skips a few beats. When Gross gets back to his foxhole, he finds his partner dead from a mortar round blast. Five prisoners have been taken so far.[8]

Sergeant Hanlon comes up to me with an order: "Rich, your turn for guard duty." Guard duty means manning a Browning automatic rifle (BAR). I am a bazooka gunner. Hanlon can tell I am puzzled. "I need someone who knows what he's doing," he adds.

I head with Hanlon to the southeast corner of the field, along the main road outside of Sainte-Marie-du-Mont. We find the opening, and I shimmy through the tight space with considerable difficulty and noise. Then, sliding down to the other side, I find Boz manning the BAR. I haven't seen Proppe since he'd been ordered to make contact with the British unit to the east.

The BAR is positioned on the road. It is larger than an M1 rifle and twice as heavy. The weight of the gun requires it to be fired from a bipod. Each ammunition clip holds twenty rounds. The big gun fires at about the same rate as a machine gun, but it is more accurate and more portable, and every squad of soldiers has one. Being in the front is exciting, and guarding the camp makes me feel like a leader, but I also feel vulnerable as I look to the south. My vision is limited by the darkness and a slight curve in the road. The guard duty is dangerous; the enemy is likely only ten feet from me on the other side of the hedge around the field to my south.

The Germans can very easily see me, if they are looking or listening. If I have to shoot, or they shoot first, the gung-ho American soldiers may start firing in my direction. As I lie tiredly in the road, I still feel an adrenalin rush of excitement. This is an important job.

Then I hear the sound of marching soldiers, which makes the next few moments seem to be an eternity. I am sweating although it is cool. Surely the enemy will hear my heart pounding. Louder and louder the marching sound becomes: German soldiers have metal cleats on the soles of their boots to prevent excessive wear, and I am sure I am making out the sound of metal on pavement. These certainly are not American soldiers. By the sound I can tell they are just beyond the curve in the road, but I can barely make out movement through the thicket. I wonder if I should fire.

I haven't fired a BAR since basic training in California. I look back over my shoulder, down the road, knowing that other guns are pointed my way. Bracing myself as best I can, my face sore from grimacing, I squeeze the trigger to let the gun rip up the enemy. Nothing happens. The trigger doesn't move. I've forgotten to switch off the safety.

Composing myself, I set to pull the trigger again when a thought crosses my mind. I speak aloud: "I know that sound." And then I follow with, "I hate horses."

I've been hearing the sound of loose farm horses meandering down the road. They are trying to get away from the loud noises of the fighting further ahead. Horses haven't been on my good list ever since I was kicked by one as a kid. But if I had fired, the American soldiers behind me might have fired, too. Who knows what might have happened then? My heart races with relief.

After my stint on guard duty, I go back to my foxhole. I can't sleep the rest of the night. The next morning, Monday June 8 (D+2), 2nd Battalion breaks camp and heads south along the road from Sainte-Marie-du-Mont to the Carentan road.

The battle is developing like a big free-for-all ahead of us. Imagine a game of dodgeball with no team boundaries, no rules, and many places to hide. That's what the Allied armies are facing. Overall, the invasion is going much more slowly than planned. Yes, there are unexpected crack German units in the area, and the enemy does inflict heavy casualties on the Allies the first day, but the main reason for the slow development of the invasion is the hedgerows.

The 327th slowly but steadily follows the narrow road. Enemy soldiers are frequently reported in the area, hiding in the hedgerows. Several dead paratroopers are still hanging by their parachutes, having been caught in trees. The sight is unsettling. Constantly aware of the dangers ahead, we continue our forward movement, slowly. At any moment we could be attacked. Also at any moment we could be called up to the front lines. Soon, I figure, I'll be able to use my bazooka or carbine.

Reports from up ahead indicate that our bazookas can get stuck in the hedgerows as the bazooka men try to make their way through. Imagine carrying a four-inch-diameter pipe that is four and one-half feet long into a tangled mess of undergrowth during a raging battle. Obviously, this news worries me, and I am determined not to get stuck.

Artillery barrages occasionally scream overhead. Although we are dragging from lack of sleep, the artillery explosions shock us back to alertness. Some of the shells come from battleships stationed miles away, while others are from artillery set up near the beaches. The big shells from the ships make a whirring sound with a whistle to it, and the army artillery shells make a swishing sound. As we move toward Carentan, we come to a corner on the main road near Sainte-Côme-du-Mont.

"Dead Man's Corner up ahead!" Sergeant Hanlon growls.

"Dead Man's Corner?" someone asks as more shells scream overhead, causing explosions ahead.

"Krauts are shelling every time something moves at the corner, killing lots of guys," Sarge replies. "Seems they don't want us to get past there; they are trying to keep us out of Carentan. Go through the corner and you're dead."

Colonel Wear speeds by in a jeep but suddenly stops. A private from headquarters is asleep along the side of the road. "Fine him twenty-five dollars!" Wear orders.[9] The fine seems harsh to me. I am very tired and could use a catnap myself.

The 2nd Battalion keeps moving forward, slowly making its way toward the corner. I look around and listen intently for incoming shells as we approach the intersection. Shells have pock-marked the place. A few unexploded shells lie on the ground as well. A two-story house stands in the northwest corner of the intersection. At the intersection off to the side is a destroyed American tank, a hole in it from a Panzerfaust antitank weapon. A dead German soldier lies in the middle of the intersection, killed by artillery.

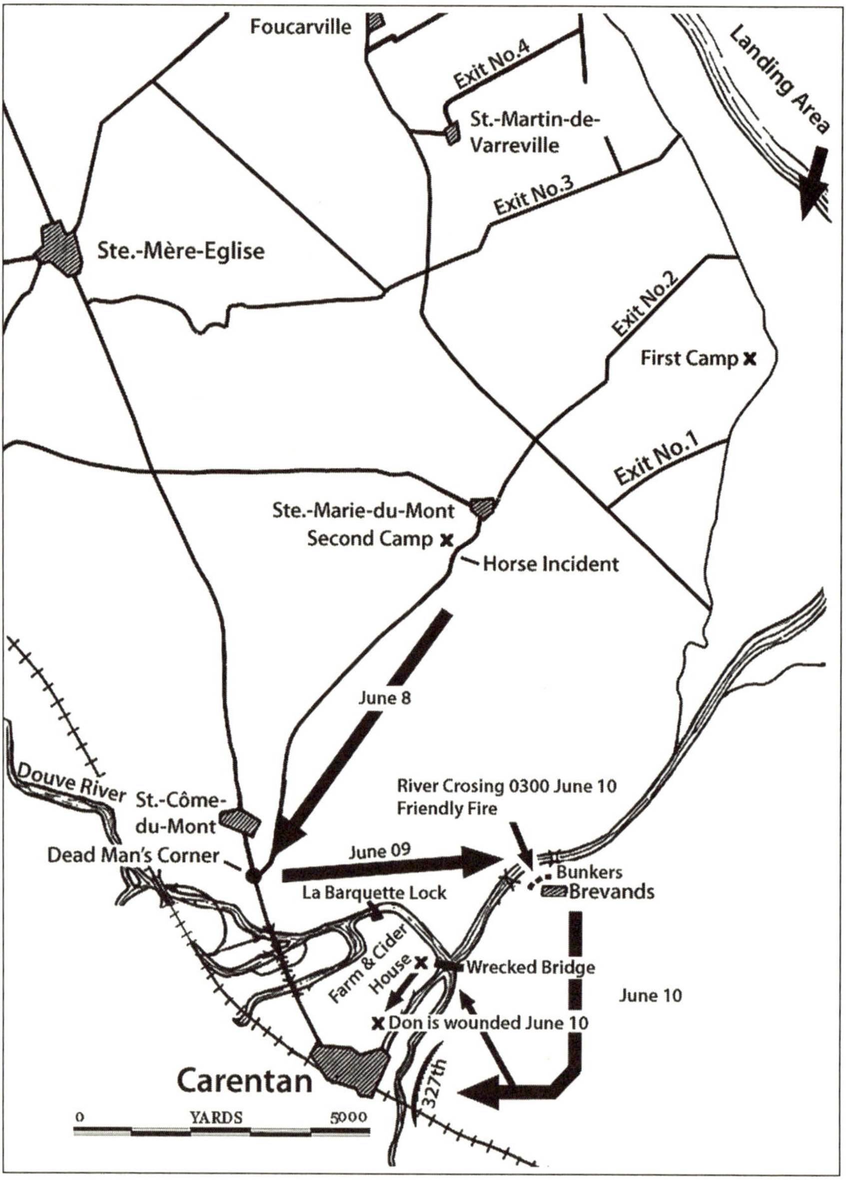

Company G's march from Utah Beach to Carentan.

This is the first dead German soldier I've seen, and it makes me feel sick, but I don't dwell on it. The guys in my squad gawk, but they don't say anything. Someone says there is a dead American in the tank, but I don't look.

After getting past Dead Man's Corner alive, we turn to the east toward Carentan, now only about two miles away. We are no longer on the main road; this side road is more of a path through an open field. We continue on parallel to the Douve River, heading east. Snipers are taking shots at us, but nothing comes close to hitting us. Not taking any chances, though, we keep our heads down.

As we continue east, Boz shouts at me, "Rich, you thirsty?"

"Yeah, I'm pretty dry," I answer.

Boz, Spikula, who is acting as my assistant bazooka man, and I, with canteens tied together and slung over our shoulders, go hunting to find water for the squad. I jump over a stone fence first with Boz and Spikula following right behind. As we land on the other side, we are surprised by a squad of odd-looking American soldiers. They all have gas masks on. Startled, Spikula shouts what the other two of us have already thought, "Gas!"

Back over the fence the three of us leap, hightailing out of there as fast as we can. After running a short distance, we stop, looking at each other, gasping for breath. "If it is gas, it's too late now, we're dead anyway," I say. We look at each other, then around at our surroundings. Then we break out laughing. Obviously, there isn't any gas, so after catching our breath we go back to looking for water.

Second Battalion is pretty close to the Germans. Enemy territory is just across the Douve River. The Douve flows west to a point just north of Carentan and then turns north toward the English Channel. Wanting to keep us on our toes, Germans across the canal pop up and fire at us, keeping the air filled with gunfire. We never do get any water.

The 501st captures the locks at La Barquette on D-Day. Allied commanders believe the locks to be of critical strategic importance. At low tide the marshlands around Carentan are below sea level. Whoever controls the locks can flood the marshlands to the east and north of Carentan, which could be used to drive out an enemy or, at least, keep a barrier between themselves and the enemy. Royal Air Force scout planes observe the Germans practicing this maneuver, and Allied command decides it might be a good tactic to use this against them. The surrounding area in and around Carentan needs to be secured to keep the enemy from retaking the locks.[10]

Company G continues to make steady progress toward the Douve north of Carentan. I never sit down in the open, but always stay behind a tree, fence, or building. Still I have no word about Proppe.

We move through a small bump in the road named Peneme. There's not much there at all. Marching along, we come to a place where enemy prison ers have been held. I decide to glance at the pile of discarded items dumped by the German prisoners. Much to my surprise, I find a German pistol, a Luger, in the grass. It's a pretty good souvenir, I figure, so I keep it.

The Germans are making their presence known just across the river to our south, sniping at us and hitting us with mortars, although nothing really comes close to me. We arrive at the Douve River late on D+2 and dig in for the night. When we wake the next morning, overlooking the Douve, we learn that the enemy is on the other side. Company F is on the left flank, and Company E is to the south of us on the right. Further to the north is 1st Battalion. All together the front is about two miles in length.

Carentan

Starting at dawn on June 9 (D+3), 2nd Battalion prepares to advance toward the mission objective of Carentan. We will cross the river and sweep to the east and then south to attack Carentan on the east side. This is our first real battle assignment, and the guys are more than ready. Progress has been slow. Right now we are waiting until dark to cross the river. Rubber boats are being sent for the crossing.

June 9 is almost spent, and night begins to fall. Niland tells us there are still Germans in the bunkers across the river.

In the evening light I can see a few trees up ahead along the riverbank on both sides of the Douve. Aside from these trees, the area is mostly open fields. The Douve is about forty or fifty yards wide at this point. There are three sod-covered enemy bunkers on the other side of the river about twenty yards from the river's edge. Sergeant Hanlon comes over to me carrying a Springfield rifle and several rifle grenades. "Rich, hit the bunkers," he orders, while handing me the rifle with a rifle grenade attached.

I know why Hanlon doesn't want to use a bazooka. The warhead of the bazooka would probably deflect off the bunker's low, sloping roof. Hanlon hands me four or five more grenades. Again, he thinks I'm the best man for the job.

I look around from my vantage point, which is behind a few trees. The area I have to fire from has no cover to hide behind, but I do as I am told, despite the inherent risk of being in the open while firing. Walking quickly, I find an area from which I think I can get a pretty good shot. I don't see any German soldiers. Quickly, I place the butt end of the rifle on the ground, raise the front-heavy weapon, estimate the degree of elevation needed to land the grenade on the bunker, and fire. The grenade takes off, streaking across the river, and hits a bunker on the side. A pretty good shot, I think to myself. I quickly reload and fire again. This time I am even more on target. My training must have been pretty good after all.

Expecting return fire from the enemy, I quickly go through all the grenades, each of them hitting the target. I can just make out the slits in the bunker facing my direction, and I wonder if anyone will fire at me from them. The doors to the bunker are apparently in the back. The ground slopes down from the back, so if the Germans are leaving, I can't see them.

After I fire the grenades, we wait some more. Then at 0130 on June 10, 1st Battalion begins to cross the river on the rubber boats. Explosions sound across the river to the north of us about seven hundred yards upriver.

As we continue to wait, word spreads that Company C has been mauled by friendly artillery fire. We quietly absorb the gravity of the situation. At 0300, it's our turn, but there are no boats for us. "Move, move, move!" Hanlon and Hidalgo bark, ordering us down the riverbank. We wade across.

I hold the bazooka high as I step into the water, careful not to get it wet. More artillery explosions rock the area ahead and the water a distance to the right. There is no return German fire, at least not yet. About halfway across, the water is about chest deep. Several others and I are in the lead. After coming out of the water, we regroup again and check our weapons.

We are told unofficially that some of the artillery shots were too short and the river crossing started too soon for C Company. Officially it is said the soldiers hit enemy mines on the opposite shore.[1]

The enemy is nowhere to be seen. The Germans have escaped out the back of the bunkers and over the hill. With the Germans gone, several squads move ahead toward the bunkers. I walk up to one of them and look in. German soldiers apparently like cabbage, because the place sure smells of it, along with gunpowder, maybe from my grenade shots. The place is a mess. Fresh cheese is sitting on the table. They must have left pretty quickly. If I hurt anyone, they were at least well enough to get away in a hurry.

After leaving the bunkers, G Company moves through Brevands at about 0800. Tired and wet, we then move east and south of Brevands toward Catz, with 1st Battalion in front. Colonel Wear is planning for 1st and 2nd Battalions to attack Carentan from the east along the main highway through Saint-Hilaire-Petitville.[2] As we head south toward the highway, we are marching in two parallel lines. We seem disorganized; companies and even battalions are intermixing confusedly. The pace is terribly slow. Sporadic gunfire can be heard up and down the line, especially ahead to the south. An incoming German shell screams toward us, so we scramble into the ditch. The ground shakes. The dust settles. We reform the lines and move ahead, passing by medic Scherrer, working on a soldier.

Suddenly, I can make out a grayish green camouflage uniform. I raise my carbine and am just about to pull the trigger when I see the German soldier is making his way toward us with his hands held high. Apparently, he has been hiding in the ditch with the intention of surrendering. A couple of guys check him for weapons, and then Delbert Blankenship takes him back to the main part of the company. Forward progress is still very slow.

Night is falling on June 10. At 2200 hours, the column turns to the southeast as we approach the village of Catz. An assault line is formed for the push forward. Our heavy machine guns spray the area ahead of us, and the enemy fires back determinedly. We seem better organized. As we move forward, on the north side of the Carentan–Isigny road, the enemy hits 1st Platoon hard with small arms fire and artillery, causing G Company to pull back after suffering sixteen casualties.[3] Company G is placed in reserve and E (Easy) takes our place. We in 2nd Platoon are separated from the advance and head toward the northwest while 2nd Battalion continues toward Saint-Hilaire-Petitville. By midnight, we halt just short of the Canal de Vire et Taute, where the canal, the Douve River, and another canal, the Bassin á Flot, converge. The enemy is on the other side of the canal, right across from us. The enemy line continues south toward Saint-Hilaire-Petitville. We hear fighting to our south (our left flank).

At morning light I can more easily see that we are on the east side of the canal facing west. In front of me is a bridge over the canal. We cross the bridge and immediately come to the Bassin á Flot, a mile-long canal that is capable of holding larger boats. At this point the two canals join the Douve River, which turns north toward Utah beach. We are looking at a wrecked footbridge over the Bassin á Flot just south of where the canal and the Douve meet. Colonel Harper is present and is examining the situation. He looks more like a scholar than a tough soldier. We find out that late yesterday Wear was relieved of command of the 327th, and Harper replaced him. This was a result of the friendly fire incident while Company C crossed the Douve. At this time, the decimated 1st Platoon joins 2nd Platoon.[4]

The bridge is in bad shape. Whether it has been wrecked by the Germans or the Americans I cannot tell. Some pillars are still standing, and time is needed to place planks onto the pillars to allow soldiers to cross. Evans orders my squad over the bridge anyway. He wants us to determine enemy strength. I sling the bazooka over my shoulder and carefully pick each step and handhold to keep from falling off and into the water, where I'd drown. The squad precariously crosses the bridge, careful not to get hurt by the jagged metal. The German prisoner held by our platoon doesn't seem to be much of a threat; he seems content to be with us. First Platoon is now guarding him.

Looking to the south, I see that the west bank of the canal rises steeply from the water. This dike is covered by trees that continue all the way into Carentan. We move three hundred yards along the top of the dike, with squad scout Frank Delarosa intently looking for signs of the enemy. I am hyperalert and anxious as we quietly make our way. Seeing ahead through the brush and trees is difficult. We go another fifty yards before turning back to report to Evans. On the way back I notice a home and a single-story building to the west of the canal, and behind them is an apple orchard. Carefully, we assault the building, which is full of apple cider. Boy, does the cider taste delicious.

Once back at the bridge, we find that it has been bolstered by engineers, and plywood has been added for a better walkway. We report to Captain Evans, who is with Colonel Harper. The officers are conversing in front of us, then Evans turns to us.

"No sign of the enemy, sir," Delarosa reports.

"They ain't there at all, sir," chimes in another. "Great apple cider though."

Colonel Harper, now in charge, has a funny look on his face as he asks, "Apple cider?"

"Yes sir, over there," says Delarosa.

The colonel and Captain Evans head over to the building for some cider. They are talking seriously on their way back.

Shortly after the apple cider break, the whole company begins to cross the bridge. We know the Germans are going to put up a fight for Carentan because of its strategic importance, but it appears that they are not heavily guarding the town, at least not where we are. We are ready for action, feeling more excited than nervous.

Most of G Company is across the footbridge when suddenly the air is filled with the sound of enemy mortars exploding in the water. The shells are coming from Carentan and fall near the footbridge, but not close enough to cause any casualties. The enemy obviously knows we are coming. At 1000, G Company forms an assault line to move down the west (right) side of the canal as we face south toward Carentan. Company A of the 401st (part of the 3rd Battalion of the 327th) is on the east side of the canal, just arrived from being in reserve at Le Rocher.[5] We are under the command of the 401st. A mortar squad is set up behind the apple cider building. Niland reports there are German Mark III tanks in the area and mines near the Bassin á Flot marina to our south on the edge of town. On opposite sides of the canal, both companies move forward.

Cautiously, we advance, seeing only trees and brush and hearing only the rustling of grass and twigs breaking as the company moves. Evans again chooses my squad to be out in front. We make it past the area where we turned back not that long before on our scout patrol and advance another one hundred yards. Startlingly, the Germans open up with murderous machine gun and rifle fire, taking us completely by surprise. Machine gun fire rips into our line and mortars pummel our positions; everywhere soldiers are falling. Our attack stalls. I crouch low and look around for something to shoot at, but I can't make out where the fire is coming from. Because of the trees, I can't find anything to fire my bazooka at.

The intensity of the battle makes the happenings around me surreal, not at all what I expected. The smell of gunpowder stings my nose. Still not able to get a clean shot because of the trees, I head back from our front line for further orders from Lieutenant Hibbard. Bullets whistle through the leaves as branches fall among us. As I approach the main body of the company, I hear some of the guys yelling, even above the noise of battle.

"Why the hell did he do that?"

"What were we going to do with him anyway?"

"Better him dead than us killed trying to protect a Kraut!"

"What are you talking about?" I ask.

"Blankenship shot the prisoner," a soldier replies.

"What?" I am surprised.

"Blankenship shot the damn German!"

My head swirls. No one says any more. We have a battle to fight, and things aren't going well. Still, many of the guys, including myself, are pretty upset by this. Even though I can understand why my fellow soldier chose to kill our prisoner, I am furious and sick to my stomach. Most of us feel we should be treating others, even the enemy, as we would want to be treated should we be captured. Still, we all know that when the prisoner was taken, we were engaged in a combat operation, and everyone was needed to fight, not watch a German prisoner. No one really knew what to do with him when we were under attack, so one of the guys in the squad decided to shoot him.

Not finding Hibbard, I make my way back to the front line. Brap, brap, brap! The enemy is again firing fast and furious in our direction. Zing, zing,

zing! Thump, thump, thump! The enemy fire is homing in on us. Behind us to my right I can see Germans popping up from the marsh and shooting at the mortar squad behind the cider house. Around me are dead and screaming, wounded soldiers. Blankenship has been hit in the hand by machine gun fire. He is howling as if he is horribly wounded. I'm sure it hurts, but he doesn't get much sympathy from the rest of us, partly because of the stressfulness of the situation and the severity of other wounds, but also because we are still upset by what he did to the prisoner.

The fighting rages on. Enemy machine gun fire continues to rake the area. I am still waiting for orders. From where I am positioned there is still nothing to shoot a rocket at. Lieutenant Niland from headquarters orders Frank Delarosa to find the exact placement of the enemy machine gun. I am still near Niland when Art Rutherford runs up to the lieutenant.

"Delarosa's dead; that machine gun got him!" I can barely make out the words over the noise. I crawl forward, still assessing the situation.

Niland comes up behind me, shouting, "Let's get that gun! The mortars can't clear it out because of the trees in the way!" We head about twenty-five yards or more along the top of the dike, ducking in and out of the trees and brush, which hide us a little from the gunfire. I still can't see the machine gun, although I can hear it, and I am not sure that Niland can see it either, but we keep on going.

The smoke that the machine gun emits when it fires eventually gives away its location. Except to reload, its shooting is almost constant. The gun is hidden at the bottom of the dike on the east side of the canal, firing at us from across the water. To get a shot at it I will have to go down the dike and sneak into the open, hoping not to become a target.

The bank is nine feet almost straight down. I take the bazooka off my right shoulder and keep the carbine on my left. The machine gun fires away toward the top of the bank as I slide down it. There is a large tree standing by itself along the water. At the bottom of the dike, I come to a stop, staying on my feet. I still can't see the enemy position through the trees. I can't see Niland but can hear him up on the dike. He will have to load the rocket for me.

Where is he?

Now the bullets are hitting all around me, sounding like popcorn popping as they hit the ground and trees. The large tree behind me rattles and splinters. Most of the bullets are hitting a little over my head, and others are kicking up sand and rocks.

"Rich, Rich get the hell out of there!" Niland screams.

Not needing an order, I spin around and am starting to head back up the embankment, flinging the bazooka up the incline at the same time. I can run much more quickly without the weapon weighing me down. The bank is too steep to just run up, and I am weighted down with gear. My legs feel like rubber as I scurry up the bank.

Getting to the top of the dike, I hit the ground to stay low, below the fire. Suddenly I feel pain like a hot iron sticking me in my left leg. I have been shot! Adrenalin pumps through my body, and my leg hurts. Instead of heading back toward the rest of the squad, I get up and start running along the dike in an attempt to outflank the machine gun, getting in a number of steps before diving for cover again. I want to find whoever has shot me.

"I'm gonna get them for this," I think. My carbine is still in my hand as I look for something to shoot at.

Niland screams again from behind me, "Rich!"

"The sons-of-bitches got me!" I scream back.

"Rich, what are you doing? Get the hell outta here!" Niland yells back. That brings me to my senses. Getting up to head back toward the squad, I stumble and fall after a few steps. I look down at my throbbing leg, which by now is bleeding heavily but not gushing. I need to get help. I crawl on my belly through the trees along the canal. Intense, incredible fighting is going on all around me. I hear more cries and see more dead bodies. The whole situation seems blurry. I start to call out for the medic but stop when I realize many others need him much more than I do.

Through the gunfire, I hear badly wounded soldiers moan and scream: "Medic, medic. Help me! Medic, help! Someone help. Help, Help!"

One of the men I see is mortally wounded. He is bleeding profusely. "Mama mia, Mama mia," he cries. I don't know who he is; he's not in my squad. No one can get to him because of the murderous gunfire. Gradually his cries get softer. Nearby, Simpson is hit in the shoulder.[6]

I continue on my belly, because some of the bullets are just inches above my head. I find Sgt. Jewell Hayden crouching behind a tree.

"Rich, where the hell do you think you're going?" Hayden screams.

"I'm hit, damn it!" I yell back.

"Get the hell out of here, then!" he orders.

Bark is flying all around as bullets splinter it from the trees. I can hear the zing of the bullets as I make my way back toward the Douve. Through the brush I can make out the house back near the orchard. Gunfire is coming from the south and from the west. I want to get under some cover to recuperate. The house faces toward the south, which makes the front door vulnerable to enemy fire. There is no way to get to it without going into the open for a small distance. Desperately wanting to reach better protection, I crawl through an opening in the brush into a garden on the east side of the house. Thirty feet of garden separate me from the house. As I crawl down the garden path, bullets continue to zing above my head. I make it to the steps and up the porch and bang loudly on the door, not expecting anyone to still be there.

Suddenly, the doorknob turns, and a French man with thick, dark hair pulls the door open and drags me in, quickly shutting the door behind us. I hear a gasp and then see a woman cover her mouth with her hand. There in the corner with her is a young boy. The French family is trying to stay safe from the battle. Their eyes are wide with surprise and fright. I look at them as they stare back at me. Then the man steps forward and offers his hand, putting his other hand on my shoulder as he bends down toward me.

"American, American!" he exclaims in a heavy French accent while wildly shaking my hand. The woman quickly follows. The fact that they don't speak English quickly becomes apparent. They nervously look toward the door and bend over some as if to keep from getting hit by bullets.

By now, my head is beginning to swim. I am getting weaker. The blood loss isn't great, but when coupled with the exhaustion and trauma, I am feeling woozy. The woman begins to clean and dress my wound with cloths. I begin to worry that the family is in peril because I am here. The Germans probably won't be happy with them if they are caught helping me. We gesture, trying to understand each other. A girl from Wayland had given me her picture to take with me. I pull the picture out of my wallet. I think the couple thinks the girl is my fiancée, and I don't mind.

After the bandage is applied, I motion toward the back door. The family has risked enough. The man helps me to my feet, and I go outside and sit on a back porch chair. He goes back in the house. After I sit there a few minutes, Walter Burton comes crawling along the side yard. He crawls over to me. "Burton, what happened?" I ask, already knowing.

"Rich, looks like the bastards got you too. Now what do we do?"

Burton and I are both bleeding and in a fair amount of pain. His right leg has been shot in almost exactly the same location as my left leg. Between us we have two good legs.

"I think we're in the clear as long as we stay behind the house," I say.

We help each other up and, locking our arms around each other's shoulders, make our way toward the Douve River. The house protects us from German fire all the way back to the river. Each step is painful, but we make it to the riverbank, where we find a medic with the red cross on his helmet. I am shaking with fright and shock.

The medic opens my bandage, shoots me with some morphine, and puts a fresh bandage on. The eight-inch wound has opened my flesh to the bone. I get queasy, and things begin to spin. The medic quickly bandages Burton and helps both of us into a wooden rowboat.

"You're on your own, pals," says the medic. He pats our shoulders and then quickly disappears toward the fighting.

Together we row across the Douve, where more medics have established a first aid station. There I receive more shots of morphine, and the last thing I remember is being placed onto a stretcher. Next thing I know, I am waking up on Utah Beach, waiting for a ship to take us back to England.

After having the wound cleaned and dressed again, I am carried on a stretcher to an LCT (landing craft, tank), which is serving as a hospital ship. Things aren't spinning anymore, but I am awfully tired. The orderlies carry me on the stretcher toward the water's edge. The big ship is practically ashore. A medic motions with his hands quickly.

"Better hurry up. May already be too late," the medic says. "She's about to leave with the tide," he adds, referring to the LCT.

Guards wave us into the open loading door, and my stretcher is placed on the tank deck, which is below the top deck. In a matter of minutes, I am on my way to England. I drift off, in and out of consciousness. Waking up in the big, open tank deck, I see a sailor who looks pale and nervous.

"A U-boat torpedo just missed us," he is saying. A German submarine has just taken a shot at the LCT, barely missing.

I drift in and out of sleep again, so I don't remember much more about the trip back across the Channel. I do remember waking up in a hospital in England, where there are clean sheets and very pretty nurses. Right away the medical staff prepares me for surgery. I still have the Luger in my pocket, and an orderly notices the pistol as they are getting ready to knock me out.

"Better take good care of that! It'll be stolen for sure," the orderly advises.

"I'll take care of it for you," a friendly and pretty nurse remarks as she takes the Luger.

"Where you from soldier?" the surgeon asks.

"Iowa, I'm from Wayland, Iowa," I manage to reply.

"She's from Burlington," the surgeon tells me, pointing to the pretty blonde nurse who took my Luger. Burlington is only about forty miles away from Wayland.

I lose consciousness at that point, and I don't remember anything more until waking up in the ward with my leg hurting. There on the bed is the Luger. I never see the nurse again. I hold the Luger all the time because I am worried that someone might steal it.

As I am being wheeled down the hall in a wheelchair, another soldier sees the Luger and makes an offer to buy it: "Give you three hundred for that beauty." Not giving it much thought, I sell the Luger right then and there. Since I am planning on going back to my company, I figure I can find another. Three hundred dollars is a lot of money. Someone will probably steal the pistol, anyway.

✪ ✪ ✪

Back home near Wayland on June 12, Lillie Rich (my mom) receives a call from Jim Holub, the Wayland railroad agent.

"Mrs. Rich, may I speak to your husband?" Jim asks quickly.

"He's not here right now. Forrest is at work," she responds.

"Can I leave a message for him?"

"Sure, what's this all about?" she asks, wondering if the message is about me.

"Telegram, I have a telegram addressed to Forrest Rich."

"Can I pick it up?" Mom asks.

"No ma'am, it's addressed to Forrest Rich."

"Anything you *can* tell me?" My mom's voice rises. She is beginning to fear that there might be bad news. "I think the army comes to the home when a soldier is killed," my mom says quietly to herself, trying to remain calm.

"Just tell Mr. Rich to call us when he gets home from work," Jim says.

For the next several hours my mother wonders and worries about the telegram. To get a telegram now, right after D-Day, is probably not good news. For a mother of a soldier, the wait is gut-wrenching.

My father gets home a little after five, finding Mom in tears. As calmly as she can, she tries to explain the message. Not completely understanding what she is saying, Dad calls the agent at the depot.

"Hello! This is Forrest Rich!" One has to speak loudly to be heard on the phone. Other families can also listen in on the conversation, should they happen to be on the line.

"Frosty, we have a telegram for you from the United States War Department," Jim informs him. Frosty is my dad's nickname.

"Can you tell me what it says?" Dad asks.

"You can come down to the depot and get it," is the only response.

"Okay, I'm on my way," Dad answers, with my mother standing right beside him anxiously waiting for the news.

My parents, along with Albert, jump into their truck. The trip to the Minneapolis and Saint Louis Railway depot from our small home south of town is about four miles. My parents don't say anything along the way. As they walk into the depot, the agent recognizes them right away.

"Let me see, here. Ah, yes, here it is," Jim mutters.

Dad takes the piece of paper from the agent, turns, and walks away, studying the telegram. "Regret to inform you Pfc. Donald J. Rich was seriously wounded in action on June 11, 1944," Dad reads aloud.

"That's it? That's all it says?" asks Mom.

"Yes, that's it." Dad quietly speaks.

As Dad repeats the words, Mom begins to sob. Both are quiet for a long time. Their oldest son is seriously wounded. That's all they know.

✪ ✪ ✪

Across the ocean, after a couple of days in the hospital I begin to feel well enough to write my parents. I have no idea what, if anything, they know about my being wounded.

June 14, 1944

Dear Mom and Dad,

Sorry I haven't been allowed to write after they moved us to the seaports and airfields where we would take off for France. After I was wounded I was moved back to England to the hospital, where we are now allowed to write. I was hit in my left leg by a machine gun bullet. Don't worry. I will be OK in the hospital for about six weeks till my leg heals. Getting good care, lots of nice nurses.

Love,
Donald

For the first few days after the surgery, I have to get around in a wheelchair. The pain isn't too bad except when I get up. One afternoon I hear a commotion down the hallway: "Krauts! There are dirty Krauts in here!" Immediately, guys jump out of bed and run out of our room and down the hallway into another large recovery room. I get into my wheelchair as fast as I can and head down the hall, too.

In the corner of the room are about half a dozen wounded enemy soldiers being cared for in the hospital. American soldiers are pressing against their beds and pushing nurses out of the way, trying to get to the wounded Germans.

"Get back! leave them alone!" I hear a nurse yell.

There is more shouting, and I can hear some German being spoken excitedly. Military police officers scamper into the room and push through the crowd.

"Break it up! Break it up!" the MP officers shout.

The wounded Americans, glaring at the wounded Germans, say some things about "Krauts" that are not particularly nice and turn away. I roll my wheelchair up towards the bed of the closest German, look at him, and then roll away, not sure what I am doing or why I am even there. He looks scared.

The guys in the hospital eventually get bored, so some of the guys in the room decide to play a trick on an older nurse who rules the patients with an iron fist. She is a good enough nurse, just way too serious and too bossy. One of the wounded soldiers somehow has a box of marbles with him. We rig the box so that when the nurse comes to check the patient, the box will fall and marbles will spill all over the place. The soldier next to me rings the bell, calling for assistance. The nurse comes in with a stern look. As she leans over the bed, a soldier yells, "Booby trap!"

The crash is loud and effective. Marbles roll all over the room, creating an obnoxious racket in what has been a perfectly quiet hospital room. The nurse charges out of the room. Some orderlies pick up the mess of marbles. Later, the nurse comes back in, showing no emotion at all. I'm not sure many of us still think it is funny after seeing her subdued reaction.

I take six weeks to recuperate in the hospital, during which I'm gradually allowed to put more weight on my leg. I ask about the Screaming Eagles and G Company, but all I get in response is that there are lots of casualties. Later I am told the 101st Division has returned to England.

Market Garden

THE 101ST AIRBORNE IS DESIGNED TO GET INTO AND OUT OF ACTION fast. But because the resourceful enemy uses the hedgerows to stymie Allied attacks, the Normandy campaign doesn't go as quickly as had been hoped by the top army brass. The 327th Regiment is in France from June 6 to July 13,[1] and by the end of the campaign the troops are utterly exhausted and greatly depleted in numbers. Many young men don't make it back at all and are buried near the beaches of Normandy. Others, like me, are wounded. I am in the hospital most of the time my buddies are fighting and at times dying. Getting any useful information about my regiment, company, and squad is almost impossible. Until the Screaming Eagles get back, there isn't much news at all. I can't wait to be with them again.

Upon getting back to England, Sergeant Hanlon and other squad members come to see me and bring my mail. We avoid talking about casualties, although I know that fighting was hard and casualties were high. They tell me how Chaplain Cosby and Lieutenant Ernest Walker from 1st Battalion risked their lives leading a volunteer patrol out fifty yards in front of our lines and fifty yards from the Germans to rescue our wounded.[2] The 327th has had a major part in the capture of Carentan. After they leave at 1030, when the lights are turned out, I sit up in my bed and lower my leg off the side. The pain is intense as the blood flows through the wound. Then with my crutches I make my way to the latrine and read my mail until midnight. I haven't heard from home for several weeks.

My wound is still draining fluid after six weeks, so the doctors decide it is best for me to spend more time in the hospital. I want to do more than sit in bed, though, so I ask the doctor in charge if I can get out of the hospital to go on a short leave. He reluctantly agrees, informing me that I will have to come back to the hospital as soon as I am back from leave. I spend the seven-day furlough in northern England, visiting several castles, but it isn't much fun: the pain in my leg and armpits, from being on crutches, makes it difficult to get around.

When I get back, my leg wound is still draining quite a bit, but there doesn't seem to be any infection. The doctors in the hospital decide it will be best if I stay several more days. My leg hurts and throbs a lot, and I am tired; I must have overdone the activity.

After a few more days of rest and therapy to regain my leg strength, I return to my squad. The army has invested a lot in our training, so an injured 101st Airborne soldier has to be in pretty bad shape not to be put back into action as soon as possible. With the severity of my wound, if I were in another division I probably would have had a ticket home. But I am a Screaming Eagle.

We don't do any heavy training, just light duty. My condition is such that if we were doing heavy training, I wouldn't be able to participate, because I still can't run or carry much weight. I'm not fit to do much of anything. My wound is healing all right, but very, very slowly. If my life depends on running, I'm sure I'll die.

Getting back to the barracks is overwhelming. I am amazed at the number of empty bunks in the long metal building at camp. Of the 149 of us in G who went ashore in France, only 85 made it back to England as a group. A total of 30 were killed or wounded the day I was hit.[3] My buddy Proppe's bunk is one of the empty ones, stripped of blankets. Even though I had heard that Proppe hadn't made it, reality sets in at this moment. I've never lost anyone close like this before. My buddy is gone, and I was not there when he was killed. I want to cry but manage to hold in the tears. The feelings of loss and sadness are extremely painful.

Out of my squad of twelve men, five are dead: Hank Proppe, killed in action June 6; Frank Delarosa, KIA June 11; Ed Spikula, KIA June 17; Art Rutherford and Gilbert Walloch, KIA June 21. When the squad was ordered to pull back in Carentan, Rutherford wouldn't, and Walloch stayed with him. From first platoon, Delbert Blankenship is KIA July 4. From 1st Platoon, Lieutenant Morrison is wounded but will recover. Sergeant Mills is wounded twice and is going home.[4]

Out of fourteen thousand soldiers who landed in France during the airborne phase of the assault, the Screaming Eagles suffered almost four thousand casualties—wounded, captured, missing, or killed—during the month of June alone. I am one of those casualty statistics. Out of all the original troops, nearly nine hundred are listed as killed in action.[5]

I question Sergeant Hanlon about Proppe.

"Proppe was killed the first day," replies the burly NCO shortly.

"How?" I ask, trying to remain respectful. Inside, I really want to know *why*. Why did Proppe have to die?

"Sniper. An enemy sniper got him," he answers quickly.

"Sniper? How?"

"Proppe was a runner for the big shots. He had some important information on artillery fire for the British. That's how they got him," he explains.

I can tell by the tone of Hanlon's voice that the conversation is over. I don't dare ask any more questions. Frankly, it doesn't matter. My buddy is gone forever. Proppe is not coming back.

The fact of the matter is that Proppe was killed while serving as a message runner between US and British forces. Other than what Hanlon tells me, I never learn any more about it. I never saw Proppe after getting to the Normandy beaches, because he was already running messages. Our trio is now a duo. Boz and I don't talk about it, but we both hurt badly. I get a lonely feeling deep inside when I think about the other buddies and teammates of mine who are gone as well.

Eventually life as an everyday soldier does start to get back to normal. The 327th has fought admirably in and around Carentan, and rumor is that we will soon be sent back to the war in a drop behind enemy lines. I manage to con my way back into heavier, but still light, duty, squad-level training. My left leg, still painful, and burdened by cumbersome bandages, makes me unfit for duty, but I want to be back training with my buddies. That's where I belong. I'm thankful that no infection develops.

Company G is given plenty of time to rest, and the light training means that I do not miss out on much. Many in the company, including me, receive a seven-day furlough, and we spend it in Scotland, one of the most popular destinations for young troops. I enjoy seeing the sites, but life isn't all about trying to have a good time. We have to regroup from the loss of almost half our men.

During live-fire training I am given a British-made two-piece bazooka. This newer model, which snaps together for use, won't get caught in brush as easily, increasing the bazooka gunner's chances of survival. Before we fire the new bazooka we have to stop and snap the tube together, and while this can be annoying, its advantages more than make up for the disadvantages. The newer bazooka also has much improved range and accuracy, and it is also very light compared to the older model. Still, two men are required to use it; we snap it together, one loads the rocket, and then the other fires.

In a change in tactics, I am no longer assigned to 1st Squad of the 2nd Platoon. The army thinks it better to make up a section of bazooka gunners that will support assigned platoons, as needed, within G Company. Bazooka gunners will still be under command of G, and my main duty will be to support G, but I'll fill in wherever I am needed.

A big day comes when we receive two months' worth of pay, but I don't feel like spending much of it. Grieving from the loss of comrades, such as Proppe, takes the fun out of life. We are also issued new clothing, which includes jump boots like the paratroopers wear, so there is no longer as big a distinction between paratroopers and glider troops. Actually, the veteran paratroopers are behaving a lot better towards us glidermen, having fought and died alongside us fighting the same enemy.

Replacements for the captured, killed, and severely wounded began training the day we left on D-Day. As the unofficial bazooka squad leader, I am responsible for the new replacements in the bazooka section. The new guys try to blend in, but the situation is awkward. The replacements are proud of their airborne patches but know they haven't paid their dues yet. They want to belong, and some are annoyingly arrogant and cocky. Most of the veteran soldiers don't want anything to do with them. The new guys are anxious for action, but those of us who have been in France are not, because we have seen and experienced too much.

James Mize is assigned to the bazooka section from 1st Squad. Mize is likeable and a good soldier. He and Louis Simpson introduce me to a good-looking and confident new guy, Jack Sherman. Sherman is assigned as a runner between the squads and company headquarters, and he works with Simpson. A buddy of Sherman's, Jim Shaw, is assigned to the bazooka section as an assistant.

Chuck Fisher, another replacement, is assigned to battalion headquarters. Fisher is a blond-haired guy whose father was an aide to Gen. Douglas MacArthur. He also has a brother who was killed when the Japanese sank the USS *Juneau* in the Pacific.[6] Fisher likes to mix things up, but he is really likeable. Bert Sparks, another replacement, is also likeable but isn't really cut out to be a combat soldier.

"Keep Sparks close to you," Hibbard advises me. "Someone with experience needs to keep an eye on him."

"How is he different from the other replacements?" I ask.

"During training he accidently unloaded a BAR at other trainees," Hibbard informs me. I truly hope his inexperience won't get us both killed.

A lighthearted look at the frustrations of bazooka gunners like Don.

The new guys all look so young. I later find out Sherman is one month my senior.

Officers took high casualties in France as well. As a result, new orders forbid map reading in the open, as this helps the Krauts figure out who the officers are; they try to kill the guy looking at the map. The Germans seem to fall apart and retreat in confusion if their leader is killed, so they think we will also fall into confusion if they kill our officers. They haven't caught on yet that we have someone else ready to step up and lead.

First Lieutenant Evans gets promoted to captain and becomes easier to get along with. Evans seems military through and through, and as a lieutenant he was hard to get along with. He acted as if we couldn't do anything right, nit-picking us on seemingly everything we did.

Before the invasion we developed into a well-oiled team. Now, things are different. Getting used to all the new men from top to bottom is a challenge. The situation is helped as recovering wounded, like me, are reintegrated into the units, providing needed experience. A few Screaming Eagles who were captured by the Germans and then managed to escape prison camp are also "volunteered" back into their units. Company G now has twenty percent more men than it had during the invasion. Officers training the replacements in airborne tactics work to instill an aggressive attitude among them. I am disappointed that I don't get promoted officially as the bazooka

John Sherman and James Shaw (*top*) living it up in New York City. Courtesy John Sherman collection.

John Sherman (*bottom left*). Courtesy John Sherman collection.

Charles Fisher (*bottom right*). Courtesy Thomas Niland collection.

section leader. It seems that the Southerners get preferential treatment from Captain Evans.

Sherman, Simpson, and I get a pass off base. I don't really know Sherman at all, but as we take in the sights I do notice that he is behaving himself. I figure this is because he has a girlfriend back home. Simpson, on the other hand, has a way with the British girls, and before long he is off on his own, a girl on each arm. Later, we meet again.

"How'd it go? Have a good time?" I ask Simpson.

"I love England," Simpson quips back with a winsome grin.

We are standing by a water fountain, and Simpson bends over to get a drink. What happens next surprises Sherman and me: a British girl walks up to Simpson and slings her purse down hard on his head while he is drinking. "Hey, what the. . . ." Simpson quickly jerks around to see which one of us has hit him. The girl, along with a friend, goes storming off. Simpson puts his hand to his mouth and spits out a front tooth. He has a puzzled look on his face. Recomposing himself, he smiles again with the same winsome grin, minus a tooth.

When we get back to base, Simpson leaves us to clean himself up. Sherman and I look at each other and laugh.[7] We wonder what it was all about, but decide we really don't want to know. Simpson is one of a kind and certainly has a way with the girls, but we aren't sure what that really means.

Scherrer, the medic, is getting really serious with his British girl. We tease him some. He comes back from leave and tells us he's married. We don't believe him until later, when she shows us the inexpensive wedding ring.

Friction between glidermen and paratroopers begins to build again, probably because the troops don't have enough to do. A few paratroopers still feel we are inferior soldiers because we don't jump; they don't mind letting us know their unwelcomed personal opinions. Paratroopers originally got paid more than glider troops, because brass perceived that there was a higher risk for them, and that difference angered some of the glider troops. Finally, the army allows the glider infantry to receive regular airborne pay, which amounts to an extra $37.50 per month. Still, though, the money isn't as important as recognition for us glider troops. We are now on equal footing with the paratroopers in the eyes of the top brass, or at least we think so, and we have uniforms to match.

One thing that really puzzles me is the way the US Army gets away with transporting racial segregation into England. African Americans are relegated to cleaning, burial, and other similar duties. Rarely does one hear of a black unit getting into combat, although we do hear of one, an artillery unit, that is getting a reputation as a crack outfit.[8] Still, some wonder why the US Army, supposedly a shining light of democracy in a world of dictatorships, ironically brings racial segregation to England.

As a result of the segregation policy, our leave trips off base are limited by assigned black days and white days. African American soldiers are given one day to be out, and whites are given the next day. Supposedly this is done to keep black and white soldiers from fighting. Violators of the black day/white day schedule are supposed to be fined.

On a trip to Scotland, Boz and I meet a couple of local girls and decide to stay an extra day, which means that we will be traveling back through England on "black day." We decide the girls are worth the risk of a fine. On the way home, we hop a train bound for Reading and make it back without incident. At the camp gate we walk right past the military police and we aren't stopped, much to our relief.

On the day we get back from Scotland, the Screaming Eagles are ordered to prepare for a combat drop somewhere near Paris on August 17. Knowing I still can't get the medical okay for combat, I don't ask for clearance, but instead decide to circumvent the system. I meet my squad at the airport as they are preparing to leave. I don't have my steel helmet or a rifle, but boy, am I eager to go. Quickly, they brief me on the plan. The 101st is to trap the German 7th Army by blocking the roads that the Germans are using to escape from General Patton's Third Army. Patton, very popular with American soldiers, is greatly feared by the Germans, who think he is crazy. However, just as we are ready to go, we're ordered to stand down, because General Patton's forces have already overrun the drop zone.[9]

Another operation is planned using the 101st. We prepare, along with the 82nd Airborne and other airborne units, for a drop into Belgium to support advancing British armor forces. Again, the operation is cancelled at the last minute because British General Montgomery's forces also overrun the targeted area.[10]

On September 4, General Montgomery cancels another plan, which calls for airborne troops to secure bridges over the Meuse River in Belgium in advance of the penetration of British armor into German-held territory. General Monty feels the mission will be compromised by a lack of maps and intelligence data in the targeted area.[11] The Brits are always sticklers for detail, even if it means causing more delays and problems.

Being on again and off again is emotionally hard on the troops, including me. To pass the time and to keep us fresh, we train by marching, marching, and more marching. When not marching, we spend a lot of time in the barracks, where tensions continue to increase between replacements and experienced troops. One replacement soldier, who is older than most of us, and whose name I don't bother to learn, has a very arrogant attitude. He thinks he already knows everything he needs to know and therefore doesn't need to train with us. He is a legend in his own mind, but in no one else's. I do get to know the replacement who sleeps on the bunk below me a little bit, although we don't really become buddies. He is a nice enough guy, but more like a necessary teammate than a buddy. Keeping Shaw and Sparks from getting killed is going to be enough to do. I miss Proppe.

The war in Europe is going so well, and the enemy is believed to be in so much trouble militarily, that after the many false redeployment alarms rumors fly that very soon we might drop on Berlin to end the war in Europe. Some think we may be home by Christmas.

A more realistic new plan calls for the Brits to invade northern Germany through Belgium and the Netherlands. Command estimates that German resistance in Belgium and the Netherlands will be light, because German troops there are believed to be in disarray, and the enemy forces in the area are deemed to be of low quality, mainly older men.[12]

The Netherlands, although flat as a pancake, has many canals and small rivers that make transportation through the area dependent on bridges. The British army will need to cross bridges at such places as Grave, Veghel, Eindhoven, and Son, and the Waal River at Nijmegen and the Rijn (Rhine) River at Arnhem. Both of these wide rivers are potentially major roadblocks if the enemy controls or destroys their bridges. But once British armored forces cross the Rijn, they can race through the northern Netherlands and into Germany. In order for the operation to be successful, someone will have to secure the bridges and important crossroads to keep the British tanks moving towards Germany.

The highway chosen as the route for the British armor is not a long stretch of road. Heading north from the Belgian border into the southern Netherlands, the compressed gravel road, with a few stretches of brick, is wide enough for two cars to pass each other easily, although large trucks and tanks will have to be very careful. The highway shoulders are well made, but away from the shoulder the ground is soft and marshy in many places, making it necessary for heavy vehicles to stay completely on the road.

The 101st Airborne Screaming Eagles are one of the divisions assigned to keep the road open for the British tanks. The problem for the airborne troops in securing the highway is that there aren't enough soldiers and equipment to guard the entire road. This means that long stretches of highway between

Veghel and Grave will be entirely unprotected from German attacks on the British armor most of the time.

The plan to get the British moving is code-named Operation Market Garden. "Market" is to be the airborne portion of the assault and calls for the division to take the main highway and bridges. It is to be handled by the Screaming Eagles, the 82nd Airborne Division, the British 1st Airborne Division, and the inexperienced and lightly armed Polish 1st Independent Parachute Brigade, which is attached to the British division. Polish soldiers are known for their ferocity in battle; they are eager to take revenge for what the enemy has done to their homeland.[13]

The British armor is to push from Belgium into the Netherlands in the "Garden" part of the operation. The risky airborne assault to keep the road open is to begin on September 17, barely leaving the division enough time to prepare for action. Two whole German armies are to be trapped on the left flank during the northward push by the Allies. These armies have the potential to wreak havoc, but it is hoped that they are already depleted and will not be capable of putting up much of a fight.[14]

Planners feel that the Market Garden assault has a significant amount of risk. If the British armor doesn't succeed in pushing through, the outnumbered and outgunned airborne troops could be destroyed. An airborne division operating behind enemy lines isn't equipped to hold positions for more than forty-eight hours against an armor-supported enemy. Each airborne division is assigned an area of about twenty miles along the highway to secure and protect during the operation. The British armor, led by the Guards Armoured Division, has to get through to the Rijn at Arnhem quickly, within the forty-eight hours.[15]

The staging area for Market runs about sixty-four miles from north to south along a highway that would later come to be known by the Screaming Eagles as Hell's Highway, for good reason. To the far north of us, the British 1st Airborne, along with the smaller Polish brigade, is to land near Arnhem and capture key bridges on the lower Rijn River. The US 82nd Airborne Division will strike into the middle of the staging area in order to secure bridges from Grave to Nijmegen.[16]

The 101st is to land in the southern part of the staging area. Our targets are bridges in and near the Dutch cities and towns of Eindhoven, Son, Sint-Oedenrode, Best, and Veghel. Screaming Eagles paratrooper and glider landings will be relatively easy in the flat fields around the target areas. Our glider training is finally to be used in combat. And there is no doubt that this operation, unlike the previously planned missions, is going to take place.[17]

The division is alerted for the operation on September 11. The units are issued a warning order to be prepared for departure within twenty-four hours. Equipment that is not going to be taken with us into battle is packed away and secured. Kitchen personnel are ready to go by sea, and battle equipment is moved to the airfields. British pound currency notes are exchanged for Dutch guilders in case we need to buy anything in the Netherlands.[18] Sergeant Hanlon briefs us as we prepare to go: "The enemy will outnumber us. The division isn't large enough to completely secure the highway. We will take bridges and crossroads. After securing the targets, patrols will be set out to engage the enemy and keep them guessing our strength. Speed and precision are necessary."

Paratrooper drops are to be in daylight, not during the dark. The parachute regiments parachute into the Netherlands on September 17. The 327th follows with glider landings on September 18, 19, and 20, holding in reserve for the parachute regiments, as needed. There aren't enough towplanes to get us in on the first day with the paratroopers.[19] My glider will go in on the second day (D+1).

On September 16, Company G pulls out of Camp Ranikhet at 0845 in trucks, moving to an airport at Ramsbury, England. We stay at a tent camp near the airfield. On September 18, we load 181 men into fifteen gliders at Membury Airfield near Hungerford, England, for the flight to the European mainland. Captain Evans, ever the stickler on detail, has the company officers divide so each is in a different glider. At the end of the runway, the gliders and tug planes are lined up in two rows. Second Battalion is readying eighty gliders. Brigadier General McAuliff and his party are loading in the first two, and Colonel Harper is in the third.[20]

"What do you think about these greenhorns?" Boz asks loudly, also sending a message to the replacements. Boz is helping me, knowing I am the only one on the flight who has had proper glider training. "I hope they don't get us killed!" he adds. We continue to load the supplies, mostly by ourselves, to ensure it is done right. This is the first flight for the replacements, and they don't know how to properly pack and balance a glider for safe flight.

Boz steps up into the glider with a heavy load of several boxes. "Ah! My back!" he exclaims. The look on his face tells me he isn't kidding. He steps out of the glider, sits down, and leans against it.

"Better get that checked out," I tell him. "If you're as hurt as bad as you're acting, you'll be harder to babysit than these greenhorns."

"No, I'm fine." He stands and tries to load another box. "Ah!" he exclaims again.

"Take Boz to the medic," I say to the replacements. A couple of them lift him, putting his arms around their shoulders, and half carry him to the company medic.

They return a short time later. "Boz isn't going anywhere, at least not today," they inform me. "He's staying behind."

After finishing the loading, I head off to find Hanlon, wanting to find out what is up with Boz. On the way I see a glider whose nose is painted with shark teeth. I chuckle about this, but I can't really decide if it is funny or scary.

As I walk up to Hanlon, a guy snaps a picture of him sitting on the ground relaxing with the guys. Hanlon tells me a soldier from company headquarters will take Boz's place. Captain Evans wants headquarters personnel, like the company officers, to ride in separate gliders to prevent them from being killed or captured together.[21]

On the side of another glider Hanlon and some others from the squad paint the words, "Look Hurmin, no motor!" Hurmin is a new nickname Americans have for German soldiers; it pokes fun at Hermann Göring, the second-in-command of Germany.

At 1130, McAuliffe's glider takes off into overcast skies and a ceiling of four thousand feet.[22] One by one the towplanes take their turns, catapulting the gliders into the air. My head snaps to my right from the force of the take-off as the towline is stretched to its full length and pulls on the glider. The already loud sound of air rushing by the canvas becomes deafening as we pass through the towplane's propwash. Coming out of the wash, it is still hard to hear, so as a group we say little. I don't want to talk, and the replacements seem too scared to talk, or maybe they are just thinking to themselves.

Once airborne, the towplanes and gliders circle above the airfield until all are up and ready to fly across the Channel. By 1205, Company G is fully in the air. The second group of forty gliders prepares to depart as the first group of forty clears the skies. We make our way over the English coast; the landscape below is beautiful. We are flying at fifteen hundred to two thousand feet.[23] The flight over the channel is uneventful and takes three hours and fifteen minutes. In spite of the good weather, some of the gliders from other companies go down over the English Channel. The vomiting starts, but my stomach is still okay. Helmets are passed towards the replacement soldier sitting by the door, who empties them into a bucket and periodically opens the door enough to empty the bucket in flight.

The flight path takes us over the coast of Belgium and the Schelde Estuary. I can see mile after mile of fields the Germans have flooded by

The inscription, "Look Hurmin, no motor," was intended as mockery of Hermann Göring, Nazi leader of the German air force. From Rapport and Northwood, *Rendezvous with Destiny,* courtesy Battery Press.

Towplanes and gliders lined up for the Market Garden flight. Courtesy Charles Day collection.

destroying dikes that normally hold ocean waters back. The Germans have done this in an attempt to prevent our invasion through the Netherlands. We meet sporadic gunfire once we fly over the coast, likely diminished somewhat because the enemy can't put up as many antiaircraft batteries because of the flooding.

The latrine bucket is passed around the glider one more time before we land. We all chuckle as the young soldier who dumps the contents out the door is hit by the contents when the wind blows it back into the glider. The flight is fairly smooth, and only some of the guys are airsick. The antiaircraft fire starts to get heavy; some of it comes very close, startling us with each explosion. I think only about living through this. Occasionally I can see German soldiers firing up at us. Sherman tells me later that gunfire came up through the floor of the glider and out the ceiling, sounding like popcorn. When the bullets came through, the guys sat on the wooden stocks of their rifles for a little more protection.

I am scared for my life as the explosions continue to pound angrily around us, tossing the glider violently several times. Were we the next lucky German shot? One glider goes down, but it is not one of G Company's. Germans try harder to kill us as we near the landing area near the city of Eindhoven. Some of the towplanes are hit, but most of the glider pilots are able to disconnect. My glider and towplane make it to the landing area and set up for release at about four hundred feet. Even with the good weather, the ride is rough. The German antiaircraft explosions are increasingly intense. To say I am scared is a major understatement.

Close to the landing zone, the glider cuts loose from the C-47 and breaks in a typical pattern, careening toward the airfield. As we descend, the pilot approaches the landing field from the south. It seems we are dropping rather than gliding. As we get closer, the pilot spots a waterway in the field that was to serve as the runway. If the glider hits the ditch on landing, the impact will immediately kill us all.

The pilot pulls the glider out of the landing approach, leveling out and causing the sluggish glider to nose up a bit, gaining what seems to be only a few feet of altitude. This is both exhilarating and scary and causes butterflies in my stomach. The pilot sets up a new landing approach and then again lowers the aircraft's nose. None of us in the glider say a word. Most of us simply look down at the floor and quietly pray, some to Jesus, others to Mary. Again the pilot sees another waterway ahead and pulls out of landing a second time, only this time we are even lower, and the nose doesn't come up quite as much. Still, no one except the pilot says anything; he is talking to

Troops deploy from a glider after landing. Courtesy Charles Day collection.

the soldier in the copilot seat. This time the aircraft glides in a little slower; our altitude is not very high. The third time, we lower a bit as we approach the field for a landing. "Boys, this is it!" the pilot exclaims. "If we don't get down, there won't be a fourth try. We don't have enough airspeed!"

We are going to have to land this time even if there is a ditch in our way. As the glider slows down, each bump seems bigger than the last as we bounce along in the rough air. The glider bounces hard on touchdown and then skids bumpily through the field, and after what seems like minutes (but in fact is only a little more than ten seconds) it comes to a stop right at a waterway. Its nose is hanging over the edge of the ditch.

"Whew, glad that's over," I say, out loud. Then suddenly the glider lurches forward, knocking us around. "What the hell? Wow! What was that?" Another glider is suddenly parked right beside our glider. We stagger out of the glider door. Our right wing is gone, knocked off by the other glider.

Our pilot is the last out. He is very upset. "Can't you fly better than that?" he yells at the crew of the other glider. "You've got the whole field to land in, and you run into us. Look at that wing." His grumbling goes on and on. I think it's a little funny, seeing he had a hard time putting our glider down where he wanted to.

I look around. The landing zone is a flat, open field, rectangular in shape, about a mile across by two miles long. Discarded parachutes and supplies are everywhere. White chutes belong to the soldiers, while colored chutes are from a supply drop. After exiting the glider as quickly as possible, the other men and I, along with others from several nearby gliders, set up a perimeter defense until it is determined we are not under attack from the enemy. Small arms and mortar fire can be heard in the distance, but nothing near us. We have landed about a mile from where the company commander, Captain Evans, is finally located. I have to walk one hundred yards to find a place where we can cross the drainage ditch. Soon we march off, under Lt. Stanley Morrison's calm leadership, toward the main 2nd Battalion assembly area near Wolfswinkel. The crew members from all fifteen Company G gliders are accounted for.

Nearly all the gliders have enemy gunfire damage. One crewman has to put out a fire in a glider when mortar ammunition is hit by small-arms fire. Two men are killed by shell fragments from antiaircraft fire.[24]

We are briefed on the situation for the 101st. The 502nd Parachute Regiment is having serious problems with enemy forces at Best, which slows down the operations. On the positive side Son, Sint-Oedenrode, and Veghel are now in American hands. Major stretches of the highway are also under American control.[25]

As we pass time talking, many stories circulate among the soldiers. General McAuliffe, one of the top leaders of the 101st, had the misfortune of having his glider's tug plane hit by antiaircraft fire, causing the loss of an engine. We are thankful they were able to land safely. While still airborne, Colonel Harper was shooting at Germans from the glider with an M1 rifle. Another glider was safely landed by a soldier who took over after the glider's pilots were killed by enemy flak fire. The only flight training he'd received was watching the pilots fly the glider during training and then during the mission before they died.[26]

Operation Market Garden is proceeding, but not without difficulty. The British Guards Armoured Division (the troops we are to open the road for) is advancing up the road on its way to invade Germany. The Guards come within fifteen miles to the south of Eindhoven at the start of Market Garden but are stopped by German pressure. The Son bridge is blown by the enemy. Eindhoven is still in German hands.[27]

Soon after getting organized, Sergeant Hanlon tells us to get ready to support the 502nd at Best, just to the west a couple of miles, but we end up staying right where we are. The rest of the day and night for G Company is spent organizing patrols to protect the perimeter of the landing zone, plan-

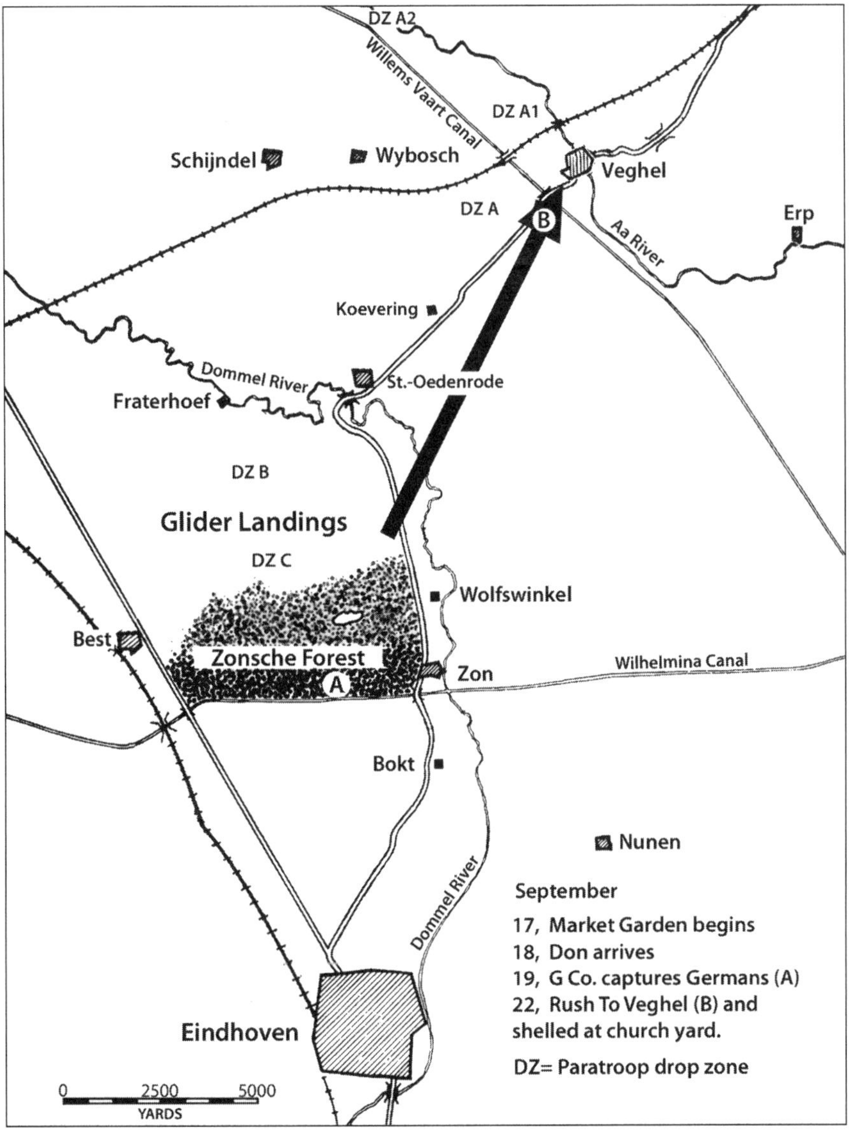

Company G in Operation Market Garden, September 1944.

ning, and cleaning our weapons. We hear more reports of the battle going on at Best, where the Germans are apparently making their main challenge.

Members of the Dutch underground, dressed in the blue overalls commonly worn by livestock farmers, greet us. They are wearing orange armbands to signify their membership in the Dutch Resistance. We are getting quite a warm welcome from the Dutch people, and we are proud to help them.

Niland comes around, inspecting the perimeter and, as always, assessing what the enemy is up to. With him is Charles Fisher, the replacement soldier who has just turned eighteen. This scrappy, blond-haired kid is wide-eyed and scared like most of the replacements. Niland points out a telephone wire heading out into the darkness. On the other end is a guy in a foxhole whose job it is to alert command if the enemy is confronting us. Niland says to Fisher, "Follow the line to the foxhole and relieve the guy at the other end. Remember, the Krauts can also follow the line to where you're going." Fisher heads out in front of the perimeter and disappears into the night.

Niland turns to me. "Keep an eye out. Fisher's green," is all he says.

At 0500, Niland comes around again. "Rich, let's go get Fisher and see if he's still there," he says. "I told him you'd replace him five hours ago."

The two of us walk about two hundred yards to a foxhole with Fisher in it. Fisher is looking the other way, toward the enemy positions. Niland jumps into the foxhole. "Nice job, Fisher," Niland assures the young man. "You stayed. Now I know I can trust you." Then we all head back.

The next day, September 19, the weather isn't nearly as good for glider landings. Rain and fog hamper visibility and make life miserable. In addition, the Germans, unknown to our commanders, are benefiting by using a map and schedule they found in a crashed glider. Knowing where and when other landings will be made, they hit incoming gliders hard with antiaircraft fire on their landing approach. Many gliders crash from the weather, accidents, or enemy fire.[28]

Later, more reports come in that Eindhoven is in American hands and that the British Guards are moving into that city on their way north to Germany. Eindhoven locals excitedly mob the American soldiers. Some of the most affectionate greeters are women who have "collaborated" with German soldiers and are trying to avoid the retribution of villagers by showing support for American soldiers. This tactic does not work, and most of them have their heads shaved in scorn by the Dutch villagers. Some collaborators are sent to jail or work camps, but occasionally a trigger-happy Dutchman with a personal score to settle kills a known collaborator. The French didn't seem quite as thrilled to see us, and the French culture was stranger to us than the Dutch. In fairness to the French, I never really got to know them, because of my wound, except for the nice family who opened their door to me and tended to my wound. I will always be thankful to them.

Colonel Allen of the 401st (organized as the 3rd Battalion of the 327th) is ordered to use his men to assist H Company of the 502nd near Best on the morning of September 19. Allen's men force two hundred enemy troops to move into hiding positions in the Zonsche Forest. Second Battalion of the 327th, including G Company, is called in to clear the forest of these enemy troops. The 502nd will push the enemy in the west of the forest and 2nd Battalion will push toward the west from a small lake, called Oude Meer, in the middle of the forest. It is planned that the pincer forces of the 502nd, aided by British tanks, and the 327th will corner and crush the enemy against the canal to the south.[29] If the operation goes as planned, the trap will keep the enemy from being able to retreat. We hope it will be that simple.

Second Battalion is finally given marching orders at 1230 to move west and get into position for the attack. For the Screaming Eagles the battle plan is going fairly well, except for the trouble the 502nd is still having at Best. The Germans, by making a big stand there, have greatly weakened their ability to attack in other areas, allowing for large expanses of the highway to remain open. The enemy manages to counterattack at Veghel, with some serious action. The enemy also has heavy artillery, which our side still can't counter, creating an ever-present danger for us.

Moving out for the attack, we leave our nonessential gear in a glider for safekeeping. The attack is to begin at 1400. I find an M1 Garand and quickly discard my peashooter carbine. We assemble at the northwest edge of Oude Meer Lake. Companies F and G are given the task of carrying out the mission, with E Company in reserve. We are told there will be between fifty and five hundred enemy soldiers for us to clear out. Company F is positioned to the northwest of the lake. First Platoon under Lieutenant Morrison is on F's right flank. Second and 3rd Platoons are on F's left flank, a short distance north of the lake. The machine gun and mortar sections also are positioned on the left flank of Company F, with the machine guns being closer to the lake and the mortars behind them. We are on the mortars' left flank. Company G is to sweep the forest from east to west in an attempt to take eight hundred yards of ground.[30]

Battalion headquarters machine gunners start the attack by laying down heavy machine gun fire. At 1400 we are underway when the firing subsides. The machine gun fire has been so intense that it starts a fire in the forest, creating a lot of smoke. We move south about four hundred yards and reach the edge of the forest with no sign of the enemy. The smoke from the blaze is thickening.

"Rich, stay here and guard the rear," Hibbard orders me.

The two columns from 2nd Platoon head south on both sides of the path, with Hibbard's 1st and 2nd Squads moving through the trees on the right side of the path and Hidalgo's 3rd Squad on the left. They disappear into the forest and smoke.

After about fifteen minutes the squads reappear. The trees and smoke are making it impossible for them to get through. They start over again, this time staying on the pathway.

At first I don't think much about being left behind, but the deeper the company moves into the forest, the lonelier and more vulnerable I begin to feel. There won't be any tanks in the forest. Basically, I am the warning guy: I am to alert the rest of an impending attack from the rear. Unfortunately, there will be no one around to warn me.

Five minutes later, I hear shots and hollering in English, German, and Spanish. From my vantage point, I can't see anything of what is going on because of the trees and smoke. The gunfire intensifies with the sound of a German machine gun and then subsides. Company G machine gunners show up and head toward the fight with two .30 caliber water-cooled machine guns and a BAR. After ten minutes, the big guns open up on the Germans fast and furious. A few more quiet minutes pass, and gunfire erupts again. More hollering is heard in all three languages and then some more sporadic gunfire and more hollering.

"Cease firing!" I know Hibbard's voice.

After another minute goes by I hear Hibbard again: "Get Sergeant Gross!"

A few more minutes pass, after which comes another round of gunfire.

"Cease firing!" I hear again, but I can't tell who it is. More shots.

"Fire anyway!" Several more shots.

Germans are coming out of the forest near me with their hands in the air. I raise my M1 and survey the situation and then lower the rifle. The enemy soldiers aren't going to fight. Headquarters guys show up and start corralling the prisoners. As I'm trying to get past the surrendering soldiers, an older one, in his fifties or older, grabs me firmly. His accent sounds more Eastern European than German. He's bawling and speaks in broken English.

"If I surrender, you'll kill me. If I do not surrender you'll kill me!" he says, begging as if pleading for his life.

"Shut up, no one's going to kill you!" I shout at him while jerking free.

I make my way down the path toward the commotion. After about a hundred yards I run into the machine gunners. Lloyd Gross is shouting in German. Then there is another shot.

"You sum bitch, keep up with me or be with me!" Hidalgo hollers.

"Look out! There's a German behind you!" I hear Hanlon yell again. I head east down the path toward the hollering. Hanlon fires his Tommy gun. The German drops to the ground dead. Hidalgo turns, looking surprised.

Hidalgo continues running through the trees along the road and runs into two Kraut officers who are completely surprised. Hidalgo and one of the Germans swing their guns toward each other and hit each other in the gut at the same instant with the barrels of their rifles. There is a long pause, no voices, no hollering. The two combatants stare each other down. The other German officer drops his rifle. It seems like a minute passes, but likely it is only seconds. Hidalgo backs away. The weaponless Kraut shouts at the one with his rifle still pointed at Hidalgo, then they both raise their arms in the air. Five more Germans are running east down the trail, running past a dead Kraut and a bicycle.

"Surrender or die you summa bitches!" Hidalgo yells at them.

Gross hollers in German. They stop in their tracks, raising their hands.

Hidalgo and Hibbard take off up and down the trail.

"Surrender or die!" Surrender or die!" "Surrender or die!"

More Krauts come out of the woods with hands held high, and an American major steps out of the woods with a group of prisoners. He's with the 377th Parachute Field Artillery Battalion and was captured earlier by the Krauts.

Second Platoon reorganizes and sweeps 150 yards south to the canal. Two German soldiers are seen across the canal where we can't get to them. Gross induces them to swim the canal and surrender.

Because of the excitement of the situation, I haven't noticed the dreadful smell. There is a dead animal rendering plant just west of the north–south trail and along the canal. Third Squad guards the road along the canal. Second Platoon enters the plant compound, which consists of a number of buildings. Half squads go through the buildings. No shots are fired as two Germans are taken in the factory building. More prisoners are surrendering, coming out of the woods. They are scared, having encountered the 502nd and British tanks to the west, the 401st, and now us.

Meanwhile, 1st Platoon under Morrison links up with us, having swept in from the northwest. They were delayed by enemy fire and were supported by F Company. German noncommissioned officers are being forced at gunpoint through the woods to tell their men to surrender, and as a result, 159 prisoners are taken.

We head back toward the lake, where G is placed in reserve at the landing zone. We have time to rehash what had happened during the day on the march, and as we walk, Jack Sherman fills me in: "Paul Thayer was the first to spot the Krauts. He dropped one with a single shot right along the trail. Back to the east they had a machine gun set up along the path where Hidalgo and the Kraut eyeballed each other. They fired at us and didn't hit anybody. The heavy MGs were brought in, but they couldn't reach the Krauts due to a hill. The BAR could get closer, but we still couldn't get to them. Hibbard took his guys through the woods on the north side of the path, Hidalgo's men to the south. The guys crawled and crouched until they got close."

A soldier who speaks some German tells Hidalgo, "It sure sounds like they really don't want to be here. They all want to surrender. At least, I think so."

Hidalgo yells out to Hibbard to get Gross to talk to them. While they wait, a German soldier stands up and is immediately shot in the leg by Grapentine. Hibbard yells, "Cease firing!" but there is no way the Krauts are going to give up now. The guys move in.

"I think I saw most of the rest," I reply.

Jack keeps on: "Another Kraut takes off on a bicycle, leaving a civilian behind. Hidalgo shoots over his head. He doesn't stop and Hidalgo kills him with a head shot. Another Kraut from the same foxhole makes for the bicycle and Hidalgo hits him in the leg. Hidalgo takes off across the trail to keep other Krauts from running. Hanlon on the other side almost hits Hidalgo with his Tommy gun. That's when Hidalgo yells at Hanlon and calls him some names. Hanlon yelled back about the Kraut coming behind him and drops him in his tracks with the Tommy. Hidalgo is sure surprised."[31]

Some of the local Dutchmen, including children, come out to greet us, waving and happy to see us. "Are they crazy?" I say to guys in the squad. "What are they doing?" I guess years of German occupation have diminished their fears. Sometimes the Dutch endanger themselves and us by their happiness and gratitude. Others, however, are scared and are desperately trying to stay hidden.

Now, having returned to the landing zone, we find that our gear is gone. "Stolen," I think. But instead of being stolen, the gear has been picked up by local Dutch people and taken by horse-drawn cart to a nearby barn for safekeeping from the weather and any Germans who might stumble upon it. The rest of the evening and night we spend guarding our supplies from bands of German soldiers and helping unload gliders that have just arrived.

We dig foxholes and cook some food. When in a foxhole, we usually don't dare to stand up because of the hazard of enemy fire. I am quickly learning that my helmet is quite the asset to have under these circumstances, and a soldier can get quite a bit of use from a helmet besides protection. A helmet can be used to dig foxholes, cook a meal in, take a bath in, or use as a latrine.

During the night we can hear fighting going on at Son, not far away to the southeast. The enemy has a bonfire lit in the area, hoping to illuminate American positions, and they are supported by tanks and artillery, which we have very little of at this point. To the south, Eindhoven is being battered by the German Luftwaffe, and fires set by the bombs light up the night sky. We find out later that two hundred civilians are killed.[32]

September 19 has been an exhausting day. Out of ninety-eight gliders, thirty-eight didn't make it to the landing zone. We have captured many prisoners. I am worn out. The next morning, the enemy hits the 327th's sector of the perimeter in an attack with tank support. The attack is directed at C Company to the south of the canal. Reinforcements are called in, and the arrival of ten British tanks forces the enemy back. The sounds of battle echo through the area. Three British and four German tanks are destroyed, and a Brit gasoline tanker explodes in spectacular fashion.[33]

US aircraft fill the sky. Gliders are still landing, and supplies are dropped by parachute near our position. German ground fire opens up on the aerial armada. Crews bail out of C-47s at such a low altitude that their parachutes don't help. The big transport planes hit the ground and explode on impact or careen along the ground and then explode. German Bf 109 fighters strafe the field, with British Typhoons and American P-51s in pursuit. German ground fire peppers the area. Then the Germans begin to withdraw.[34]

As the enemy falls back, G Company is called to complete another mission very similar to the one in the Zonsche Forest the previous day, but located further west. The rifle platoons sweep westward, parallel to each other, for two kilometers without meeting any resistance.[35]

Sparks and Shaw seem to be working out all right as bazooka assistants in the section, but Sparks concerns me because of his poor reputation as a soldier. Since we haven't yet seen any real bazooka action, I really don't know what will happen in fighting involving bazookas. Shaw's buddy Sherman seems confident as he delivers orders to us. He is from Michigan, where he has a serious girlfriend named Phyllis. He worked in a factory before being drafted. Sherman hangs around to visit with Shaw before heading back to company headquarters.[36] The replacements have a comradery of their own, although they are ignored and treated badly by the veterans. I listen to their conversation.

"Hey buddy, keeping the Krauts off the highway?" Sherman asks Shaw.

"Just playin' cowboys and Indians," Shaw replies, referring to the hit-and-run tactics of the enemy.

"We've got to keep Rich here safe, being he's such a young kid," Sherman says. "Don't want to see him get hurt by them Krauts again." Sherman likes to remind me he is almost a month older than me. I am getting to like the two of them, but it seems awkward, since they are replacements. The sting of Proppe's death at times still fogs my mind.

In the afternoon we make contact with the 502nd. Mission accomplished. Instead of returning to the landing zone, however, 2nd Battalion sets up a defensive perimeter at a clearing in the forest near where we started in the morning. G Company's position extends from the canal north toward the west edge of the landing zone. We stay in this position until September 22.[37] Several times I join patrols making sweeps through the area, making sure there are no enemy troops coming back in. The Germans apparently have one of the same problems we do: not enough men. Orders stress that we are not here to kill Germans. Only those enemy soldiers who are threatening to close the highway are to be attacked. We are thankful that the Dutch continue to be our eyes and ears, telling us what the Germans are up to.

To the north, the 82nd Airborne has also achieved most of their objectives, except for one: the bridge over the Waal River at Nijmegen is still in German hands. This is costly, because it causes the British armor to halt their advance. The British Guards cross the bridge with a few tanks, then stop, refusing to go on. I can't imagine an American commander doing such a thing as abandoning his own troops. This also puts more pressure on the 101st to keep the road open. After a fierce battle on September 20, the 82nd finally captures the bridge. Even further to the north in the Netherlands is where the real troubles for Allied forces start. The British 1st Airborne Division lands on September 17 in an area where two crack German panzer divisions are refitting after long deployments along the Eastern Front. The Germans are seasoned and battle-hardened troops.[38]

The Brits succeed in securing the north bank of the Rijn River at Arnhem, where the bridge is located, but can't accomplish the task on the south bank. Furthermore, British airborne reinforcements are delayed by weather and combat losses. The British try to air drop supplies to their comrades, but the drop lands in the German-controlled zone. By now, the situation is becoming desperate for the 1st British Airborne. Airborne divisions are only supposed to be able to hold out on their own for two complete days; they are now on their fourth day and in a very bleak situation.[39]

In contrast, at the 101st staging area the Germans are in disarray and have no idea that they in fact have sufficient numbers to take the 101st head-on, so they don't. They continue to use hit-and-run tactics to destroy bridges. Another tactic used by the enemy is to capture and hold small villages for short periods of time in an attempt to slow up the northward movement of British tanks. Knowing the Allies need to cross the Rijn at Arnhem, the Germans funnel reinforcements quickly to that area, causing more problems for the beleaguered British troops. The situation for the Germans is like holding onto a rope for dear life: that rope hold is at the bridge over the Rijn River at Arnhem.[40]

The Screaming Eagles are beginning to experience an unexpected problem. The German troops in the area are not used to US Army tactics that involve flanking maneuvers in an attempt to attack from the rear. This is because either they are not experienced enough or they have come from the Russian front, where the Russians attacked head-on, sacrificing men instead of weapons. Because of our tactics, far more German troops are surrendering than anticipated. They are so uncomfortable with the unfamiliar situation of being confronted from both the front and the rear that they often surrender in spite of having superior numbers and artillery.[41] Occasionally, though not often, captured enemy soldiers are released by US units engaged in trying to keep the highway open, because there simply is no place or way to properly keep prisoners.

On Friday, September 22, the 327th is again alerted to expect more action. Intelligence from the Dutch underground tells the Allies that a German attack is to take place along the highway near Veghel to the north. The enemy is building up numbers on both sides of the highway. Second Battalion leaves the Zonsche Forest area at 1000. As the British armor have priority along Hell's Highway, we have to take secondary roads close by. We start on foot for Veghel, where we will be under the command of Brig. Gen. Anthony B. McAuliffe.[42]

Niland leaves early in a jeep to scout out Veghel with Fisher and a couple other guys, Mike Panic and William Feeney. When they return, Niland reports that he doesn't like the views the enemy will have of our movements from the church steeples in surrounding villages.[43]

The amount of damage and debris from battles along the way to Veghel is surprising. Destroyed trucks, jeeps, transports, and tanks are strewn about.

Bodies and fresh graves, along with sporadic rifle fire, are rather unnerving things to see and hear. Most of the dead are British and German soldiers. When we reach Sint-Oedenrode, word is given that the enemy attack on Veghel has already started. The road is cut, and not only is the British armor stopped, but it is engaging the German armor and taking heavy losses. Two companies from the 401st (3rd Battalion of the 327th) are immediately loaded into trucks and rushed to Veghel. The 401st becomes fiercely engaged with enemy infantry supported by German Mark IV tanks. British armor and the Screaming Eagles don't work well together because of lack of trust in each other and lack of joint training.[44]

We begin to double-time it on foot toward Veghel. Enemy artillery falls around us on the march past Sint-Oedenrode, prompting us to take a different route across open country, which is pretty hard to do when fully loaded with seventy-five pounds of supplies and weapons. With several more miles to go to Veghel, our officers protest to command, thinking we'll be too tired to fight if we keep up the pace.[45] My legs hurt and I feel weak, largely because of lack of food. The older guys are having some difficulty keeping up.

Second Battalion reaches Veghel an hour or so before dark, with G leading the column. More than forty enemy tanks are reported to be in the area, as well as sizable numbers of German soldiers. We expect to engage the enemy at any time. As we cross the Aa River bridge and make a slight turn to the left, we face a very large, beautiful Catholic church and see some locals clearing out and going into buildings and houses as we march up the street. They seem to know something we don't.

Another group of Dutch citizens is standing together, looking at us from a main intersection. This small group seems quietly excited although somewhat nervous about our being present, and their warm greeting makes me feel pretty good. Behind this group is a young couple dressed in full-length black leather coats.[46] In contrast to the others, the two do not seem glad to see us at all and keep looking back over their shoulders as they scurry down the street away from us. I wonder what is wrong with them, but I decide that maybe they have never seen Americans before. I suppose that we are quite a sight. We probably look like we need a bath, at least.

"That doesn't look right to me," Sherman says. "I don't like it."

"Feels like we're being watched," Denis Parsons adds.

The battalion is ordered into a reserve position in a large open area, about the size of three football fields, next to the big church, which is located right in the middle of town. I am fifty feet west of the church in the open field. We are being arranged in the field by company, and G is closest to the church building. Some of the battalion soldiers are still out on the street. Seemingly out of nowhere, shells whoosh in, and the ground rocks with three successive explosions. The heavy barrage continues like clockwork, with shells literally walking up and down the field three at a time, one salvo after another. The shells pound our position. Men scream with fear and pain between explosions. In between salvos, some try to make a run for a bridge located over a full drainage ditch (to the west), wanting to get away from the carnage. A smaller and closer footbridge crosses a canal north of me.

I count out the time between incoming salvos and estimate how long it will take me to get to the bridge and then safely in one of the houses on the other side of the ditch. There is no way I can make it to that bridge between shell bursts. Frantically, I make futile efforts to dig a foxhole in between bursts, hoping to get it deep enough to hide my body. Dirt flies in the air from the explosions, sounding almost like rain when it hits the ground. Metal shrapnel zings through the air. Captain Evans is close to me and digging like a madman in suspenders, straight down. Joe Slish, just to the south of me, is also digging and making good progress. His body workouts are coming in handy for him.

The Germans' 105 mm shells, incoming from the southeast, are chewing us to pieces.[47] The church takes several direct hits, and I am protected somewhat by its roof. But when a shell hits the roof and skips off, landing nearby, I go back to frantic digging. A scoop of dirt is all I can get in before the next round hits. Medics are bravely running from one wounded man to the next. Medic Henry Scherrer, jumping up, runs by me toward someone screaming in pain. Blam, blam, blam! The shells hit nearby, and Henry falls head first and doesn't move, not more than twenty feet from me. His head is to the side, and I can see blood trickling from his forehead. Blam, blam, blam! Whoosh! Wham, wham, wham! The cycle repeats. Sherman is much closer to safety than I; he gets up and runs for the footbridge over the small canal on the south perimeter and makes it. I get two or three shovelfuls dug between explosions. As I lie there I scrape dirt and pray. "Keep on digging," I tell myself as the explosions rage on.

The barrage is utterly terrifying, and there is no way to fight back. We are so helpless. I think each round has my name written on it. I don't expect to survive. The barrage continues as if it will never end. The sound from the exploding shells and the resulting concussions are unbearable, penetrating right through me. I try to shrink as small as I can when I hear more incoming shells, but there is nowhere to go, nothing to do but dig in between

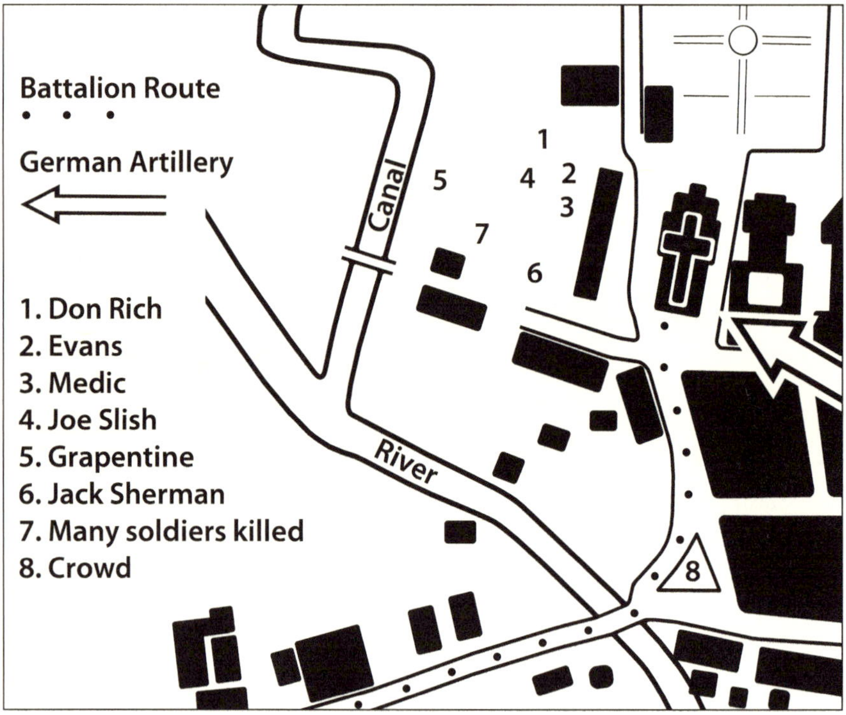

The shelling at Veghel, the Netherlands, September 22, 1944. Second Battalion approaches Veghel from the southwest, continues to the church, and begins digging in in the yard to the west of the church.

each salvo. After the explosions come screams from wounded and dying US soldiers. There isn't much anyone can do. The shelling lasts about thirty minutes, then stops as quickly as it began. Soon, darkness settles in over the decimated battalion as the smell of gunpowder and death covers the area. Company G alone suffers twenty-one killed and wounded: a lot of men.[48]

Sergeant Hidalgo comes around coaxing men to get up and leave the area: "Come on, guys, let's go, up and at it, let's go!" Then, with more emphasis, he speaks louder and faster: "You sum a bitches, move!" He still doesn't seem mad; it's just his usual way of talking. Hidalgo is a paradox. He is so much a serious soldier, yet he knows how to be compassionate.

Niland comes over. "The bastards knew we were here!" he says angrily. "They must have seen me look the place over from the steeples. The artillery is just too accurate not to have it planned out."

The battalion makes camp in another field within the village limits, but because of shell shock and just plain fright, some soldiers don't want to move.

I'm one of them. For some reason, and I really don't know why—probably because of emotional shock and numbness—I stay in the decimated field. I can't sleep, anyway; the sounds of the explosions play over and over again in my mind. My hearing is funny. Voices seem distorted, and I can't make out what is being said.

That awful night eventually turns into morning. Early on, Colonel Harper makes an appearance, assessing the situation. I overhear him say the battalion lost eighty men. Captain Evans believes the enemy had someone in the village directing the fire.

Sherman comes up to me and tells me his experience: "During the night I could hear the sound of marching soldiers. Click, click, these were not US soldiers. Then there was a lot of hollering. Some of the fellows were yelling, 'Get 'em! Kill the damn Krauts! Shoot 'em!' while running toward German prisoners who were being marched right by our bivouac. One of the soldiers guarding the prisoners yelled for our guys to back off. Then there was more hollering by our troops. I said, 'Back off! Leave them alone!' The guard moved his hands toward his rifle. He meant business. Good thing Hidalgo was there. Calmly he says, 'All right, guys, break it up. Leave the sum a bitch Krauts alone.' The guys turned and went back to their foxholes."[49]

At daybreak, Hibbard, ignoring the carnage around him, says in a matter-of-fact tone, "Rich, gather the weapons. We're going to need them." I look about me, seeing weapons scattered around. Some guns are on the ground with no dead soldier near them. Others are partially under dead bodies.

I walk over to Scherrer's body. On his forehead he has only a little blood coming from a small hole caused by shrapnel. His eyes are open. I wonder why he had to die and others of us made it out alive. He had to be the nicest guy in the company. With a heavy heart I look around and see what is left of Sgt. Joe Slish. His eyes are still open as well. Slish's body-builder physique is literally blown in half at his waist. Nearby is Sergeant Grapentine, whose body is riddled with holes throughout. He looks like a sieve; I can't begin to count the holes. All three of these men bunked in my barrack back in England. I am sick to my stomach but manage to hold it in. A Dutch Catholic priest is there as well, praying over the dead.

We get word that the Dutch underground took care of some collaborators. One was shot by a group of Dutch underground soldiers while she walked out of a church building with her hands held up behind her head. Possibly this was the woman I had seen dressed in black; she may have been responsible for providing the Germans with the information on our location. Some other guys report seeing a German soldier in the steeple there as well, saying that the German had even taken a few shots at them. Still, the German artillery had a clear view for a long way to the northwest and southeast and could have spotted us themselves.[50]

A squad of African American soldiers is assigned the duty of burying the dead. The look of horror on their faces tells the story. Even with their dark skin, they look pale from the ghastliness of the sight. Watching them, all I can think about is the image of assistant squad leader Joe Slish, with only his head and shoulders left, and my other comrades. We are down to 158 able-bodied men of the 181 who left England.[51]

Soon we are moving again. We have orders to defend the southeast outskirts of Veghel. Another group of prisoners is being held under guard as I walk by. They are given some of our K rations, and they stare, wondering what to do with the boxes. The fear in their eyes clearly shows they don't trust us, and they can't read the writing to know they are being fed. I feel kind of sorry for them.

During the day the enemy makes several attacks on Veghel. The 501st, 506th, and 401st hold off a determined German tank attack on the southeast approach to the village. The Dutch underground fighters are moving among us. I am definitely not comfortable being around non-American fighters armed with rifles and machine guns, but they are very happy to see us. Company G is in reserve on the west side during the attacks, which are from the north, east, and southeast. Later in the afternoon, at 1700, we form an assault line about six hundred yards to the south of Veghel to mount an attack along a road heading east toward Erp. We are to meet up with the 501st on that regiment's right flank. There is so little advance notice that we receive instructions as we are marching. The only action is occasional sniper fire from the enemy.[52] I am still numb from the shelling. No one talks very much at all.

On the morning of September 24, G leads the final advance on Erp, which is taken without resistance at 1200. The German tanks that have been shelling us are gone. The enemy infantry withdraws upon our arrival. They are still doing hit-and-run attacks. The locals arrange for us to stay in homes, which is a comfort we haven't experienced in a long while. However, a Brit company relieves us, and we are moved in reserve back to Veghel. I am really starting to not like Brit commanders.[53]

The enemy during this time closes the highway between Sint-Oedenrode to the southwest and Veghel, which takes us until September 26 to clear. The Germans keep up the pressure on Veghel from the northwest. Next, we are sent to Dinter to clear the area northwest of Veghel where the German SS

Lloyd Gross (back left,) Hugh Evans (in suspenders), and Louis Simpson (at Evans's right shoulder). Courtesy Screaming Eagles of WWII Foundation, Eindhoven, the Netherlands.

is harassing the British—an area that we earlier relieved. The Germans leave without much of a fight. Lieutenant Niland interrogates prisoners in the town schoolhouse.[54]

Company G moves around a lot in anticipation of enemy attacks, but we are not involved in any real fighting. We move from Dinter, located seven miles northwest, to Veghel and then southwest to Eerde. Gradually enemy pressure in this area diminishes.[55]

I become better acquainted with Sherman, Shaw, Sparks, and Louis Simpson during this time. There isn't time for much fun, although we do visit with the locals some, as they are right there with us. When I dig a foxhole in someone's flower garden, they take it well, preferring to have me there as opposed to a German soldier.

Toward the end of September we have more free time. My cousin Jay Hill comes by to visit. He tells me how he got a job to serve as a bartender at a local bar converted into an officer's club. What he doesn't tell me is that Lieutenant Hibbard and he got into a fight at the bar.

Later on, Simpson comes up to me with a big grin on his face. "That crazy cousin of yours punched out Hibbard," he says. "Hibbard had too much to drink at the bar and said something about your cousin being big and a slob of a bartender, so your cousin punched him. Hibbard didn't know enough to quit and swung back. Punched him a number of times before the fight was broken up." Sherman and Simpson get the inside scoop on officers, because they work with them.

I don't believe it until I see Lieutenant Hibbard walking around with sunglasses, which he typically doesn't wear. When he takes off the glasses to wipe his face, I notice both eyes are swollen and black. Jay blackened both of the officer's eyes.

When I next see Jay, I ask, "Don't you know better than fighting with an officer? A lieutenant at that. . . . Are you crazy?" Soon we both are laughing, me thinking about Hibbard's sunglasses. I like Jay and Hibbard.

Meanwhile, in the northern section of the Market Garden area, British forces at Arnhem are still completely surrounded by superior German forces and in a hopeless situation. The British Guards become bogged down again near Nijmegen. American paratroopers urge the British on toward Arnhem with the 82nd in support, but the Brits stop the advance for the night. They are too tired, their commanders say. The Brits also have concerns about the ability of American airborne troops to support the tank advance, even though they had been fighting alongside tanks. Despite the hellish attacks their British comrades are taking at Nijmegen, the Guards just won't budge. The British paratroopers at Arnhem, nicknamed the Red Devils, have so many wounded that a temporary truce is called to transport British wounded to a German-held hospital. Only 2,163 make it back across the lower Rijn River.[56] Market Garden, which was supposed to be an easy operation, has turned into a bath of British, Polish, and American blood.

On September 28 the US 101st Division is placed under British command. The British don't tend to do anything quickly; they slug it out day by day with the enemy. Occasionally we get back to the rear of the fighting line, where we wash up the best we can, considering the circumstances. Our fighting skills are very much needed by the British, even though, as an airborne division, we aren't really equipped for prolonged action like this. We control both Hell's Highway and the canals and bridges on and around the highway. The Germans hold surrounding hills along the highway and constantly barrage us with artillery, day and night. Life is lived moment by moment.

Market Garden is a failure, at least in terms of meeting the main objective. The British Guards don't make it across the Rijn, even though the Screaming Eagles, 82nd Airborne, and British airborne troops are courageous in their persistence in taking on an enemy with superior numbers and firepower. The British Guards also perform bravely.[57] I, however, lose a lot of respect for British commanders; they are too tentative, which results in the loss of too many British and American lives. I also get the feeling that the British commanders use us to help fix the messes they create. In my opinion, the Brits are good soldiers, but they are crippled by inept commanders.

The rest of our stay in the Netherlands basically consists of trying to hold and expand the corridor along Hell's Highway. Because the British armor doesn't get across the Rijn River, a very long fall and winter stares the Allies in the face as we endeavor to keep the Germans at bay.

Stuck on the Island

As the calendar moves into October, enemy action in and around Veghel becomes quiet.[1] However, trouble for the Allies in the Netherlands continues as the enemy fights tenaciously to keep the war out of their homeland. The biggest problems continue to lie twenty miles to the north of Veghel, in Arnhem and Nijmegen, where the Screaming Eagles are assigned to hold off German attempts to regain control of the west. Arnhem is the place where the British took so many casualties at the start of Market Garden. The enemy still has to keep the Allies from crossing the Rijn River, for if the Allies do cross, the German homeland will be vulnerable, and the war will end quickly as Allied forces pour into Germany. The enemy is doggedly determined to push Allied forces out.

The center of where the opposing armies are smashing against each other is near a very small village, Opheusden. Called by American soldiers "the Island," the land around Opheusden is located between the Rijn and Waal Rivers, thus giving the impression that the area is surrounded by water. It is basically a ten-mile-long lowland marsh, which likely had been underwater in the past. The tiny village itself has maybe a hundred buildings. The surrounding land area is very flat, and both of the rivers are held back by twenty-foot-tall dikes. Drainage ditches and raised railroad tracks slice the area in between. The Island seemingly has no military value except for the fact that opposing armies are slugging it out there with incredible brutality. Basically, an artillery duel is going on between the British and the Germans. The Germans use the drainage ditches and trees along fences to advance close to Allied positions without being seen. The Allies need more troops to keep the German infantry from overrunning the artillery batteries.

General Montgomery has a reputation of battling things out without any real objective, and we are under his command, but we aren't happy about it. The Germans have an advantage over the Allies, as they hold the hilled area to the north of the Rijn, giving them an excellent view of what we are doing. They are not giving up, trying to kick the Allies out of the Island and away from their homeland.

The 506th Regiment of the Screaming Eagles joins the British forces in holding on to Opheusden and pushing the enemy back. British Typhoons drop bombs on enemy positions in an attempt to help even up the advantage the German army has in artillery. In the several days prior to the 327th's arrival, both the Brits and the Americans have been beaten up pretty badly by the enemy in fierce fighting, particularly on October 5, but still the Allies do not give in.[2]

Niland tells us that the area is muddy from excessive rainfall. The rivers are running full but not flooding. The prospect of living day-to-day in wet clothes and weighted down by muddy shoes seems miserable, since we are in the open twenty-four hours a day. There is also a risk that the enemy will flood the area by destroying the dike system.

Colonel Harper receives orders to have the 327th Regiment engage, encircle, and destroy the enemy in and around Opheusden. Colonel Allen of the 401st (3rd Battalion of the 327th) is ordered to move his men in advance of the 1st and 2nd Battalions of the 327th on October 6. To replace the exhausted 506th and British soldiers, the 401st moves toward Opheusden. Colonel Allen locates his troops outside of Opheusden to the east but refuses to advance his men any further. The scene in Opheusden is one of utter confusion, and there is no way to distinguish among British, German, and American forces, so he doesn't see any reason to go any further and waste his men. After an argument with Col. Robert Sink of the 506th, Allen moves his men within half a mile of the village and sets up defenses. The Brits and the 506th withdraw during darkness. The 401st doesn't have enough soldiers to fill an entire defensive line, so gaps have to be covered by gunfire from a distance, an almost impossible task.[3]

Before dawn on October 6, the enemy attacks the 401st with three hundred men in an attempt to run through the open areas of the thin 401st line. Light from burning buildings exposes the enemy, and a fierce American counterattack causes the Germans to retreat. Another enemy attack comes near dawn, this time again with three hundred men, now supported by tanks. This attack succeeds in breaking through the US lines before heading east. Another tank attack comes from the west at 1330 but is wiped out by the 401st after intense and close fighting. With enemy units attacking from the west and some already breaking through American lines, the situation is bad for the 401st, but they manage to hold their position.[4]

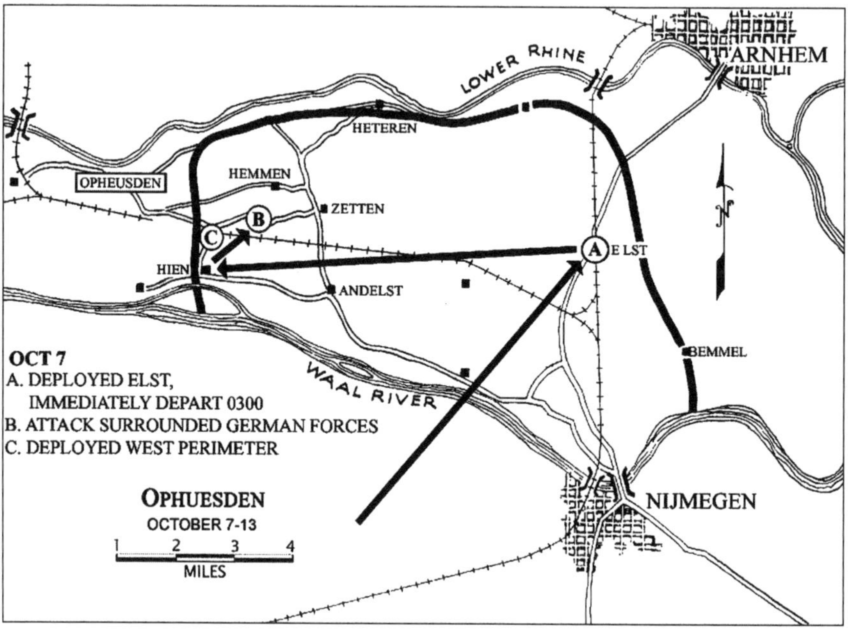

The "Island," October 6–8, 1944.

Second Battalion marches out of Eerde, west a mile and a half, where we leave the area by truck. Arriving at Elst as the sun is going down on October 6, Company G immediately begins to set up positions to relieve the Brits. Before we complete setting up, however, we are ordered to Valberg, where we are shelled, and then on to a really small place named Hien, less than two miles south of Opheusden, at 0300 on October 7. Orders are given for us to build a defensive line, which we complete in about an hour.[5]

While it is still dark, 2nd Platoon is ordered to check out German activity in Dodewaard, not more than half a mile to the north. Hidalgo gets us started. We hide in the deep drainage ditches just outside out of town to keep out of sight of the big German guns to the west.

"What the hell?" Hibbard says quizzically as a British armored vehicle drives wildly up and down the road near us. "Crazy Limeys!" he adds. They are trying to make the enemy think there is a large armored force outside of town. Before long, German machine guns open up, making quite a racket but missing the armored vehicle as it skids almost out of control. Soon British soldiers come running down the road, away from the invading enemy troops. The sight is almost comical. The sun is about to come up, and in the early light the first thing I see is a dead British soldier, missing his right foot.

"Look at the sum a bitches run!" Hidalgo says, chuckling.

Simpson arrives to inform Hidalgo, "Captain Evans wants us to retake the town."

We advance up the ditches next to the road and into town, going from house to house. There is some rifle and machine gun fire but nothing for me to do with my bazooka. A small number of Germans run away like rabbits.

"Look at this place!" Sparks says. The town is amazingly devastated from all the artillery attacks.

After taking the town back in short order, we regroup in the ditches outside Opheusden while the Brits move back in. A little while later the same commotion starts again with German machine gun fire, and soon the British are once more running down the road in retreat. Again Simpson shows up with orders, and again we move back into the village without much action, although we do capture six enemy soldiers this time. With interrogation, the Germans indicate they are just a small-sized squad that has been able to make the British run after making some noise by shooting their guns. The British officer in charge is summoned. Evans shows up, too.

In prompt military manner, Captain Evans speaks to the British officer: "Next time you run away, I'm going to shoot the first British soldiers I see running out of town." He is so matter-of-fact that I am surprised and humored. A few hours later the Germans put up a bunch of noise, but no British soldier runs away.

According to reports, the enemy soldiers that earlier broke through the US lines now number about 150 men, having taken tremendous casualties from the 401st during their breakthrough. They are surrounded behind US lines north of the Hemmen-Dodewaard railroad station and a mile and a half west of Zetten. Second Battalion is given orders to dislodge them.

The attack gets underway at 0845. Company G leads the way against the trapped enemy. The attack is northward along the Hemmen–Dodewaard road. First Platoon spearheads, followed by the machine gun section and then 2nd Platoon. First Platoon is to clear buildings, with 2nd Platoon ready to assist. The bazookas are in a reserve position awaiting targets. Sniper and artillery fire is a risk to all of us.[6]

The landscape in the immediate area is as flat as a pancake and dotted with orchards and houses, from which the enemy hits us with sniper fire. Especially intense enemy artillery fire comes from the high ground across the river and to the north; the Germans can easily see us from there. Six men from 1st Platoon go down.[7]

"Keep low, Sparks!" I remind my assistant. Don't get killed now, I think to myself. We come to an area in the road south of the railroad track that has six or seven buildings. Sniper fire increases in intensity. I have my bazooka and carbine, but there is nothing to shoot at. Fighting is heavy. We clear the buildings to the railroad track and take twenty prisoners.[8] I don't go into the buildings, as Evans doesn't want his bazooka gunner killed needlessly.

Leaving the buildings and heading north, G is pounded for ten minutes by enemy artillery, which holds up our advance. Captain Evans, seeing that G will continue to be fully exposed in open terrain, asks for and receives permission to change tactics and swing around through the orchards to the east before we get to the railroad tracks. Second Platoon takes over the lead, with 1st Platoon now in reserve. In the orchard we get hit again by artillery for six minutes.[9]

Several soldiers are still down from the shelling. We press on to the tracks and swing left 400 yards north of the track just west of the Hemmen-Dodewaard rail station. The company continues west a half mile and stops. We turn north and form a 350-yard defensive line. The 506th presses the enemy from the opposite direction, and they try to escape, running right into Company G and the 401st. The surrounded enemy force is in a desperate situation as they are squeezed together. They begin to surrender en masse. An army surgeon, Captain Warren, fearlessly walks into the enemy lines and somehow convinces the enemy to give up their fight. Fifty dead German soldiers are lying on the ground, and we take more than two hundred prisoners.[10]

Battalion command orders us to hold the east–west railroad line, covering about eight hundred yards. Company E is on our left flank facing west about a mile west of the railway station, with F in reserve. Gradually enemy fire diminishes, and F and G both are placed in reserve. Later, the 327th relieves the 506th along the line between the Waal and Rijn Rivers on the west end of the perimeter, with Companies G and F still in reserve. Dom Gentile is dead, his body maimed beyond easy recognition. He was killed in the apple orchard. Company G has 143 able-bodied men on duty.

Hidalgo calls Larry to identify Dom's body. My heart sinks. The Gentile twins are very likeable. Larry is extremely upset and in a daze. Captain Evans orders Denis Parsons to keep an eye on Larry so he doesn't hurt himself. Seeing Larry in so much emotional pain is hard to take, but I stuff it and concentrate on staying alive myself.

The Screaming Eagles now have almost the entire task of holding onto the Island. This task would be difficult for any division, let alone one that has already suffered over twenty-three hundred casualties since September 17. The 327th now has its mission: it is in charge of holding the west line of the Island, Dodewaard to Opheusden, from German attacks. British and American artillery are placed behind in support. There aren't enough men to cover the length of the front, so individual companies are placed around roads leading to the front, and machine guns, bazookas, and BARs are placed to cover the gaps. At times the gaps are more than five hundred yards wide. A railroad track runs through the south end of our line.[11]

The terrain in front of the 327th is very flat. Woods and farm buildings dot the countryside, and connected drainage ditches crisscross it in every direction. The ditches are three feet wide and seven feet deep, thus allowing enemy troops to come up to our positions completely protected.

October 8 brings heavy rains and fog, and the weather is miserably cold. The enemy doesn't launch anything major against us, although constant artillery barrages keep up. During a break in the weather, British Typhoon fighter-bombers hit German artillery positions, which quiets the artillery down some.[12]

Lieutenant Niland shows up at my foxhole. "Rich, ready to go on patrol?" he asks. "We're heading across the river to see what the Krauts are up to." I am reluctant to go, as the patrol is heading over the river. I couldn't swim if I needed to, but I agree to go anyway.

Sherman comes up later. "Evans cancelled the patrol. Staying safe, Kid?" He winks at Shaw.

"Niland's going to be the death of me yet," I reply.

"Easy Company says the Krauts are dug in five hundred yards to the west," Sherman says.[13]

After a night of periodic incoming artillery, daylight arrives to even heavier enemy artillery attacks, which pick up the pace throughout the day. Company G is in reserve behind E. Strong enemy patrols come at the 327th following a heavy artillery barrage. Sparks and I are together as a team in the same foxhole, which measures three feet deep and five feet or so across. We hunker down during the barrage, which reaches its heaviest tempo at 1700. I'm never going to get used to this. I try and shrink myself, in my mind, anyway.

The enemy artillery, after hitting the front lines, directs its fire more at G in reserve. The enemy brings up eight tanks,[14] but they are out of effective range for me. There are no distinguishing sounds, just an intense roar that shakes my inner being, even more amplified on close hits. I can't

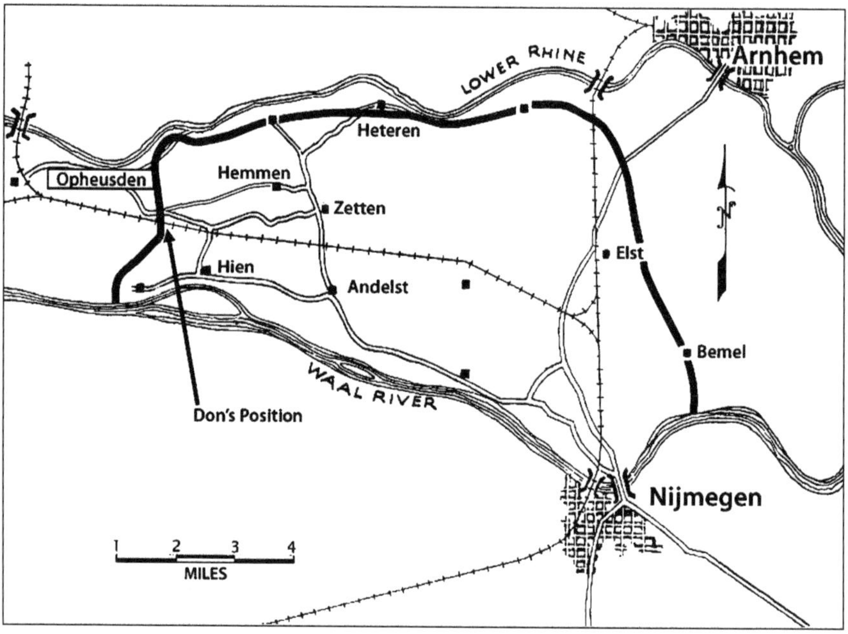

The "Island," October 9–12, 1944. October 9, 2nd Platoon of G Company clears Dodewaard several times; October 10, G Company moves up to the line; October 11, Don destroys an enemy machine gun; October 12, Don is wounded by artillery.

even hear myself think, and my head is pounding. There is nothing to do but wait it out. I try to block out what is going on and experience no real emotion, consciously trying to keep my composure. Head down, I glance up occasionally. The ground shakes as the artillery keeps coming, one after another.

Finally, the barbaric artillery onslaught relents and is followed by a dead silence, except for the crying and screaming of wounded young men on both sides of the line, many of them on the verge of death. At least things seem quiet compared to the explosions.

Then the moment of silence is suddenly broken by a loud whistle and hollering: large numbers of German soldiers, supported closely by the tanks, are attacking our much depleted regiment. Two enemy Mark IV tanks are approaching Easy Company's right flank.[15]

"Ready, Sparks!" I shout. "They might come through the line."

"Ready! Let the bastards come," Sparks retorts.

The view from my position gives me an excellent vantage point. The enemy soldiers are screaming at us. BAR gunners zero in on the approaching Germans. M1 rifles fire away. Company G waits to see if the guys in front of us will hold. Along our front, especially to my right in front of 1st Battalion, the Americans come out of their foxholes and meet the enemy head on. Grenades are thrown back and forth. Bayonets clash. The German tanks are close to each other as they approach Easy's flank. The lead tank is hit by a 57 mm antitank gun and is knocked out. The second tank turns tail and flees back to enemy positions. The Screaming Eagles hold.[16]

Throughout the evening the enemy mounts smaller attacks. They blow whistles and then they come, but none break through. I can hear them cursing from the other side of the dike. Company G readies to move up to the front line so that Easy can move into reserve.

Shortly before 2400, the whistles blow, and here they come again. Wham! Wham! "Boy, that is close!" Wham! Wham! The explosions continue; dirt falls on me. We can hear enemy troops screaming in pain throughout the night during lulls in the action. Company G replaces Easy on the front.

I set up with the bazooka to guard the most logical tank approach, which is on the left flank. I think I can make out a big barn off to the left, but I'm not quite sure. Mortar squads are placed on both sides of the tracks. Simply put, we don't have enough heavy weapons to cover everything.

At 0130 on October 10, G's defensive lines on the front are completed.[17] I am in my foxhole, waiting for orders. Mel Barton is in a foxhole to my right with a BAR. Bert Sparks is with me. Out in front of me, darkness covering an open field is interrupted by the flashes of gunfire and artillery explosions.

After just fifteen minutes in my position I hear, about fifty feet away to my left up the track, Lieutenant Hibbard hollering: "Machine gun at the railroad station! The Krauts are aiming to pin us down; they're attacking along the tracks! There's a sizable force over there!" If the enemy pins us down, they could drive right through us. Barton moves the BAR around to hit the enemy's machine gun, but his big gun is jammed.

A group of Germans has penetrated our lines on the north side of the track. The brick railroad station is located about thirty feet directly to my right and ten feet lower on the other side of the railroad track, but I can't see any more than a dark outline of a building. "Rich! Get the gun! Get it, dammit!" Hibbard yells. Sparks loads the rocket into the bazooka. Barton fires his rifle as fast as he can toward the building, but he has no target, as it is too dark. I stand up and ready the bazooka. "Get 'em, Barton, get 'em!" Hibbard shouts.

"How'd they get in there?" I murmur to myself. I can't see a thing. If the enemy machine gunner opens up, I'll be dead in an instant. Barton quits firing. In the dark, since no one can see anything and no one is moving, it

Don took out the enemy machine gun near Opheusden at night.

becomes strangely silent. Standing up, protected some by the foxhole, I wait, holding my breath. God, please don't let me miss, I pray silently. I can hear some stirring near the building. They are trying to reload fast to get us before we get them. There is more quietness. Then the German gunner pulls the bolt on the machine gun, preparing to fire: Click, clack.

Instantly, I pull the trigger, aiming where I hear the bolt click. Whoosh, the rocket slams through the building, lighting the night around us. A brief but agonized scream pierces the air, then silence. I duck back into the foxhole.

How many are there? How many are left? Lying down for a while, I still don't hear anything coming from the area of the building. There is gunfire further away, coming from both sides of the battle lines. Are they waiting for me to move? My heart is pounding so loudly that I know the enemy will surely hear it. I take a grenade from my coat. Pulling the pin, I toss it toward the machine gun. No explosion. How dumb can I be? I think. After seeing some replacements die as a result of grenades going off in their coat pockets, I'd put tape over the safety lever to keep from accidentally killing myself. I throw another, Boom! Then I throw another, Boom! Throughout the remainder of the night I throw several grenades over the embankment, some exploding and some not because I had forgotten the tape again. I am terrified, expecting a German grenade to come into our foxhole. Intense fighting continues and then dies down. We get hit hard with artillery.

During a lull in the fighting, Lloyd Gross, frustrated that the enemy is using the ditches for cover and getting so close to us, decides to go over the dike next to us and disappears into the dark. The enemy is out there, and so is Gross. I can see him once in a while lit by the glow of a burning barn three hundred yards to the west. He leaps and dodges from hole to hole and ditch to ditch.

A couple of hours later, completely out of breath, he comes sliding down the dike. "What the hell have you been doing?" Hibbard demands to know.

"We need to site the machine guns better. I'm tired of the damn Krauts getting in here," Gross responds. Gross has his knife in his hands, staring at it.

Gross then tells us the bigger story. He went out into the field in front of G's position to better line up machine gun fire. Jumping from hole to hole, he comes face to face with an enemy soldier. He pulls out his knife to kill him, but the enemy, in his native language, says, "Don't shoot. Don't shoot." When Gross hesitates, the German adds, "I am dying." With the burning barn providing a backlight, Gross can see the man has a severe neck wound and is bleeding profusely. Fearing there are other enemy soldiers around, he leans back against the dirt on the side of the hole.

"What religion are you?" the German asks.

"Catholic," Gross responds.

"I am Lutheran," the German says. He is obviously becoming weaker. Then he asks, "Do you have a family?"

"I have some nephews. They gave me this knife," Gross answers, thinking about his earlier intentions with the knife.

"In my pocket is a picture of my wife and four kids," the German says, his blond hair shining in the light of the fire. Gross wants to leave, but the fire is too bright; he'd be spotted.

"Nice family," Gross says. He thinks of his nephews, who are probably about the same age. Maybe I should put him out of his misery, he thinks.

"Would you pray with me? The Lord's Prayer?" the German asks, almost begging as his strength is leaving him.

"Our Father who art in heaven, hallowed be Thy name, Thy kingdom come. Thy will be done on earth as it is in heaven," they speak together.

Then Gross puts his arm around the man who is no longer an enemy. Quietly, the German loses consciousness. His breathing stops.

Gross leans back against the wall of the hole and waits an hour as the fire dies down. Then he makes his way back to the 327th.[18]

At daylight the Germans withdraw, and I can get a good view. There is the enemy machine gunner; the round from the bazooka rocket went right through his lower body before traveling clean through the brick building. He is dead. There are no other Germans around. To the left of the station and on the other side of it are several American soldiers in a foxhole. I easily could have thrown a grenade at them in the dark. Thank God, I didn't.

I am pretty shaken up. Sure, I'd blasted areas where enemy soldiers were before, and I had also fired my gun at a distance. At times I had shot in the dark at shadowy figures, but others with me were doing the same. Back in France, I fired at bunkers but still didn't know the results. This is the first time I know that I have killed someone. I am sick and want to leave.

Sparks and the others in the squad go over and loot the dead German's body.

"Rich, look, a P38 pistol! You want it? Your kill, your gun!" Sparks asks about his newfound treasure as he looks it over with a smile. I can tell he wants it.

"No," I mutter as I look away.

First squad has captured some enemy soldiers who broke their lines. The intelligence gathered from the prisoners helps Hibbard put together a patrol squad. I am part of the squad, and we head toward the German lines. We walk up to a big barn that has been badly damaged by a bazooka rocket hit, and then we go back to friendly lines for the rest of the day. We do not encounter the enemy. They are long gone, except for their fallen comrades. There must be close to 150 German bodies, some piled on top of each other.

A medic is standing near a culvert under the railroad track bed. He isn't right mentally. He has a pistol in his hand and repeats over and over again, "Ain't nobody comin' through here. Ain't nobody comin' through here." Sparks says he's been guarding the culvert like that all night.

Sherman comes by with ammunition. "The Brits are impressed," he tells us. "Said, 'You Yanks need to stand up and fight through the artillery,'" he goes on in a British accent. "'Won't happen though. Too much to handle.' Our officers said, 'Yes they will!' E held firm. No ground was lost." The British constantly underestimated our ability and willingness to fight.[19]

After a hellacious attack by the enemy at Opheusden, a medic was in a state of confusion: "Nobody is coming through here!"

I find out Leonard Green is dead, too. Green was in my original squad. That's five of the original twelve dead. I think back to what Eisenhower said to us before we landed in France: half won't survive. Five dead out of twelve is pretty close to that. Evans somehow finds out where Dominic is buried, and Larry is allowed to visit the grave. Company G is down to 126 soldiers.[20] The smell of dead German soldiers is getting repulsive.

The Germans again ask permission to pick up their wounded. Colonel Harper gives permission. Just in front of us, under the protection of the Red Cross flag, enemy soldiers bring in a stretcher. By now I am somewhat numb to battle, so I'm not paying much attention to what is going on around me.

Several groups of German soldiers indicate they want to surrender. They try to come toward us, but the Germans launch mortar rounds to keep them from actually doing it.

Move in the daylight, and you get artillery coming your way, as the Germans have a clear view of you. I am hungry and just want to eat in peace. I am angry. Sparks and a replacement are in the foxhole with me. In front of

After Don took out the machine gun, the enemy paid him back with a mortar attack.

me is the big culvert under the railroad track, the medic still guarding the entrance on the other side of the track. The culvert isn't big enough for me to get into, but there is a place to sit down by myself. Deciding to eat under the cover of the culvert, I grab my K ration and then start up out of the foxhole. I hear the "fump" sound of a mortar being fired, but I don't hear the explosion right in front of me. I'm not moving.

"He's dead," Sparks says to whoever can hear. He tells me this later. Apparently, they drag me and the replacement, who was hit too, back to the medic tent, where I begin to regain consciousness and my senses.

"Where am I?" I ask, still groggy from the concussion.

"I thought you were a goner, buddy," Sparks replies, moving his mouth like he is speaking loudly. I can barely hear him. The replacement isn't doing very well.

Sparks and the guys then take off for the front. I can barely make out anyone's words. There aren't enough men to get me back to the hospital, so I lie in the tent, and gradually my senses and more of my hearing come back. Focusing visually and mentally isn't easy, so I shut my eyes and try to rest.

Behind the front lines, Cousin Jay hears about my injuries, and he drives his truck right up toward the front lines in the dark, loads me up, and takes me to the field hospital. Because of the heavy artillery attacks, truck drivers usually don't drive forward to pick up wounded, but when Jay got word that I was wounded, he risked his life to come get me. Not everyone would do that for someone, and I am very appreciative. Still, I think he is crazy for coming. Jay also hauls back the replacement hit by shrapnel from the same shell. I never find out about his condition.

I recover for twelve hours behind the lines, then I am put back up in the front. My hearing does not return to normal for several more days. I go right back to the same foxhole, where the guys are glad to see me. My eyes become fixed on a metal K ration container. Right through the middle of the container is a hole made by shrapnel from the mortar round. This is the one I was holding when the explosion occurred.

Lieutenant Hibbard comes around to see how I am doing. "You should get a medal for taking out the machine gun," Hibbard mentions. "I'd say the Krauts are trying to repay you for ruining their plans. By the way, the bastards brought up the mortar that hit you on a stretcher when they came to pick up wounded. They hid it in the shell of the burned barn over there. We won't be so nice next time they want to pick up their wounded."

Niland, Panic, and Fisher have been missing for a couple of days on an intelligence gathering mission. When they finally get back, Niland reveals they'd been scouting the area to the northeast of Opheusden when they had to hide in a brick factory as a German unit moved into the area to stay for several days. They were stuck there until the Krauts left. Panic says that he was hiding in a tube while the Germans checked out the building, when a cat jumped in with him and scared the daylights out of him, almost causing him to holler.[21]

Toward sunset, while I watch from my foxhole, someone drives an army truck right through our lines, with lights on but pointed down. Out in the open where the German artillery can easily fire at it, the truck stops at several farmhouses before coming back. Whoever it is guns the engine for all it can do, making quite a sight. Then the truck makes its way back right next to my foxhole. The driver, with a rifle strapped to his back, steps out and hollers, "Hey Don, how ya doin'?" It is Jay again.

"Are you crazy?" I reply, somewhat embarrassed.

"We needed some food," Jay continues. "We were out. I grabbed the cook and told him I knew where we might find some, so here we are. Hungry, Don?"

I sure wish Jay was with me in the foxholes. We'd be unbeatable. Later, I hear Jay has wrecked his truck and is banged up but basically okay.[22]

At 0300 on October 13, during a heavy rainstorm, we pack up and are relieved by the 502nd. We march south to positions on the north side of Dodewaard. Easy Company is on our left flank.[23] Instead of allowing us to sleep, Captain Evans orders us to clean our weapons. Easy is hit with random artillery, causing several casualties.

Twenty-four hours later, without any rest, we move north two miles. Arriving twelve hundred yards east of Opheusden, we replace the 401st on the front line along a big dike that runs northwest to southeast. Easy sets up three hundred yards to our south. The 401st saw action earlier in the day.[24] The weather is absolutely miserable: cold and wet.

Quickly, Company G sets up a line of defense, not wanting to give the enemy any time to exploit the situation. Barton and I dig a pretty good foxhole on the east slope of the dike that rises about six feet high from where we are. The dike is higher back toward the northwest and lower to the southeast. Opheusden itself is on higher ground than much of the surrounding terrain. The dike offers some protection from enemy artillery. The guys behind us in reserve are even more exposed than we are. The terrain to the north of me is flat, with a slight rise in elevation less than half a mile from us because of another dike, which is holding back the Rijn River, also north of our position.

From the north side of the river the enemy can look down on us if we aren't keeping low on the south side of the dike. The land north of the river rises to more than one hundred feet several miles from the river. This gives the enemy a huge tactical advantage. Several buildings are scattered through the area, but not many, because of the threat of flooding. A couple of villages and more farm buildings are on the other side of the river to my right. Enemy sniper and artillery fire keeps us from moving much during the day, and runners between squads and command can't be used during the day because the enemy can see us too well. To our left lies a large gap of four hundred yards between us and Company E.[25]

First Platoon covers the road and dike. That approach makes 1st Platoon more exposed to the enemy than 2nd Platoon is. Receiving orders from Lieutenant Hibbard, who is behind the dike, I lead the bazooka section out to the dike to set up. We are supposed to keep the Germans from advancing tanks through line gaps at either end of our line.

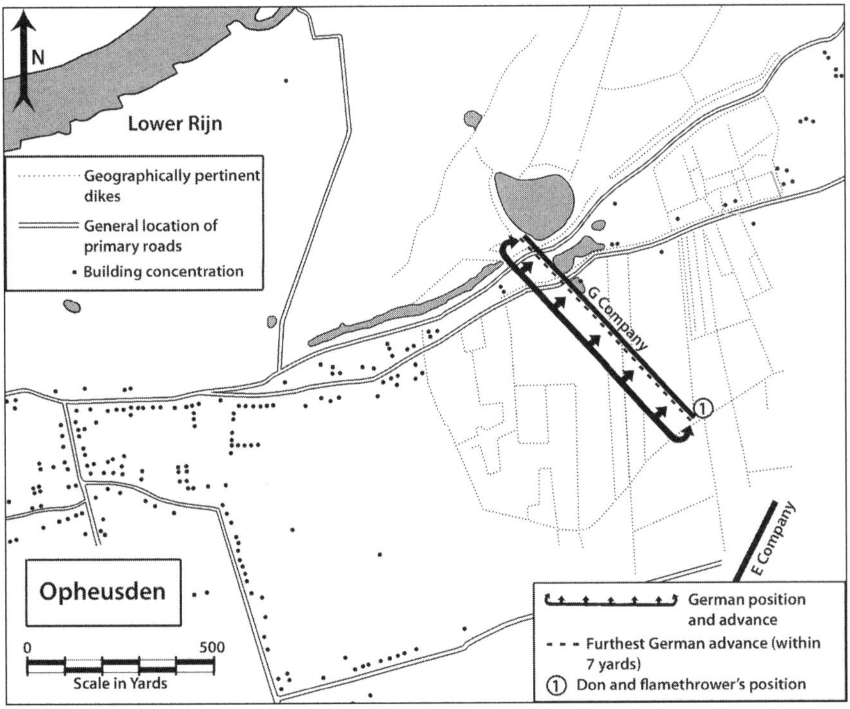

The "Island," October 14, 1944.

"You take the left flank toward Easy, and I'll take the right at the road," I say to a replacement from New York City. I motion to his partner to follow him and bring Barton with me, carrying the bazooka. Without a lot of thought, I notice the right flank is less exposed to artillery, but there are two roads that the enemy can approach from in that area.

"The hell you will!" The New Yorker shouts at me. "The right flank is much easier!"

I am a little flustered. I haven't thought about which side is easier to handle, but I thought I was taking the harder approach.

"Okay, it's yours!" I snap back. He isn't like fellow New Yorker Proppe was. I really don't like him. Gross is on the right flank with his men in the light machine gun section, which includes Parsons. Heavy machine guns are on the left flank closer to where I am setting up.

Throughout the day, October 14, the enemy peppers us with artillery and mortar fire, then at 1630 the Germans cut loose with an intense artillery barrage for thirty minutes.[26] The incoming artillery fire is hard to take, but I'm not scared. The artillery explosions move from around us to behind us a couple of hundred yards, shaking up our reserves. The enemy has moved to within seventy-five yards of our line. We hear hollering in German begin as they lay smoke across the attackers' positions. They come at us hard and furious, using drainage ditches to get close to us. Three enemy companies are making a three-pronged attack right against G.[27]

The Germans come at us along the entire front but concentrate more on the right, where they are supported by six tanks. The tanks are beyond the range of my bazooka. The only slackening in the fighting occurs when the Germans occasionally regroup before another attack. I think about the guy from New York demanding to face six German tanks. Two of the tanks are hitting our right-flank machine guns with automatic fire.

No tanks are approaching the left flank that I can see, so we fire away with our rifles. The noise is so loud and the situation so intense that I can hardly tell what is going on around us. The enemy troops are protected by drainage ditches right up to our positions. American and British artillery comes in from behind, and artillery hits all around us, sometimes too close for comfort. The ground shakes, dirt is flying. Metal whistles shrilly through the air. After a while I can't tell whether German or Allied artillery is falling.

After failing to dislodge Company G on the right flank, the Krauts try to concentrate one of their companies on our left flank, where I am the end of the line. Easy can't fire directly at them, as they would hit us. I look to the right. Evans is fully exposing himself to direct machine gun fire at the enemy. The machine gun fire rips into the Germans. British artillery is focused on the enemy in front and to the left of me. The Germans launch artillery again. The artillery shifts to further behind us. The Germans blow another whistle, mustering the assault on our positions and make a run past our flank. The whole scene is almost unimaginable. Artillery hits us. Then they keep coming, we fire back, and artillery hits again, sometimes British, sometimes American, and sometimes German. Louis Simpson and Sherman drop off more ammunition. The runners get knocked off their feet by the explosions and get right up again. We fight on and on. Barton and I continue what seems like our own little private war with the enemy. My rifle is almost too hot to handle. I think it glows red at times. The enemy is so close that we throw hand grenades back and forth at each other. Barton and I fight on like a machine.

The battle grows into a constant roar, with smoke all around us, as the sun is just starting to go down. Lieutenant Hibbard comes up behind Barton and me, yelling, "Keep it up boys! Keep it up!" He is screaming almost in my ear, but I can barely hear him. At times the German attack bogs down, and they pull back to regroup. During the lulls I think I can hear the enemy cursing. Then comes another whistle, and here they come again. Enemy potato masher grenades again fall in our positions. Sometimes we throw them back before they explode. Simpson tells us the company is almost out of ammunition, and the German artillery is making it impossible for resupply. I look at my ammo and notice that I am almost out, having gone through all the ammunition clipped to my belt and the three bandoliers hanging around my waist. Smoke is everywhere. Judging by the flashes, the enemy is almost upon us, and I have only a few more rounds left.

A shell hits very close to Barton and me, dropping both of us to the ground. I hurt all over, but I notice that Barton doesn't get up. In the dark he looks dead. He is breathing, though. I feel a tap on my shoulder. Whirling around and pointing my rifle, I almost shoot Simpson. "Simpson! My God, I almost killed you!" I scream at him, my heart pounding. Simpson has a surprised look on his face: he kind of grins and then sees Barton, and the smirk leaves his face. "Get the medics!" I scream again. Simpson tells me battalion was able to get a jeep and trailer loaded with ammo to the front, and he drops off my new supply.[28] Then he is off to the next hole. For the first time in a while I feel real emotion. Barton is badly hurt. I have several morphine syringes in my pack. I take one out and give him a shot to kill his pain.

To my left, a soldier named Ed, from 2nd Squad, is manning a BAR. He is one of the older soldiers, in his upper thirties, I think. He is close enough that I can hear him scream, "They've broken through! They've broken through! Run!"

The guy is freaking out. Finally, he bolts and runs away from the approaching Germans, waving his hands wildly and still screaming. Wham, Wham, Wham! The artillery continues. Then I heard a shrill sound. I know I am in trouble and drop to the ground. Suddenly, I feel as if I've been hit by a baseball bat on the side of my right shoulder. My head is spinning, my hearing is distorted, and the ground moves from the concussion. I am on top of Barton, and he isn't moving anymore. My first thoughts are, I've killed him. I've killed Barton!

I grab my rifle and begin firing again. Finally, at 1830, with darkness covering the battlefield, the Germans break off the attack, except for German artillery, which hits us to cover their withdrawal from our front. British artillery hits them back in an equally measured response.[29] I lose complete track of time and decide to check Barton over. His breathing is labored, and I know this means he's in bad shape. He stirs some, obviously in pain, going in and out of consciousness. I still have several morphine syringes in my pack, so I take one out and give him another shot to kill his pain. Later, without incoming fire, and with the benefit of the first light of dawn, I am able to better check him over. He has a wound in the center of his back and is semiconscious. He's lost a little blood, but not nearly enough to kill him, at least not yet. He is badly hurt, though. The medics show up now that the shelling has stopped. "Help Barton," I plead. "He got hit hours ago and isn't doing very well!" The medics take a look.

"Get up soldier, you're not hurt!" one medic yells at Barton. "Get up!"

"Hey! Knock it off! He is hurt, I know he is!" I speak sternly to the medic, stunned by his assessment. "Look at his back!"

The medic turns him and sees the wound. "Let's get him back," he says to the man holding the stretcher. They hurry Barton away.

Leaning against the side of the foxhole, I survey the scene. Dead Germans and some Americans are scattered around. The Germans haven't breached our lines as Ed thought, but their bodies are on the ground about twenty feet or so away. Looking away as I try to process everything I am seeing and smelling, I glance to the bottom of the foxhole. There are the morphine syrettes I used on Barton. They are still full. I forgot to break the seals on the syrettes, so Barton didn't get any morphine for the pain. Also lying in the foxhole is a six-inch-long fragment of metal, which must have been the one that hit me. I notice some more of the varnish has melted off my M1.

"Boy, my shoulder sure hurts," I say to no one in particular as I move my arm around, trying to assess the damage. The pain is pretty sharp, so I head toward the medical tent back by the company command post.

"You've got a pretty good bruise, but the skin's not broken. You'll be okay," a medic says after he pulls my shirt down off the shoulder area. I guess the New Yorker bazooka man is right. It was tougher on the left flank.

I turn and head back toward the foxhole. On the way back, medics are still helping the wounded. A burial detail is picking up dead American soldiers. About twenty feet from my foxhole a dead enemy soldier remains. He has a flame-thrower on his back, with his hand on the nozzle as if he was ready to torch someone, maybe me, when he died. There are two more flamethrowers farther away.

Lieutenant Hibbard motions for me. He is rounding up a squad to do a short patrol to survey the situation and check on the Krauts. The newly formed scout squad sets out over the field, which is strewn with dead German soldiers. I'm not in the lead, nor am I bringing up the rear, thank

God. We continue several hundred yards and return. The enemy has suffered so many casualties. I try to eat, but I'm not very hungry. The lack of hunger is from both the visualization of the sight before me and the awfulness of the British fourteen-in-one food kit. Oh, the British food is bad, even by army standards.

In the afternoon, Lieutenant Niland pieces together a larger patrol. The officers are discussing Ed, the guy who broke from his BAR position and ran back to the company post at the farmhouse. Their conversation is interesting. It seems the officers were convinced at the time that the Germans really had broken through. They were getting ready to hightail it out of there when they radioed battalion headquarters for more information. Headquarters told them to hold; the Germans still hadn't gotten through. Ed is taken to a hospital and then arrested.

Niland's patrol is made up of a random mix of squads: a couple of mortar guys, a BAR team, a couple of us bazooka men, and the rest officers and riflemen. Crossing the ground that had been held by the Germans gives me a vulnerable feeling. Getting close to the river, we turn toward the west. Perhaps they have snipers or scouts keeping an eye on us. Scattered guns, dead bodies, and mortars are everywhere. Deeper we trudge toward the enemy lines, and we must have gone at least a mile when Niland stops us. "Rich! You hear the gunfire?" Niland asks. At first, I think he is crazy. "Sherman! Do you hear it?" Niland says. Sherman and I both kind of look at each other, somewhat stupefied. There is no gunfire. Then I get it. Niland doesn't want to be here, either.

"Yes, sir!" I respond. "Enemy gunfire, sir! Coming from the trees over to the west!"

Niland signals to the guy with the radio, then speaks into it: "This is squad leader. Taking incoming fire. I'm requesting permission to withdraw."

"Get out of there, then. You can't take on the whole lot of them," command answers.

We turn and head back much faster than we came. Once inside our own lines I feel better, a lot better. Fourteen-in-ones are passed around. Boy is that food bad. The oxtail soup is basically watered-down grease with bones in it. I never did like tea. And the hardtack meat is almost impossible to chew and tastes awful.

During the night, one of the guys, hearing my voice, says, "Hey Rich, Hibbard needs to talk to you!"

"What's with these guys, can't they find someone else for patrols?" I wonder, not too excited about what I might be asked to do. "What's up now?" As we head toward Hibbard, the guy sent to fetch me mutters something about command wanting to take care of the enemy artillery that has been blasting away at us.

"Rich, you can sight azimuth, can't you?" Hibbard asks rather directly, already knowing the answer. Azimuth, as I mentioned earlier, is using calculations of trajectories to determine the distance and location of enemy artillery. I guess Hibbard thinks I am pretty good at it.

"Yes, sir, I was trained," I answer.

"Go out as far as you can from the front line and watch for German artillery," he orders. "Do your measurements. When you have enough information, report back to us."

"Yes, sir!" I reply.

"How'd I get myself into this?" I ask Private Sparks when I get back to the foxhole, before heading out.

With a flashlight, pencil, paper, canvas, compass, and my M1 rifle in hand, I crawl forward, heading northwest toward the river. Artillery is incoming periodically, although it is not heavy. I crawl into a foxhole; I figure it is about three hundred yards in front of the American lines. I feel extremely vulnerable in my front-row seat; I certainly don't want the Krauts to attack now. Here I am with a pencil in hand and no one to protect me as I watch the enemy artillery firing. Across the river I see flashes followed by echoing booms. The screeching of shells pierces the quiet night, followed by Wham! Wham! up and down the line. Under the night sky, the booming and flashes of the artillery being fired and the subsequent sounds of the shells passing overhead help me to draw a map that the British artillery can use to aim and shoot back. To make the math calculations I turn on the flashlight after pulling the canvas over me so I can't be seen by the enemy.

For three days and nights this continues. Finally, I take the map to G Company headquarters. Company G has been placed in battalion reserve. The stench of dead Germans is appalling.

"I'm putting you up for promotion . . . again," Hibbard mentions.

Simpson comes by with news about Barton. Mel has shrapnel lodged next to his heart, and his left leg and arm are permanently paralyzed. We've been through so much loss; the usually talkative Simpson is matter-of-fact about Barton.

Headquarters organizes a night patrol of four across the river on a rubber boat. They come back with Kraut prisoners. The next night, officers and NCOs of the 327th draw straws, with the men drawing the shortest straws to go across the river. Five different groups are selected for the successive five nights based on the length of the straws. Lt. Fred Row, Sgt. Gilbert Chin from headquarters, and two others draw the shortest straws for the first night. Niland gets a longer straw and doesn't go with them. Not one of them comes back. The succeeding nights of patrols are canceled.[30]

The Brits bring up 201 pieces of artillery and literally pulverize the hill across the river where the Germans have located their artillery. At least for a while we have a respite from the German artillery attacks. Without their artillery support, the Germans make smaller attacks the next day. We drive them back quickly, inflicting heavy casualties on the enemy. I am getting numb to all the killing, and it really isn't bothering me nearly as much as before. What is noticeable is that the enemy isn't hitting us as hard with artillery. Maybe I helped.

The guys are living like animals in a hole, afraid to come out. Names don't matter much. Losing buddies is hard, so I don't try much to make new friends. I've already lost too many buddies. I have lice in my hair, my teeth are loose, and my gums are bleeding. I am a mess.

During an afternoon, while we are hunkering down in our foxholes, Sparks hollers at me, "Rich, here comes that crazy buddy of yours!" I look back away from the line, and I can identify the walk anywhere. Jay's flat feet give him a particular gait.

"Don, you okay?" Jay asks as he gets to my foxhole.

"Doing just fine," I reply. I think about chiding him for risking his life to come see me. After a short visit he heads back to his unit.

Why are we here slugging things out with the enemy for what seems like no apparent reason? We can tell that the Germans are running thin on men, because the numbers supporting their companies are less than half strength. We have hit back at them hard.

On October 21 the company is moved to Zetten.[31] While in reserve I get to stay in a couple of nice houses on the east side of Zetten, about three miles behind the western front lines. I draw guard duty a couple of times. Basically, I walk around and watch for enemy patrols, which sometimes slip through our lines. American orders are to keep all lights out. No fires, not even matches, can be lit, because in the dark enemy artillery spotters can see them and fire away at us from miles away.

British artillery units are in the area. A British soldier, also on guard duty, walks by me carrying a lighted flashlight. "Hey, turn that thing off!" I snarl at him. "I am tired of being shelled!" He turns off the flashlight and walks off. About twenty minutes later we cross paths again, and his flashlight is on. "Turn the light off!" I say urgently to him. "The Krauts will see us." Again, he turns off the light. But about twenty minutes later we run into each other again, and again the flashlight is on. "I'm tired of talking!" I yell at him. "Next time I see you with that light on, I'm shooting. I'm not going to get killed because you're too stupid to keep the light off!" He turns the light off, and I never see him again that night.

A couple of nights later, a British colonel is being driven around the village in a jeep with its lights on. I flag down the driver.

"Sir, no lights!" I say. "Company orders."

"The Germans have their things to do and I have mine," the officer responds indignantly. "I'm going to leave them on!"

"The Krauts will put your lights out for you then," I snap back at him. Raising my rifle, I yell, "Turn the lights off!" They drive off. I see them a couple more times that night, driving around with lights in full blaze, right in sight of the German guns, which are across the river on the high ground.

By now the battalion discovers something very important. The Dutch have a jam factory near the Rijn River. Soldiers loot the factory and pass jam around. This makes the British hardtack a bit more tolerable to eat. The Germans seem to know about it, too, as they left some trash behind.[32]

The Germans eventually withdraw even further, and except for artillery firing, most of the action stops. Finally I get the chance to get to the rear and even take a shower. The company strips down and proceeds to walk through the row of showers, never stopping, just moving on down the line. The showers are set up with cold river water, and G Company cleans up as much as river water will allow. My old clothes were so dirty that the wind couldn't get through them. When I took them off, they were so caked in mud that they stood up by themselves. After we are given clean clothes, it seems I am going to freeze.

We listen to a local German-controlled radio station at Arnhem; a lady speaking English invites us to cross the river and join the Germans. "Arnhem Annie" is what we call her. Occasionally German artillery shoots leaflets into our lines asking, "Why fight for the Jews?"

On October 25 we are back on the front line near Opheusden. We move into new positions during the night, but we need morning daylight before we know what the area is like and whether it is suitable to set up camp. I completely lose track of time; we usually have no idea what day it is. Things seem to have settled into permanent defensive lines, where many skirmishes take place. German soldiers hide in the drainage ditches and will kill us if we are not alert. The enemy still controls the high ground across the river and still has heavy artillery there. During the day we are sitting targets if we don't keep our heads down, but moving is more dangerous. As the trees defoliate with the approach of winter, our natural cover begins to disappear. This also makes the enemy more visible, and we capture some German soldiers.

On November 3 we are back in Zetten.[33] Sherman, on a run, comes around. "Hey Rich," he says. "Remember that British colonel that had his own things to do? Well, the Germans put his lights out! Bed Check Charlie got him." With his hands, Sherman demonstrates an airplane swooping down, while he makes gun sounds with his voice. The Germans send over an airplane about 2300 every night to drop a few bombs and maybe look over our positions as best they can in the dark. We name these airplanes and pilots "Bed Check Charlie," as if they are making sure we are going to bed on time.

On November 7, we are again at the front, this time one and one-half miles northwest of Opheusden, where the front eventually settles into a routine. Patrols continue and are hazardous, not because we might run into enemy soldiers, but because of mines and booby traps set by the Germans. Later, we are placed under Canadian command, and at least the food they feed us is better than British food.

While I am on the front, we get word that those of us who want to take communion will be relieved long enough to do it. I realize communion is something special, but I really don't understand the meaning of it. Some of the guys probably go just to get away for a while. Being a new Christian, I want to help, so I assist the chaplain. We kneel just behind the lines, with the sound of war ringing in our ears. I think a lot about God during this time, but with daily fighting I don't have time to study God's word, although I do have a small army-issued Bible. Still, I am firm in my promise to God to go home and serve Him if I live through the war. Seeing so many of my friends and buddies die, I also want to try to do with my life some of the good they might have done had they survived.

Tiredness and hunger are constant companions. In the Netherlands the army does a better job of getting water to us than in France, so thirst isn't as big a problem, especially with all the canals and waterways nearby. Unfortunately, we are constantly soaked. We continue patrols ahead of the front lines. The Germans we capture are a hungry bunch. Some of them are tough SS troopers, others are older soldiers, some are just kids, and there are also

The soldiers have Communion just behind the front lines at Opheusden.

Eastern Europeans who have entered German service in order to get out of prisoner of war camps. Even though they are the enemy and have killed many of my buddies, we take pity on them and give them some of our K rations.

The Germans across the river have been sniping at us periodically just to keep us on our toes. We begin a deadly game with them.

"What are we doing now?" I asked Sergeant Hanlon.

"Hide and seek," Hanlon replies.

"What?"

"You'll see."

Hanlon leads us up on the riverbank, where we show ourselves momentarily and then duck back down, trying to draw enemy sniper fire from houses across the river in a small village. When the enemy fires at us, we fire back with M1 rifles, because we don't have real sniper rifles. This continues for several hours before we take a break. We do this on and off for several days before the officers tire of it. No one in our squad is ever hit.

On November 15 we are again pulled off the front line. Both Hanlon and Hibbard put me up for promotion to sergeant. Captain Evans turns down my promotion, saying he already has too many sergeants. Still, I am in charge of a bazooka section.

Exchanges with the enemy continue to wind down, to the point where we feel little danger. When things seem relatively safe, Sparks, Sherman, Simpson, and I venture out and "accidentally" kill a Dutch farmer's cow with a club for a feast. The steaks are good, and there is some time for visiting. Lloyd Gross stops by and sees our steaks. A machine gun crew he knows did the same thing to another cow, only in their case the Dutch farmer came by. They scrambled to find an excuse and even found someone who could speak Dutch, hoping he might be able to explain things. Soldiers can get in real trouble for stealing from the locals. The conversation went on and on, with the Americans speaking in English and the farmer in Dutch. "Well, what the hell do you want?" the farmer finally asks in perfect English.

November 22, we are back on the line, this time one mile east of Opheusden. The smells of the battlefield are horrible. Bloated, dead horses, cattle, and pigs are scattered about the countryside, as are dead enemy soldiers. Seeing so many corpses is difficult. Many of the famous Dutch windmills have been destroyed. And the marshland often has a musty smell, although it may be natural. When we first went into the Netherlands, the weather was warm and sunny. As we get further into fall, it still rains almost every day, but now it is getting colder, especially at night. Foxholes are like cold bathtubs. Thankfully, I have a couple of pairs of socks. With weather turning colder, keeping feet dry is imperative. I take off the wet socks and place them in my helmet liner so my head's heat will dry them while I wear the dry pair.

The days are trudging on. Time seems to stand still, and I have no idea what day it is. The usual artillery duels and foot patrols go on and on.

"Rich, do you hear that?" Sparks asks.

"What in the world?"

I am dumbfounded. From the distance to the east of our positions comes a loud buzzing sound. It's very peculiar, and I haven't heard anything quite like it before. The sound is passing overhead with a buzzing roar to it. Sparks points up.

"There. There it is," Sparks says with a boyish gasp.

"That's a German V-1," I reply. We've heard of the flying bombs but have never seen one before. Orange smoke trails it as it speeds away.

On November 25, G is relieved by the 51st Highland Division and ends up back at Zetten.[34] On November 27 we march six miles to Nijmegen and cross the Waal River in assault boats to load into trucks bound for Camp Mourmelon, France.

By now we are utterly exhausted. Much of what we have done in the closing weeks of the Battle of Opheusden seems pointless. On the way to Mourmelon, Niland tells us that the enemy was told at the start of the battle for Opheusden that they were facing a small, worn-out, and hungry airborne unit. They were surprised by the tenacity of our defense of Opheusden. An entire armor-supported enemy division and more has been wrecked by the Screaming Eagles. We leave the Netherlands with 106 men out of 181.

Back Into Battle

THE SCREAMING EAGLES LEAVE THE NETHERLANDS AFTER SEVENTY-two days of being cold, wet, and hungry and of fighting to survive. Getting back to base at Mourmelon, France, for some badly needed rest is a welcome relief for the entire division. Seeing the faces of buddies not seen in a while is good, too. We've all been fighting our own small, personal war in the Netherlands and do not really comprehend what is going on even close to us. Soon, the realization that many guys didn't make it back sets in. A feeling of numb despair hangs over the camp. A few soldiers even commit suicide after surviving the killing madness in the Netherlands.[1]

The camp, once used by the German army, is a wreck. Along with being old and outdated, the facilities have been trashed by the Germans, who didn't want anyone getting any use out of them after they left. During the first several days of our stay here, we fix the place up. There is a lot of cleaning to do.

In a short time, life returns to a semblance of relative normalcy. Word is that we'll be here for a while to regroup and recover. Many guys are gone on leave or pass. The army even holds drawings for thirty passes back to the United States for some lucky soldiers.[2] Some of the guys offer up to one thousand dollars for a ticket back home. A thousand dollars is a lot of money, so I don't even think about doing it. Others get a pass to Paris, but I don't. Some of my buddies who aren't lucky enough to get a pass to the big city go anyway, without army permission.

We spend some time doing light drills just to keep busy. It is nothing too serious, because we are not well equipped, and we are very tired. Gambling among soldiers is a popular way to pass the time, but I prefer to keep my money.

German prisoners of war are processed through Mourmelon. Some of the prisoners are treated badly by replacement soldiers with no combat experience. This is vastly different from the treatment they get from experienced soldiers. They are our enemy, and yet there is a certain amount of respect and pity for the German soldiers. The new replacement US soldiers still walk around with a swagger, as they have not yet experienced the trauma of battle against an enemy we veterans have grown to realize isn't very different from us. The older replacements are now a part of us. For the most part, they are ordinary guys caught up in extreme circumstances like the rest of us. The new guys are confident in their training and uniform but have no experience to back it up.

Friction among the replacements leads to arguments, and sometimes fights break out, just as in England. The replacement bazooka men are no exception. Since I am one of the few bazooka gunners still around with the Screaming Eagles after the Normandy invasion and the Netherlands, I have seniority and am often asked to break up the fights. "Rich go break 'em up," Lieutenant Morrison says with a grin.

"No, let 'em fight," I reply matter-of-factly. "They'll learn soon enough their buddies are not the enemy." Usually, alcohol is the underlying problem.

We eagerly anticipate the Thanksgiving holiday, and we are promised a really good meal. Apparently, though, the food is prepared under less than ideal sanitary conditions, and many soldiers become ill afterward. The day following Thanksgiving, football games between units are organized, which helps to pass the time. USO shows are available, featuring such stars as Marlene Dietrich and former major league baseball players.

I spend some of the time watching movies in the makeshift tent theater, where we see lots of news clips of the war effort around the world. In the Netherlands we didn't hear much about the rest of the world. Now, in France, we see not only news clips but also drama movies with John Wayne depicting US war efforts in the Pacific theater. Occasionally, I go to see a western cowboy movie.

Boz makes it back to the company, having recovered from his back injury. "I heard it was pretty tough," Boz mentions when I see him, referring to the fighting in the Netherlands.

"Yeah, it was tough," I reply. "Dom was killed."

"How's Larry?" Boz quietly asks, thinking of the dead twin.

"Seems lost . . . isn't fit to fight . . . walks around in a daze," I say. "The Krauts will kill ya for that. Barton was hurt real bad. Paralyzed, they say," I continue.

"Damn, I wish I'd been with the guys. Hurts bad not to have been there," Boz says sadly. I think he is going to break.

Left: Al "Boz' Borzymowski, Jack Sherman, and Roy Oswald. Courtesy John Sherman collection.

Right: Boz with a French orphan. Courtesy John Sherman collection.

"At least you're in one piece. Good to have ya back. How is your back?" I ask.

"The back's fine, doesn't hurt much. I couldn't hardly move for a while. I couldn't have carried anything," he adds.

Sherman, Boz, and I, along with James Oswald, befriend some French kids and have some fun with them. It's like having siblings around. The three of us are really looking forward to Christmas. The kids' parents are missing or were killed during the fighting. Boz particularly likes playing with the kids, being not all that much bigger than they are. A Christmas party is being planned by the troops for the local orphans.

Training on precision marching begins again. Sparks keeps messing up. I like him, but he really isn't cut out for this, especially the precision stuff. Captain Evans, being a perfectionist, doesn't like Sparks one bit. I come back from a training exercise, and Sparks is packing his bags. "What's up, Sparks? Where are you going?" I ask.

"Evans got me transferred to the 82nd," Sparks says with some sadness in his voice.

"What for? Why?" I sort of suspect the answer already.

"Evans thinks I'm a screw-up, that's why. That's not the official reason, but that's what it is."

I am sad to see him go, because he does all right for me. He does struggle with the weapons and gear, though. My dislike for Evans is growing stronger and stronger.

On December 18 there is a general staff meeting of officers. The officers' body language makes it obvious that something big is coming. The only real information I have is a small article in the army newspaper, *Stars and Stripes,* about a big German counteroffensive in the Ardennes area of Belgium, northeast of Mourmelon. So far, I've been having a decent rest, but blackouts at night remind us that the war still isn't really very far away. As it turns out, additional troops are going to be needed to turn back the German counterattack, and the army thinks the 101st will be perfect to help accomplish this.[3]

Immediately, soldiers are restricted to base and existing passes are canceled. The Christmas party is cancelled, too. Great efforts are being taken to resupply the division, as we are still so depleted, but there isn't much in the way of supplies available. Trucks loaded with supplies do begin rolling in, but it is too little too late. The Screaming Eagles are not even close to being in combat condition. If the lack of supplies isn't bad enough, forty percent of the Screaming Eagles have been killed, wounded, or captured in the Netherlands.[4] More replacements are needed, and we don't have time to mold together a team with those who have recently arrived as replacement soldiers. Three weeks of recovery and light training with the replacements isn't enough.

The Screaming Eagles' commanding officer, General Taylor, is currently back in the United States for meetings and to visit his family, whom he hasn't seen in more than two years. The second in command, Brig. Gen. Gerald Higgins, is in England. Brig. Gen. Anthony C. McAuliffe, an artillery expert, is now in charge. The Screaming Eagles are about to leave in the morning to secure the Belgian town of Werbomont from the advancing German army. Plans to go into Werbomont are later changed; the 101st is needed at Bastogne.[5]

Word of what is coming spreads like wildfire among the soldiers at Mourmelon. The 101st is to move out in the morning. At this time all we know is that the Germans have counterattacked and have been successful at breaking through Allied lines. Orders are given for those still in the hospital to move out with us, even if they aren't fully recovered.

On the morning of Monday, December 18, 1944, the guys in the 101st wake up to a gray and dreary day. "Everybody up—we're moving out!" bark officers at about four o'clock in the morning. The guys move around apathetically; we still need rest. Outside the barracks are huge trucks. Slowly, men gather together outside. Jeeps scurry down the roads. Officers bark orders. We look more like road workers than elite troops. Weaponry and ammo are handed out without the usual paperwork. We grab all the ammunition and food supplies we can.

"What do you think, Sherman? We gonna fight the Germans again?" I ask.

"Evans seems pretty serious about this. Not sure what they expect with us at half strength," Sherman replies.

"Maybe we'll be back in Mourmelon in a couple of weeks when things quiet down. Or maybe we'll just be in reserve and back to base before you know it." I think about the terrible shelling that occurred while we were in reserve on the Island.

Loading the 380 trucks with supplies and what little equipment we have takes most of the day.[6] Parachute regiments leave first, early in the afternoon. As a division, we especially lack mortars, rifles, ammunition, and shovels. Also missing is cold-weather clothing, including snow boots. We have no gas masks. The enemy hasn't used poison gas as a weapon yet, as they did in the previous war, but the Germans are now getting desperate and just might use it.

Not only are we tired, but, because so many officers have been lost, killed, or wounded in the Netherlands, we ordinary soldiers are also not very confident in the overall leadership core. However, I like General McAuliffe, even though I don't see much of him.

The 327th Glider Infantry Regiment pulls out at 1930. Some in our company join us just as we are leaving, having been warned by military police in Paris. Briefings on where the German breakthroughs are occurring have been taking place along the way. Officers are riding in the back of the trucks right along with us regular soldiers, because the cabs are reserved for a backup driver. First Lt. Alfred Regenburg, who has just been assigned to G from battalion machine guns,[7] is with us and tries to explain the situation. Our maps of the area show roadways, but these are not in the proper scale. We are still physically and emotionally drained, not ready for what is ahead. Our only advantage is that many of us are mature combat troops and know how to do our duty.

Here we are, the best airborne division in the world, and yet we are going to the fight by truck. Boz, being his usual funny self, jokes, "In France we went in by boat. Some of us went to Holland from the air [poking fun at himself], and now we're going by truck. Good thing we practiced jumping from a tailgate while in England."

Trucks hauling the 327th are about one-third of the way up from the back of the long, slow-moving column. The drivers look exhausted, probably from all the logistical work they've had to do since the Germans' counterattack. Fifty of us are crammed into the big truck with high sideboards, kind of like pigs being hauled to market. There is standing room only, with no cover over our heads. The weather is very cold, with low clouds overhead. We travel all night with headlights blazing. Under these conditions we are easy targets for the Luftwaffe, if they see us. The bright lights of the trucks, which normally would have been doused for security reasons, are indications of the seriousness of our assignment.

During the one-hundred-mile trip, a five-gallon latrine bucket is passed back and forth in the truck and is constantly full; it is not easy to handle because of the bumping of the truck. There is no unnecessary stopping. Orders are given to lock and load all weapons. This is not normal practice. Usually with so many guys crowded together, it is considered too dangerous to have the weapons ready to fire.

"We might get a crack at the Krauts after all," Sherman jokes.

"Maybe they're already in France, the way we're driving," I add.

Getting sleep along the way would be impossible even if we were seated: the road is too bumpy and the weather too cold. As we get closer to the drop area, the weather becomes damp, foggy, and even colder. Guys speculate on exactly where we will be deployed and what our role will be. The caravan stops. "What's up?" the driver asks as someone pounds the cab roof with his fist.

"A truck has slid off the road and is partially blocking the way," the guard explains. Some locals allow us into their houses to keep warm while the truck is cleared.

On December 19 at 0850, the 327th unloads near the village of Flamizoulle, located about four miles to the northwest of Bastogne. Company strength is 115. The regiment is among the last to arrive at the tailgate drop site. An MP motions to our truck, showing us where to stop. I jump off the tailgate, a little stiff from being cold and not being able to move around much. Mud is up to my ankles. There is a musty smell to the air as we immediately begin our half-mile march to Mande Saint-Etienne, where 2nd Battalion is to protect the 327th's regimental headquarters. The tiny village has about a dozen buildings or so within its boundaries. US soldiers are pouring through the village, moving to the west, away from the advancing German army.[8]

"Go back! Don't stay!" say soldiers from other divisions who are heading the wrong way. "The Krauts will be here any minute! Tanks! Tanks! Tanks!" They seem to be in some kind of dazed stupor. I don't think much about it, as we are told the German army is still forty miles away.

We hear that US VIII Corp headquarters is in Bastogne, which is somewhat comforting. "At least we're not here alone," Shaw quips. However, later that night we hear that this VIII Corp HQ has already been packing up and is getting out of town as fast as it can in advance of the Germans.[9]

A few of the guys grab weapons and ammunition from fleeing American troops. I am fine, however, because I have my rifle, bazooka, and a full supply of ammunition. Hibbard, Regenburg, and Hidalgo confront some of the dazed soldiers, asking them to stay and fight. Some of them seemed scared to death. Others are angry at the situation and keep heading the wrong direction. Although some stay, most do not.

Company G moves into a small brick schoolhouse at Mande Saint-Etienne. There, Regenburg briefs us on the immediate situation. The enemy still isn't all that close, or so he says—forty miles or more. Earlier in the day, the parachute regiments arrived and headed toward and around the town of Bastogne.

The daytime hours on December 19 are fairly uneventful for me. I have a bedroll, although not a winter one. I make use of it and try to get some rest after enjoying some food I stuffed into it before leaving Mourmelon. I feel pretty comfortable.

Thinking about what might be ahead, I try to relax, but there is an eerie feeling in the nighttime air. In the low areas, fog begins to thicken, but it doesn't cover the sky. To keep warm, men pour gasoline in puddles and light it. The night air is very cold.

"Sherman, what do you want to do when we're done?" I ask.

"You mean back at Mourmelon?"

"No, back home."

"See Phyll. I miss her," Sherman says, referring to his girlfriend, Phyllis. "What do you want to do?"

"I just want to get out alive," I answer. "More fighting like back in Holland, and we won't survive." In my mind I have pretty strong doubts about my survival.

Before our arrival, the defense lines at Bastogne were defended by elements of the 10th Armored Division. The 10th Armored was divided into

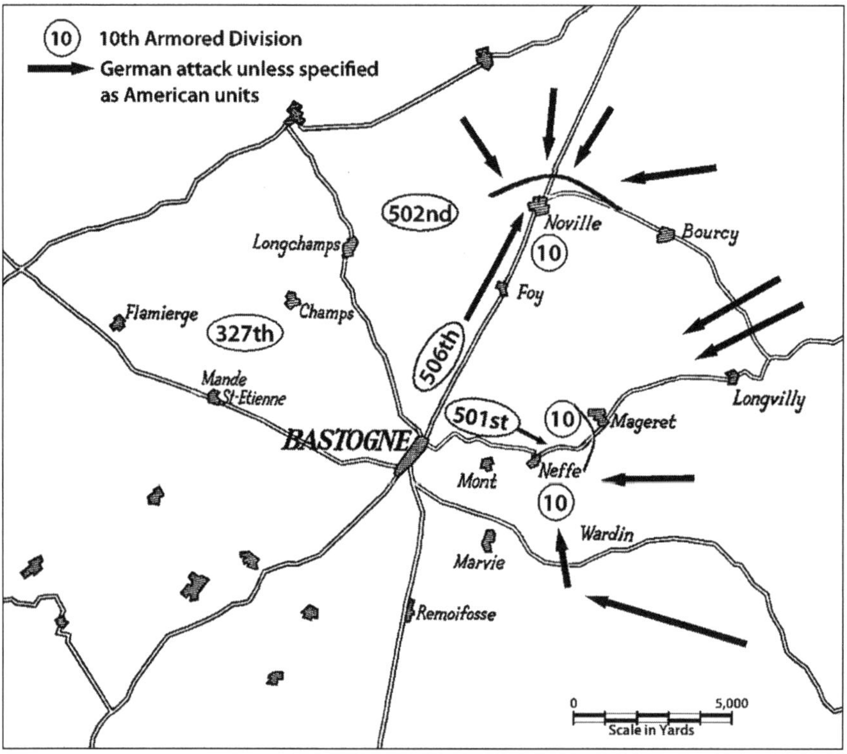

The 101st Airborne Division defends Bastogne, December 19, 1944. Company G is in reserve as the enemy presses the attack from the east and northeast.

three teams that defended three different areas to the northeast, east, and southeast of the town. A few miles to the east, the 10th engaged the enemy, resulting in heavy casualties for the Americans. Survivors had to fight their way back to US lines.[10]

The 501st heads east, hoping to impede the enemy's straight approach into Bastogne. Heavy fog blankets the area, with visibility severely limited. Sometime after 0700 on the December 19, when the fog begins to break somewhat, the 1st Battalion of the 501st is fired on near Neffe and soon later is confronted by enemy tanks.[11]

To the southeast the 10th Armored Division takes up positions east of Marvie and sets up a roadblock along the Wiltz road. About five miles to the northeast of Bastogne, the commander of a task force of the 10th, Maj. William R. Desobry, desperately tries to set up a roadblock just south of Noville at 2300 on the December 18, but a steady stream of retreating US forces keeps him from completing the task. Desobry's men search vehicles for retreating US infantrymen, wanting to press them into making a stand against the enemy. These retreating soldiers, some whom have never seen combat before, have been so badly beaten that they run and hide in cellars, and some of them bawl like babies as the enemy attacks.[12]

Also on the morning of December 19, the fog around Noville is even thicker than before. At 0830 two giant German Tiger tanks approach the northern edge of the village and are promptly knocked out. By 1030 the fog lifts, and the Americans are amazed at what they see. The landscape is covered with German tanks. For an hour both sides slug things out. Desobry asks command for permission to have his men withdraw south to Foy. The answer is delayed to give time for the 101st to arrive. The 506th finally arrives, but its weapons are in short supply.

Smoke from repeated artillery hits pours from the village of Noville. Losses are heavy on both sides. The Screaming Eagles are fighting like a cornered mad dog being attacked by a big pack of wolves. When a shell hits the street just outside the Noville command post, Lt. Col. James L. LaPrade, commanding the 1st Battalion of the 506th, is killed, and Major Desobry is wounded. General McAuliffe, thinking the situation at Noville as nearly hopeless, wants to withdraw from Noville in the evening. McAuliffe asks permission from his superior to withdraw. Headquarters' response is, "No withdrawal." The order is, "Hold at all costs."[13]

Except for the cold, biting air, the night of December 19 in Mande Saint-Etienne seems to be rather peaceful and calm for those of us "lucky" enough to be in G. We wait for orders. I can't sleep, although I am very tired. The thick, eerie fog seems symbolic of something, although I cannot put a finger on it.

Finally, after what seems like hours, I manage to doze off. Sometime after midnight I am awakened by the loud, deep rumble of what sounds like an infinite number of trucks. At 0200 word comes from Regenburg that 2nd Battalion is about to move out, although we have no idea where we are going. Some guys try to ignore the announcement and continue to sleep on, while others clean and ready weapons, but in general things are quiet. At 0400 Regenburg gives orders to deploy, and we are quickly up and about, alert and wide awake.[14]

Through the loud bustling we hear the familiar rugged voice of Sergeant Hanlon, saying, "Leave your heavy gear behind. Don't take any heavy coats, overshoes, or bedrolls. Supply will deliver them later. We can move faster without all that gear."

Even though I am a little skeptical about not needing my supplies, I drop my stuff off at the supply dump. We learn that 2nd Battalion is immediately heading to the village of Marvie to relieve Company C of the 326th Airborne Engineer Battalion, provide infantry support for the 10th Armored Division, and prevent the enemy from advancing through Marvie.

Regenburg tells us the 326th has constructed a roadblock to keep the enemy from using a bridge south of the village. Our mission is to defend the roadblock and keep the Germans from advancing to Bastogne through Marvie and area roads.[15] "Bastogne is to be held at all costs," says the lieutenant. "Watch out for English-speaking German soldiers," he adds, reminding us again, as if we need a reminder.

As we start our march, a Belgian family scurries down the road toward us. "The Germans are coming! The Germans are coming!" the mother exclaims in heavily accented English. Continuing our march toward Bastogne, we run into more retreating US forces. They seem dazed and confused. I know I will never forget the defeated look etched on their young faces.

Through our medium-weight jackets the air seems chilly to us as we march the three and one-half miles east into Bastogne. Many men grumble about the cold, but all the marching has caused me to work up quite a sweat, so I don't mind the temperature. "You'll get supplies up ahead, don't worry about it," an officer mentions. Along the path are usable weapons discarded by retreating soldiers. They are quickly and gladly picked up by guys in the company.

The column soon arrives in the center of Bastogne, which seems to be a quaint small town, although it has some buildings that reach five stories high. The town reminds me of Mount Pleasant. Nearby, we can see a church steeple. Railroad tracks run north and south through the town, which stretches about three-quarters of a mile along the tracks. The fog continues to thicken, adding mystery to the still dark sky.

Because of the fog in the early morning hours, the 327th's marching column has trouble finding the right road out of Bastogne. "Wish they'd learn to read maps," I complain to whoever might be listening. "Are we lost again?" I think maybe I should keep quiet. By 0600 we march out of Bastogne and turn to the southeast.[16] We are now arranged in a column two soldiers wide, one row on the left road shoulder and the other on the right. Ahead we hear a brief salvo of artillery but don't think much about it, as the enemy, we are told, isn't even close.

The march takes us to a foggy ridge overlooking the barely visible hamlet of Marvie, which has maybe one hundred inhabitants. Sunrise is beginning to brighten the scene. The village has fewer than two dozen standing buildings; at least, that's what it looks like through the fog, which is getting thicker still. Just to the south of me I can make out a creek running from west to east, right through the middle of the town, before continuing to the southeast. A small bridge crosses the creek in town. The creek is at the bottom of a small but fairly steep valley within the old village. To the west and north is Bastogne, where there is some higher ground occupied by Americans. I can't see Bastogne because of the fog, but I know we've marched downhill. The small bridge is determined to be a good place to set up a bazooka, as any German tank coming right through town will have to cross the creek.

Guards posted by the 326th Engineers in Marvie look at us with suspicion because of reports of enemy forces using American uniforms and equipment. The guards look as if they could shoot us pretty quickly if we give the wrong answer to their questions, such as not knowing which league the Cubs play in. Captain Evans and other officers emerge from a meeting with battalion command. Simpson tells us Lieutenant Regenburg wants to talk to those of us in the bazooka section. Before Regenburg speaks to us, the local priest is brought to Niland.

Through an interpreter, Niland speaks to the priest: "The Germans are creatures of habit. They do the same thing over and over again. In the Great War, they came right down this road (he points toward the roadblock area to the south). In the beginning of this war they came through here again. We believe they'll be right through here again. Tell your people to evacuate the village as soon as possible."

The priest looks dismissive. "I was here in the last war," he replies. "I was here in the beginning of this war. The Germans weren't a problem then. I doubt there will be problems now."

"The difference is that we aren't leaving," Niland yells. "There's going to be one hell of a fight. Get your people out, *now!*" The priest leaves.[17]

Regenburg then orders the bazooka section to stay in Marvie for further instruction while the rest of the company heads south and east of town. Soon, Regenburg informs us, "There is a bridge just beyond those trees." He points toward the tree line to the southeast about two-thirds of a miles out. "In this sector, over that bridge is the only way the Krauts can get through and take Bastogne. The engineers are blocking the road just on this side of the bridge. We'll stop 'em at the roadblock. Under no circumstances can we let any Krauts or Kraut tanks get through the Marvie sector. Understood?"

"Yes, sir!" we respond.

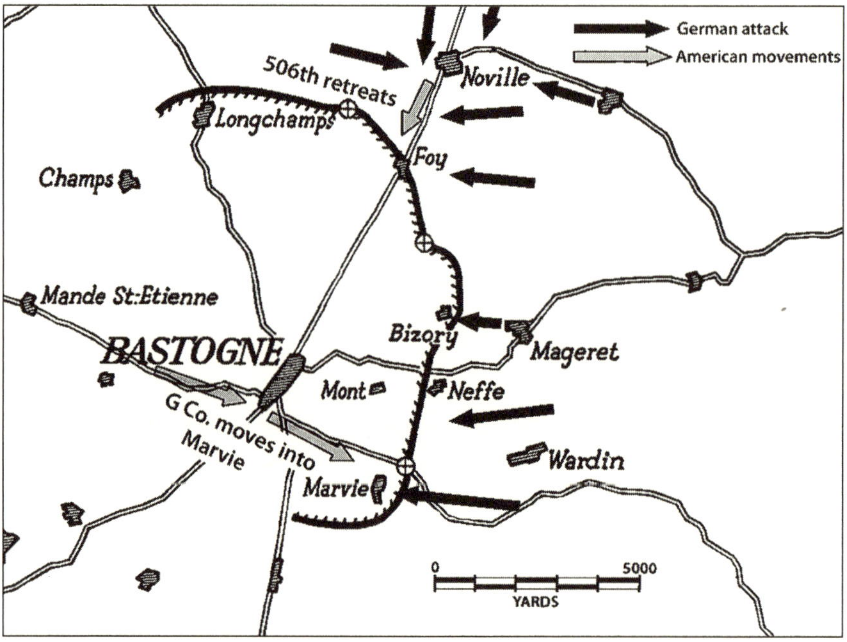

101st Airborne Division defensive lines, December 20, 1944. Company G moves to the village of Marvie and sets up defenses.

"If the damn Krauts get through, the tanks and Easy Company will engage and prevent them from advancing up the road to the east." He points again. "In the event they break through, G Company will stop them from getting through Marvie at all costs. If they get through one of these roads, they have a clean shot to Bastogne. Understood?"

"Yes, sir!" we answer.

"Rich, take two bazookas and destroy any damn Kraut tank you see," Regenburg orders. "Pick who you want and make it quick."

I take a few minutes to survey the situation. Looking around, I think briefly how pretty the scenery is. Eastward, toward the roadblock, the creek valley running from the village to the roadblock offers a good field of vision, except for several clusters of trees and some stone fences. The main force of G has already been setting up defenses, under Evans's orders, using foxholes dug by F Company, which arrived first and now is heading to the right flank, farther west.[18] I can't make out the tanks of Lt. Col. James O'Hara's task force of the 10th Armored, well hidden from view in the fog. Easy Company has a bazooka man in their defense line to the north.

Evans explains that G's positions are located from right to left (southeast to northeast) beginning with a small hill with a few houses on it that is referred to as Hill 500. From there the front line cuts across the south end of town, where two roads converge into one heading directly south. Near that intersection, G's position heads east along an ancient stone wall for two hundred yards and then turns north. Easy Company is on the left flank from the fences in front of the middle of the village running north towards where O'Hara's tanks are supposed to be located.

"Shaw, we have a good field of vision toward the road. Should they get through, we have to defend the bridge in Marvie," I say, but Shaw doesn't reply. Boz and 2nd Platoon have already headed off toward a small hill south of town and are digging in.

I turn to the bazooka man from New York and his assistant. "Take the bazooka and set up on Hill 500," I tell them. "Morrison is over there. Ask him any questions." Then I ask Shaw to stay with me.

Shaw and I set up near the middle of the defense line east of Marvie. I further assess the area, looking for strengths and weaknesses in our defenses. The woods provide cover for an advancing enemy, which is not good for us. The long, gradually sloping valley from Marvie and a decent road provide a good field of fire for hitting enemy tanks coming up the valley. The several stone fences and rows of brush inhibit the view somewhat, but they will also help to conceal us from enemy troops.

Troops from E, F, and G Companies are digging in. E Company is making the best progress.[19] Further to the left, team O'Hara's tanks are settling in. I now can barely see them, because of the fog, but I know they consist of two medium tanks and four light tanks. One of the light tanks sets up behind a barn just east of the church. I'm glad the enemy is forty miles away, I think to myself. A small squad is out in front of the line to provide protection for the guys digging in.

At 0900 the 10th Armored Division opens up with an artillery barrage aimed in the direction of the roadblock, which I still can't see.[20] The explosions echo through the valley. "Wonder what that's about," Shaw says.

"Not sure we want to know," I reply. "Target practice, I guess."

Colonels Harper and O'Hara meet with Evans and then go out to high ground to the west of Marvie to overview the situation. Second Battalion is stretched out over a mile and a half, a monumental area to cover with so few soldiers, especially if German tanks attack.[21]

At about 1115, artillery comes from the woods and hits around us—nothing spectacular or orderly, but rather random.[22] This doesn't make sense: the Germans by habit don't shell us so randomly. Evans tells us that the Germans are not close.

As I gaze across the valley, a chill shoots up my spine. "Here comes a tank!" I smart off to Evans. What I see stuns me. "Holy smokes!" Shaw blurts out. The tree line is turning a gray-green and brown color. Like an ocean wave coming out of the sea, the whole German army seems to be advancing out of the trees. I look back and can see Captain Evans, who looks just as stunned as everyone else.[23] Less than half a mile away, a German Mark IV medium tank races up a narrow farm road, making its way out of the forested area toward us. Three more German tanks soon appear out of the forest, along with six half-tracks spaced apart and advancing up the valley with infantry in between them.

"Blam!" A US 90 mm high-velocity tank destroyer blasts a German half-track that has just emerged from the woods six hundred yards away. I can make out bodies flying through the air. Just like a cowboy-era gunslinger, the tank destroyer fires off a series of shots, ducks back behind a barn, and then comes out again, firing at the Krauts. A German self-propelled gun (SP) is now leading the attack up the road that runs into the center of the village. The tanks and half-tracks are to the south (left) of the SP and trailing it.

The fog, which has not dissipated completely, as we had hoped it would by now, partially obscures the tanks. From the forested area the Germans let loose a small number of artillery shells, which land in the village. Typically, they pound us heavily before an attack. Time seems to slow as I realize that our depleted company is facing what appears to be a whole German regiment out ahead of a heavy armored division. The manner in which the enemy is advancing makes it obvious they don't yet see us. Then the 10th Armored tanks open fire, and the enemy becomes preoccupied with O'Hara's light tanks to our left.[24] One of the German tanks is hit broadside.

"Dig in! Dig in!" Evans and other officers order frantically. A 326th Engineers half-track comes toward us, speeding toward Marvie, trying to escape the enemy.[25]

The buildings and stone fences offer some protection. Men begin digging in in front of the fence or setting up behind it or in buildings. Evans is directing the soldiers, but he seems to be nit-picking about where they dig or hide.[26]

The enemy artillery fire from guns in the forest picks up and crashes around us. The enemy SP fires toward O'Hara's command post to the north of town in an attempt to hit a US half-track. Instead, it destroys a jeep and a trailer pulled by the half-track. O'Hara's command post is hit, and nearby a cow lies dead.

The German tanks get closer and position themselves for an attack on the American light tanks. My bazooka isn't much good against the front armor plate of the tanks, so I hold my fire. Shells from the light tanks bounce right off the enemy tanks. The German SP fires at the light tank behind a barn near the church and misses, and the shell explodes into a house in Marvie. The light tanks begin to withdraw. One is set ablaze. The other is hit but manages to withdraw and backs away from the fight. The enemy SP seems to get hit from three directions and explodes in a brilliant mass of flames.

The remaining German tanks now center their attention on the village, as they now know we are here. Boom-Boom! Boom-Boom! Boom-Boom! The enemy tanks are so close that the impact blasts of the shells are almost simultaneous with the sound of their guns. Easy Company, on the left flank, takes the brunt of the shells, which is good, as they are better dug in and didn't have to retreat.[27]

As the Germans get closer, another enemy tank is hit broadside and explodes. Captain Evans is directing the men, exposing himself to enemy fire. He continues to nitpick frantically about where he wants each soldier, pointing to where they should go. "Dammit, don't dig there, dig here!" he yells.

We are in for a desperate fight, maybe outnumbered ten or fifteen to one. As the enemy continues to edge closer, the engineer battalion, which we replaced, hightails it out on the north side of Marvie. A short time later, an American mortar squad flees. With the light tanks retreating, it looks like a complete rout of US forces.[28]

"Are we retreating?" Shaw yells at me.

Our situation seems to be hopeless. Colonel Harper sees the scene from the north and reports to division headquarters that Marvie is lost and has fallen to the enemy.[29]

Soldiers who are unlucky enough to have positioned themselves at the edge of the village in front of the stone fence are continuously raked with machine gun fire. Five G Company soldiers are cut nearly in half by the enemy gunfire as they shoot at the half-tracks; their bodies are now lying against the fence. The five are still holding their rifles as they lie dead in front of the stone wall.[30] Shells continue to pound our positions.

Five German half-tracks loaded with infantry still race toward Marvie, leaving the enemy foot soldiers behind. Other German tanks continue to fire into us from the forest. Blam! Blam! Blam! Pop, pop, pop, pop, blam! With the enemy shelling, the machine gun firing, and yelling, the situation

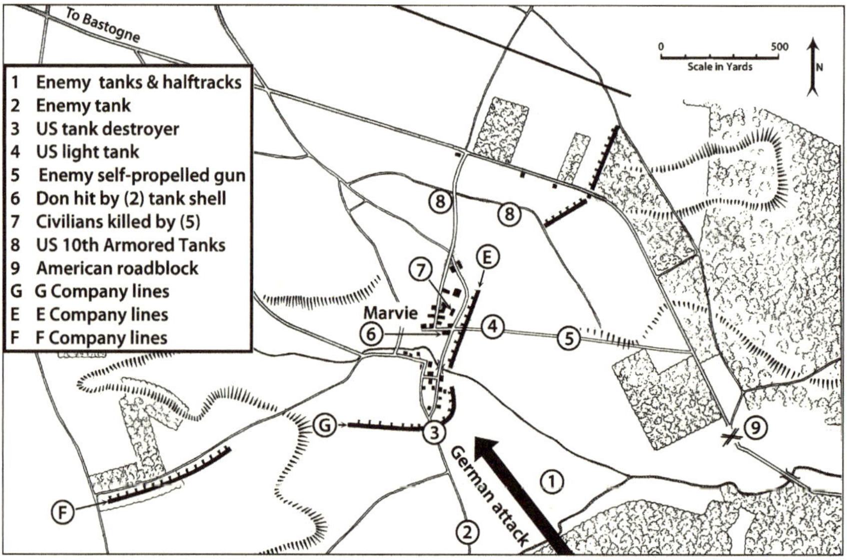

The first battle at Marvie, December 20, 1944.

seems to be in slow motion. Evans is still screaming out detailed orders: "Dig here! Soldier, dig there! Dig, dig, dig! Now! Move! Move! Move!" Evans is directing with his mouth and arms while standing in the open.[31]

"Sir, stop!" a couple of privates scream back at Evans. "You're giving away our positions!" More shells and machine gun fire hit us.

"Do what you are told!" Evans keeps nitpicking, pointing and waving. He is losing it.

"Stop it, dammit!" one of the two soldiers screams as more shells crash nearby. "I'm not going anywhere. You're giving them a target!" He's scared to death.

"Do as you're told, soldier! Move on . . ." But before Evans can finish his sentence, one of the Southerners, a guy with a heavy mustache who has been trying frantically to keep from being exposed to bullets, whirls around with his rifle and appears to fire at Evans at the same time an artillery shell comes crashing in. Evans falls backwards, his helmet flying off. Through the smoke, someone pulls him into a nearby house; he has a head wound. Colonel Harper radios to headquarters that Evans has been hit by enemy artillery fire.[32]

The remaining half-tracks speed forward toward Marvie, but some of them seem caught in no-man's land and are forced to turn and head back to the woods or move forward into G Company's positions. One is blown apart as it turns to head back towards the forest. The first enemy tank speeding up the road has reached the town's first street and heads north through the village.[33] "Let's get that tank!" I yell at Jim Shaw. Grabbing him by the arm, I head north up the street, ahead of the tank, which is still over three hundred yards away. The two of us duck into a farmhouse on the west side of the road near the church. Like many farm homes in Belgium, this one has a barn attached. "Shaw, stay down until I tell you to fire!" I order, being the more experienced soldier.

Quickly, I load the bazooka. Shaw squats down out of sight in the living quarters of the stone building, and I move deeper inside. I can hear the tank approaching. I glance out a window where there is a good view out to the street and then duck back down. The tank is closer but still almost two hundred yards away. We are slightly uphill from it. It nears the bridge over the creek.

Because the Germans' tanks have heavy armor in the front but not as much on the sides, I wait for the tank to get close. Then I glance through the door and am surprised to see Shaw standing and ready to fire, right out in the open part of the barn. The tank turret swings toward us. Then an explosion rips through the building, rolling me across the floor, and I land hard against the wall. I lose consciousness. When I start to regain my senses, I don't know where I am, what I am doing, or how long it has been. Then I remember, but glancing around, I see no sign of Shaw. I stumble around groggily and walk toward what I think used to be the kitchen. There is an eight-foot hole blown through what is left of the wall. The whole place is a wreck.

"Shaw! Shaw!" There is no response. I keep looking. "Where is he?" I ask myself. Finally, I can hear moaning underneath some rubble.

"I'm here, I'll get you out!" I shout as I grab and throw pieces of the wall and ceiling off of the pile. There are more moans, then I see a little movement. I quickly brush the smaller pieces of rubble off of Shaw. Blood is coming from his face and ears; his face is covered with dust and blood. "Can you hear me, Shaw? Let's get out of here." I speak quickly.

As I assess his wounds, I can tell that Shaw isn't mentally with me. I also realize that the world is spinning in circles. I feel sick to my stomach and I hurt all over. Gathering myself, I throw Shaw's arm around my shoulder while lifting him up. I then head down the street, dragging him along.

"Nice shootin' Rich," I hear someone say as I glance to my right at a damaged enemy tank. I knew we hadn't hit the tank, because we didn't even get off a shot before it hit us.

Denis Parsons comes up to me. "I got it. I got the tank," he says, rather matter-of-factly. Denis has a BAR in his hands with armor-piercing rounds. A loud explosion rumbles as the disabled tank is hit by O'Hara's men.

With Shaw hanging over my shoulder and his feet dragging behind me, I stumble toward the center of town. Heavy fighting continues around me. I can hear rifle fire, but I pay no real attention. Rounding another corner, I almost run into a soldier holding his stomach; I don't recognize him. I look closer: his belly is ripped open and guts are hanging out. I continue on, needing to take care of Shaw.

After another block, I see a squad of enemy soldiers setting up a defensive line. I'm thankful they don't see me; I turn right to go around them. It isn't that I am being brave; I just have to get Shaw help. I am still groggy and not thinking very clearly.

I see Fisher and Niland running up the street. Fisher is looking for a medic, too, for battalion commander Inman. He rounds a corner and runs into an enemy soldier; they fire at each other. Running to the closest home, Fisher tries to enter the front door, but it won't open. He quickly jumps through an open window into a room where a large family is present. He then comes flying back out of the house, and I hear some women screaming while one slams the window shut. A grenade goes off behind Fisher, followed by machine gun shots as a squad of enemy soldiers chases him away.

The enemy does not send reinforcements into the fray, and now it seems 2nd Battalion is gaining the upper hand. Our guys are hunting the remaining enemy soldiers down, house by house.

I continue in search of a medic and find one on the north outskirts of the village. Looking at Shaw, the medic speaks with urgency, "I've got to get him to the hospital right away. Word has it we may be surrounded soon." Shaw is in pretty bad shape, and I am quite relieved to hand him over to the medic. I'm still suffering from shell shock as a result of the explosion, and my thinking is hazy, but I refuse examination and remember that I need to retrieve the bazooka. Somehow I make it back to the house where the tank hit us. I find my bazooka: the shell explosion has bent the weapon, smashing the barrel shut.

Using the buildings for protective cover, G Company is able to mount a formidable defense against the enemy infantry in the village. Lieutenant Morrison is captured by the Germans and then later freed by 2nd Platoon.[34]

The fighting dies down, as the enemy doesn't launch a subsequent attack, apparently deciding to regroup. Several hours later, they shell us again, and several tanks come out of the woods before retreating rather abruptly. I guess they think there must be an easier way into Bastogne. The Germans suffer at least thirty killed within the village of Marvie alone. Twenty enemy soldiers are now prisoners. If they had kept coming at us with full force, we would have been broken, because Company G doesn't have the numbers left to repel a full-scale attack. We have taken quite a few casualties: twenty-five men of the company are killed or wounded. For the next several hours I walk around in a daze, startling once at 1400 when O'Hara's tankers find an enemy half-track stuck in the mud and promptly knock it out.[35] Shortly later, the Germans smoke the village and attack out of the woods, only to retreat without a fight. My head and body hurt, and my hearing isn't right.

Around 1500, Niland approaches me. I can tell he is distraught. He normally doesn't show emotion unless he's really upset. "Rich, take five men with you and protect our flank over to the west about five hundred yards or so," he says. "Morrison has Hill 500 covered." He points to the small knob of a hill about twenty feet high south of the town. "Company F has our right flank to the west of the hill; we need to make contact with F and make sure the Germans don't get through the gap between G and F. F will be on your right, starting at the woods about a hundred yards over past the hill. There should be a farmhouse to the west. Some locals have reported a German squad blocking the road to the south of the lakes, if you get lost."

"Yes, sir," I answer, and I motion to five replacements taking a break next to a nearby house. "Let's go!" I say, pointing the way.

"What's wrong with Niland?" I ask.

"Niland tried to get the priest to get the civilians to evacuate," one of the replacements replies. "The Kraut SP missed a tank and took out a house with a family in the basement. The mother and several kids survived, but the husband and a little girl, maybe four or five years old, were killed."

My head still hurts, but my thinking is clearing. I lead the squad of six west along the road out of Marvie. I don't know the names of the other guys, because they are replacements, and I don't want to know their names. One of them has a BAR. "That's good," I think to myself as I remember back to the horses near Carentan, which seems like ages ago. Hanlon, I'm sure, expects me to have a bazooka, but I can't find one to replace the damaged one.

The 101st Airborne Division surrounded.

Before we get out of town, Sherman and Fisher come up to me. Sherman is still attached to company headquarters as a runner. With Evans wounded, Lieutenant Regenburg is now acting commander of G. "Rich, the strangest thing happened," Sherman says. "After the fight, Regenburg sent me out as a runner to find Hidalgo doing mop-up detail over there." Sherman points down the hill where the Germans attacked us first. "On my way back, I heard someone say 'Hey, Yates! Hey, Yates!' I didn't know anyone named Yates, so I didn't pay any attention. I took a few more steps and thought, 'Ya know, I don't know anyone named Yates in the whole company,' so I turned and looked. Darned if they didn't have Kraut uniforms, five or six of 'em behind a fence. They looked as surprised to see me as I was to see them. I didn't know what to do, and neither did they. So I kept on walking. Ya know what sounds like 'Hey, Yates?' *Wie gehts,* that's what it sounds like. V-gates . . . Hey, Yates. Get it?"

"So?" I answer, half not believing the story.

"Means 'hello' in Kraut talk. Darned Krauts were saying hello. Strangest thing. . . ." Sherman, muttering and shaking his head, turns and leaves, and my squad goes in the opposite direction.[36] Fisher adds that he ran into Krauts in the house where he jumped through the window and shot some of them.

A few steps later, another soldier who works for company headquarters approaches me; he is coming back from being a runner, too. His gun is pointed at a squad of Germans he's captured. "Maybe they were saying 'hello' and just wanted to give up?" I say to the soldier; he has no idea what I'm talking about as he walks off. I hope there aren't any more Germans out there.

A few more steps, and we see Lieutenant Hibbard leading a squad from 2nd Platoon. I don't recognize the other soldiers from my former platoon. "So many gone," I think, as they walk on past.

"We've been attached to F," Hibbard mentions, as he turns around and notices me looking at them.[37]

We cross the creek in town as we head out to the west. We march past Hill 500, which is off to our south. I wish I could visit with Boz. "There's a house, I wonder if that's it? No sign of F," I murmur. "Come on, keep goin.'"

There isn't anyone around, no sign of either F or G. A couple of hundred yards further is a woods and another intersection. We'll be an easy target for the Krauts, I think. "Niland said there are Krauts down that way, blocking the road near the lakes," I say to the others, pointing to the south. Still there is no sign of F. On our left, the road takes us past thick woods. Another few hundred yards and we go past the woods into a clearing. I look to the south and see a farmhouse and dairy barn on the east side of the road. The house is part of the way down into a valley, with a creek further on down.[38]

"That's our place," I say as we head in that direction. Thick woods extend to the southeast of the house and up and over a ridge to the north. In front of us to the south is open, sloping farmland rising to a ridge. We walk over to the house and barn, surveying the layout. I wish we could see up and over the ridge in the distance. We make a defensive triangle around the farmstead. My partner and I set up behind the house to the northeast, thirty feet away. There are a few trees nearby. Another foxhole is set up thirty feet off the west side of the road. The BAR crew sets up in front of the house. Snow is beginning to fall, and the temperature is rapidly declining. Hurriedly we dig our foxholes and settle in as the sun is going down.

The 101st has so far held the enemy out of Bastogne. The 327th has stopped the enemy in the southeast. The 501st has formed a solid line in the east. The 506th has abandoned Noville and has had to fight their way back toward Bastogne, forming the perimeter line near Foy, only three miles from Bastogne.[39]

Fighting the Enemy and the Elements

EVERYONE IN THE SQUAD IS REALLY TIRED, SO NOBODY SAYS MUCH. I have my doubts about most of the replacements' ability to recognize danger or fight off an enemy attack. I don't know these guys and really don't want to know them. They are nameless to me; the cruelty of war keeps most of us who have been in battle from wanting to develop any more close friendships. Seeing a friend killed still isn't getting any easier. We take turns watching for any movement and pass the time in silence, watching and listening. I'm really not feeling very well because of the effects of the concussion from the tank shell.

At 2300 hours there is some movement to our southwest, but I can't make out what it is. At 2400 I notice more movement, but a short burst of US artillery sends whoever it is scurrying for cover.[1]

We made a big mistake when we left our winter gear back at the supply dump. In the early hours of December 21, the temperature continues to plummet, and the snow deepens. The temperature drops well below freezing, approaching zero Fahrenheit. I check the K rations, and among the six of us we have about three days' worth of food, if we eat sparingly. At daybreak, snow is still falling. I can hear tanks moving near Remoifosse, which is about a mile south of us, but I can't see them. I survey the terrain.

A couple of hundred feet over to the left of us is the woods. The first fifty feet or so inside the forest is fairly open. There is a clear view to the top of the ridge going south and to the west, except I can't see around the house. To the north and east of us, about seventy-five yards away, are wooded areas. The Belgian family is still in the house, which is connected to the barn; I see them come out of the barn to tend some cows. They don't seem too bothered by the war in their front yard and don't pay much attention to us.

Each of us carries a land mine about ten inches in diameter. We try burying them in the road but can't get through the surface of the frozen ground, so we leave them on top of the road. Maybe the enemy tanks won't see them.

Our foxholes, about four feet wide by six feet long, are deep enough to block the wind. I am hesitant to lie down and sleep, because I am concerned that I might freeze to death, and I am also nervous that the replacements might not be reliable enough to be left on their own. Snow is falling more heavily as the temperatures continue to drop. The standard-issue long-sleeved army jacket does little to keep me warm. The jump boots I wear aren't made to keep feet warm. I try to keep moving, mostly up and down to keep blood circulating through my feet. I have an extra pair of socks with me, which I grabbed when we left. I keep one pair dry and warm under the shelter of my helmet liner. Occasionally we hear artillery fire, but otherwise it is very quiet.

Company F is holding a roadblock to the west, behind our position, on the Arlon road, four hundred yards away.[2] They seem lonely out there, and I wonder if we look the same. It never crosses my mind that we might be in the wrong place, out too far from American lines. There is no one else around our position. The snow keeps falling. Knowing the enemy is in the area keeps everyone from sleeping. Later on during the night I can hear tank movement to my southwest, but I don't see anything in the dark. By daylight, four inches of snow has piled up. I can see enemy troops to the south, but we are out too far to do anything about it.

Later in the morning of December 21, the man of the farmhouse comes out and gives us some warm meat, which tastes very good. I think he is bold, because the Germans are known for being ruthless to civilians who aid the Americans; they can easily see him if they are watching from the woods. Eventually I venture over to the farmhouse, where he allows me to dip my canteen cup into a container filled with fresh, warm milk. The man can't speak English, and none of us can speak French, but I thank him the best I can and head back to my foxhole. After I tell the others about my amazing fortune, they follow, one at a time, except for one replacement who doesn't want to leave his foxhole. Later in the day, we hear US artillery and mortar fire trying to hit something to the southwest of us.[3] An increasing amount of enemy artillery fire hits around our area throughout the day, but nothing close. The whooshing sound and explosions echo through the valley.

At 0330 on December 22, we can again hear enemy tanks to the south, but we don't see them in the dark. US artillery pounds the area.[4]

Back in Marvie, Sherman notices that Simpson has disappeared, as he sometimes does—not to avoid duties, but because he is curious and desires to provide information to the company commander. He also seems to use

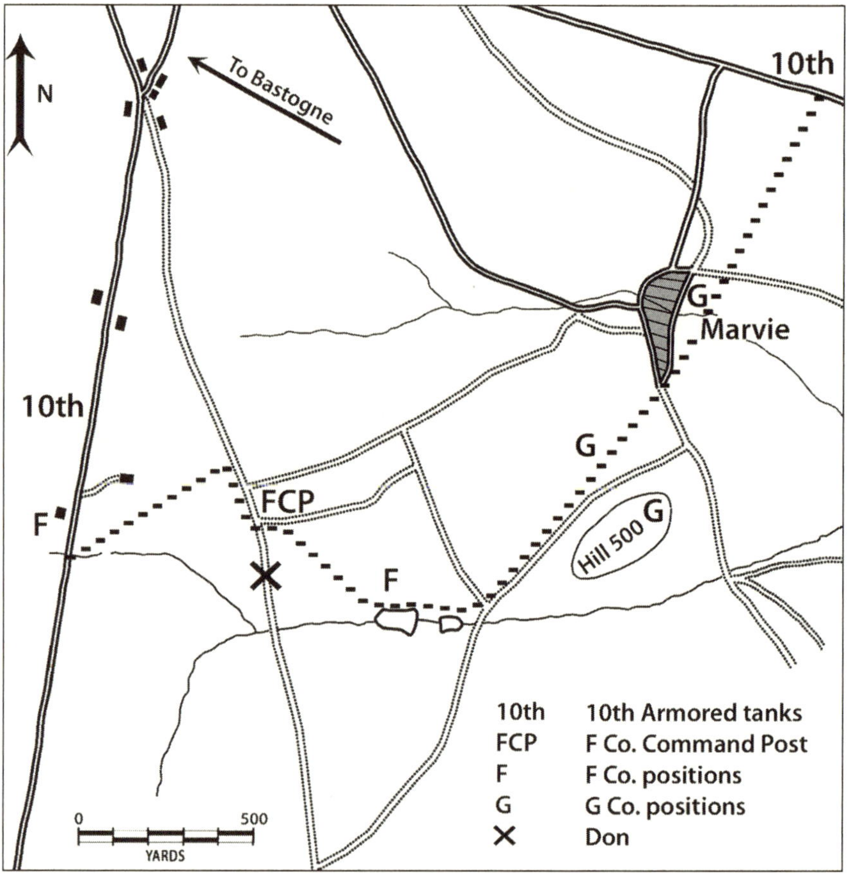

Second Battalion positions before the second battle at Marvie, December 23, 1944.

these times to regenerate himself. Simpson is very capable, maybe even the best of soldiers, but he thinks differently than most of us.

Simpson comes back and speaks to Sherman: "We're never going to get out of this alive. There are so many of them. More than we can handle. I've seen them. I've seen their fires. By the number of the fires ringing all around us, we're surrounded." Sherman looks out into the night and sees no fires. Not a one. He thinks to himself, Did Simpson really see that? How far did he go? Is he using his creative imagination? Simpson always says what he means, but he's way too smart to be here in a war.[5]

As daylight breaks, we notice a German soldier come out of the thick forest a hundred yards to the south of us. He seems to be looking for something among the sparse trees. "Hey, hey, hey, look at this!" I say, just loud enough for the other guys to hear. We ready our rifles. "Wait, don't shoot,"

I say to the others. "I wonder what he's up to." I am not sure whether the others understand.

Abruptly, the unsuspecting German soldier drops his pants. Obviously, he is looking for a private place to do his job and doesn't know we are there. Then one of the guys in the front foxhole shoots at him. As the German takes off, trying to run with his pants still down, toward the trees, the guy in my foxhole shoots in front of him, making him change directions.

"Don't hurt him!" I shout to the replacements.

Soon, we all open up, sending the German soldier first one way and then back. All of us are howling with laughter at the spectacle. We get off a few more shots before the poor guy finally makes it up and over the hill, then into the forest, to the apparent safety of the German lines. We laugh about the incident for a good two minutes. As funny as this incident is for us, it also illustrates a very sobering reality as we quiet down. We are uncomfortably close to the Germans and could easily find ourselves in a similar situation. It is doubtful that the Germans will decide to "play" with us if we get caught on the wrong side. I am feeling even worse from the concussion, and I have trouble concentrating.

At 0930 we again hear enemy vehicles to our south and west, and artillery falls on their positions.[6] A short time later, an American jeep, coming from the north, pulls up behind us. The driver has a load of sleeping bags, coats, and gloves. Unfortunately, he doesn't have snow boots, ammunition, or K rations, the three things we need the most.

The driver is quite the chatterbox. "The gear is from the supply dump. Use your ammo sparingly, we're running pretty low in Bastogne. I didn't realize that we had anybody stationed out here. What were you fellows shooting at? I heard the shootin' commotion from behind. By the way, Patton's coming up from the south, maybe a hundred miles away or so. Hope he gets here soon. We're surrounded, ya know. Drove by some of the big guns back behind. Not much more firepower left to fire," the driver says as he points towards the north, acting like he is somebody important in a big hurry. As my partner and I turn around to look at him, for the first time we notice two American 60 mm mortars set up in the valley clearing in the woods behind us about three hundred yards, well hidden from enemy forces. The driver throws off the supplies, then off he goes.

Quickly, I put on the coat and gloves. My boots come off next, and I rub my feet vigorously. I can't really feel much, because my feet are frozen. I put the sleeping bag in the foxhole. When I start to get cold again, I make another trip over to the farmhouse for more warm milk. The Belgian family is polite but unemotional about the visit. Four of the other five then make the trip, one at a time.

With not much to do but watch and wait, I notice the Bastogne area is really quite pretty, although mostly flat, with a few rolling hills. There are many areas forested with pine trees. If it were not for a war, the area would be a pretty place for a relaxing visit. Gazing around, I find the picturesque scenery of the area intriguing. Bastogne is located only twenty-two miles from the German border, with the tiny country of Luxembourg lying in between. The seven key roads that both sides want to control converge at Bastogne, making control of the town vital to slowing the German counterattack.[7] You'd never know by its peacefulness at the moment that a bloody war is going on. I'm doing my best to relax and enjoy the scenery as much as I can.

At 1130, unknown to us in the forward foxholes, less than a quarter of a mile away four enemy soldiers, including two officers (a major and a captain), come up the Arlon road from Remoifosse carrying a large white flag. "We are parliamentarians," the Germans tell the Americans. The officers carry a note for the commander of American forces at Bastogne. The German major is a very impressive looking officer, six feet four inches tall and wearing a long, gray leather overcoat and black boots. The captain is much shorter but also well dressed. Even though the four Germans are wearing much better winter clothes than those of any US soldier, the major, complaining how cold the weather is, requests to wait in a warm building for a reply to the note being delivered. So much for German toughness, especially since they have warmer uniforms. The request is not granted; there are no buildings for him at the F Company command post, 200 yards behind me.[8]

Maj. Alvin Jones, 327's ops officer, reads the letter and takes it to General McAuliffe. At headquarters, McAuliffe asks what the letter says. Someone replies that the letter is a request for American forces at Bastogne to surrender. "Aw nuts! What should I tell them?" McAuliffe replies with a laugh. McAuliffe apparently has a different view of the situation; he thinks that it is actually the Germans that are getting a severe beating as a result of the amazingly stiff resistance being offered by the 101st Airborne.

"That first remark of yours is hard to beat," replies Col. Harry Kinnard, who is standing next to McAuliffe. McAuliffe doesn't understand. "You said 'Nuts!'" Kinnard adds. McAuliffe agrees that this is an appropriate response.[9] Colonel Harper takes a note back as follows:

22 December 1944

To the German Commander:

NUTS!

The American Commander[10]

Upon returning to the field command post where the German officers are waiting, blindfolded, Colonel Harper says to them, "I have the American commander's reply."

"Is it written or verbal?" asks the German captain.

"It is written," replies Harper. Turning to the blindfolded senior German officer, he says, "I will stick it in your hand."

"Is the reply negative or affirmative? If it is the latter, I will negotiate further," says the officer in a rather arrogant tone, obviously expecting the "soft" Americans to surrender.

Temperamentally, Harper says, "The reply is decidedly not affirmative. If you continue this foolish attack, your losses will be tremendous."

The major nods his head, and the two are led to a jeep and taken back to the main road, where the other two German soldiers are waiting. Harper removes the blindfolds from the German officers and says, "If you don't understand what 'Nuts' means, in plain English it is the same as 'Go to hell.' And I will tell you something else; if you continue to attack we will kill every damn German that tries to break into this city."

The enemy officers salute, displaying obvious displeasure. The captain says, "We will kill many Americans. This is war."

"On your way, bud," says Colonel Harper, "and good luck to you."

The Germans head down the road. Harper regrets that he has wished them good luck, wondering whether the enemy might later retaliate against the 327th soldiers under his command because of his insulting tone.[11]

At about 1550 fifty German soldiers with a horse-drawn cart attack down the same road where the four Germans earlier came to deliver their message. I can hear the explosions and see gunfire, but I can't do anything about it, because the terrain greatly diminishes my vision; I can hardly see anything. There is gunfire directly to the southeast of us by the lakes as well. At 1700 the Germans press to within two hundred yards of F Company's lines just to the west, and the enemy is annihilated. Hibbard's squad, which is attached to F Company, is putting up a heck of a fight. The enemy is taking a beating trying to get to Bastogne. Sporadic enemy artillery fire hits the area. The 327th's supporting artillery unit is getting very low on ammunition.[12]

That night, the temperature plummets even lower. Ice forms, eighteen inches thick, along the sides of the foxhole. We can hear mechanized enemy troop movements to the south in the dark. At least we all have sleeping bags now, but I am even more concerned about going to sleep and freezing to death. To keep awake, I stand in the sleeping bag all night long. We take turns keeping watch for the enemy. The wind is howling, and the foxhole still blocks the wind, but it also seems to act like a freezer. Because I can't sleep, I jump up and down in the foxhole to keep my blood flowing. During the night I walk over to the dairy barn for warm milk. Steam rolls off my canteen cup as I walk out of the barn. I am very appreciative to the family, but I wonder why they put themselves at such a risk. I wonder if they'd do the same for the enemy. I want to stay and go to sleep. My head hurts and I still feel woozy.

I begin December 23 by ritually taking off my boots, rubbing my feet, and changing socks. One of the replacements is in bad shape and can't stand up at all. He is the guy who won't get out of the foxhole. His partner and I help him out and across the road to the farm family so he can warm up. The Belgian woman helps get his boots off as he lies back in a chair. His feet are a blackish gray color. After a few minutes, his feet begin to swell, and he winces in pain. After a few more minutes his feet swell so much there is no way he'll ever get the boots back on. His partner and I leave a few minutes later without him. I don't want to be gone too long, because we never know if the Germans are watching.

At 0945, US aircraft appear overhead, and Pathfinders (airborne soldiers who help find locations for future airborne drops or artillery targets) parachute into the 2nd Battalion section behind our position.[13] It is a welcome and beautiful sight. A US tank west of the Arlon road opens up on a German armored column, knocking out several half-tracks and a command car. Enemy artillery retaliates from the south.

At 1115, US fighter bombers hit targets to my south. I feel emotional at the incredible sight, a huge morale builder. A short time later I can hear a droning sound in the distance, getting louder and louder, and seemingly hundreds of American C-47 transport aircraft appear overhead, wave after wave of them. The sky is filled with thousands of parachutes weighted down with badly needed supplies. The airdrop lifts everyone's spirits. Cheering can be heard up and down the line.[14]

In the afternoon we hear more action in the distance, far to the west. The 401st (our 3rd Battalion) is being hit by fourteen German tanks supported by snowsuit-clad infantry. First Battalion, also to the west, but closer to my position than the 401st, is hit hard as well. After fierce combat between men and tanks at the foxhole level, the 401st falls back toward Bastogne. The battalion commander, Colonel Allen, shouts to his men, "This is our last withdrawal! Live or die; this is it!" For some reason the Germans break off the attack again.[15]

To my east the enemy removed the logs on the roadblock east of Marvie on the Wiltz road after the first battle. Now the Germans have machine guns set up in a crossing pattern and are keeping the engineers from rebuilding it. The Americans launch mortars at the roadblock in protest.[16] The enemy seems to want the roadblock out of the way for a reason: we are about to find out why.

At 1725 on December 23, Marvie is the next target for the enemy. On Hill 500, Lieutenant Morrison has his men divide time between being alert in foxholes dug at the base of homes to being in the homes, keeping warm. From the woods the enemy hits Hill 500 with intense machine gun fire and tank shells before mounting a frontal assault on G Company troops on the hill. The Germans want to take the town, which will make it easier for them to take Bastogne. The sounds of battle are intense. German tanks shell the American lines for about ten minutes. Because of wooded areas between Marvie and me, I can't see the action, and the sounds are muffled. Screaming enemy infantry and four tanks from two companies attack the platoon on Hill 500, splitting the American lines. The attackers are dressed in white snowsuits, making it hard to see them.[17]

A fleeing US self-propelled gun coming up the Wiltz road is accidentally destroyed by O'Hara's tanks. Command sends a US 57 mm gun, towed by a half-track, to help support Hill 500 and is just arriving as the attack unfolds. Boz is with ninety-eight American men (most from G Company) defending Hill 500. After splitting the US lines to the southwest and northeast of Hill 500, the Germans quickly surround and overrun the hill on all sides. Lieutenant Morrison reports by telephone to Harper: "Now they are all around me. I see tanks just outside my window. We are continuing to fight them back, but it looks like they have us. . . . We're still holding on. . . . I need tanks." Accounts indicate that short and stocky Morrison was calm and collected in the face of a very bad situation, but he is now missing in action.[18] A German tank runs right over the top of my buddy Boz's foxhole and stays there for a period of time. Boz can't run or do anything with a tank sitting right on top of him.

By 1800, Easy Company, which has been holding most of the village of Marvie, reports enemy troops operating to their rear. Easy pulls back, giving up the southern half of Marvie. Niland, seeing the seriousness of the situation, presses cooks, supply men, and anyone else he can find into the fight, plugging the gap in the lines. Two US 37 mm antitank guns are put in place in the vulnerable area. German tanks promptly fire and kill the gun crews. The driver of the half-track setting up on Hill 500 panics and then speeds rapidly toward the center of the village. When the half-track crosses the creek bridge during the fighting, US forces hit the vehicle with their weapons, mistaking the half-track for a German one, killing the American crew. The half-track's wreckage inadvertently creates a temporary partial roadblock in the middle of Marvie's main street.[19]

The enemy manages to advance two tanks toward the church in Marvie. The German tanks turn around and withdraw when they realize they can't get past the US half-track wreckage without heavy risk of being destroyed.[20]

Analyzing the situation further and determining that the enemy tanks are going to break through, Niland sends Panic and Feeney to set up machine guns in a two-story house across from the church. Again using his understanding of German predictability, he knows the Germans will bring in a machine gun squad in advance of a tank penetration to mow down US antitank gunners. Sure enough, the German machine gunners show up; Panic and Feeney mow them down instead.[21]

At the farmhouse where I am, the sounds of battle coming from the west are getting closer to me. First Platoon of F Company is being attacked on the Arlon road as the sun goes down. Fighting erupts again to the east of me as 2nd Platoon of Company F comes under attack. The enemy is on both sides of my position. Behind me, the woods are pounded by German artillery, with the shells going over us and hitting behind. For about an hour after dusk, fighting decreases in intensity to just sporadic fire. But at 1830 hours heavier fighting erupts again to the west along Arlon road as the enemy hurls its forces, including twelve tanks, at 1st Platoon of F Company in a furious attempt to break through to Bastogne. The Germans are stymied by the defenders, who include Hibbard and his squad. Another squad from Company F is firmly dug in just to the west of Hill 500 and holds for the time being under intense enemy pressure.

The Krauts drive foot soldiers right through F's 2nd Platoon in the woods beside me to the left. They try to drive through the gap between F and G, which is right where I am supposed to be but am not. The enemy tanks now on Hill 500 attempt to force their way into, around, and through Marvie. At 1900 the enemy again attacks along the Arlon road at the roadblock (to

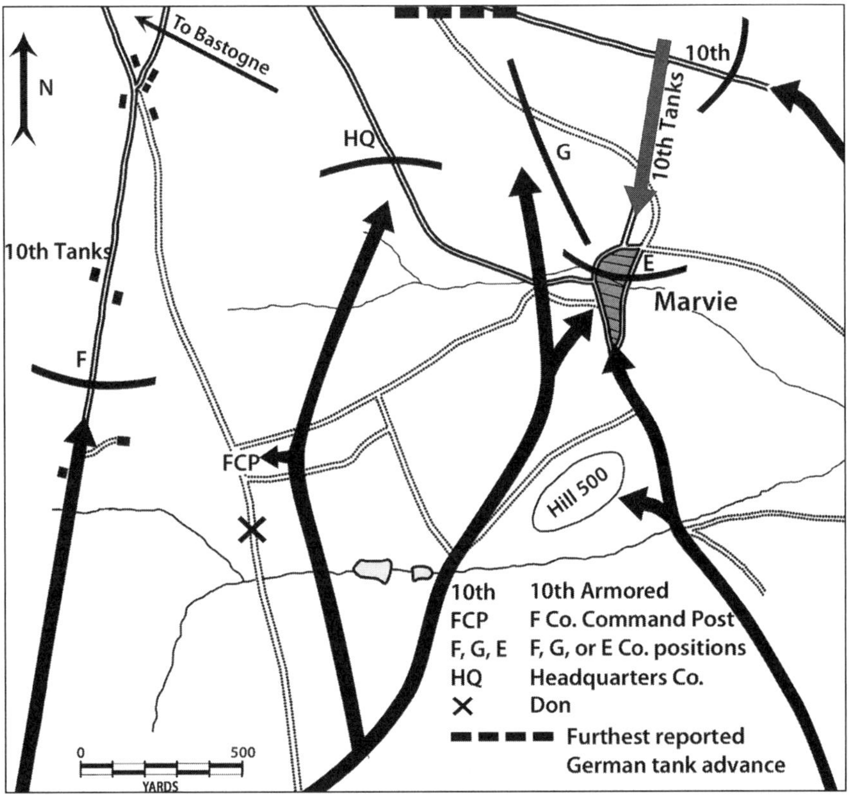

Lines of German advance and extent of the attack during the second battle at Marvie, December 23 and 24, 1944.

my west) but is beaten back in a frantic fight with help from US artillery.[22] O'Hara's tanks near the roadblock retreat to safer cover.

By 1925, four or five German tanks are operating behind 2nd Battalion's defensive lines, north of Marvie halfway between the village and Bastogne. At 2000 defensive lines falter further because of the fall of Hill 500, and the enemy infantry drives through the gap between F and G, pours through to the north, and attacks F Company from behind. Sergeant Gross and his machine gunners stay in a barn behind Hill 500, west of Marvie, as the enemy swarms the area, their machine guns sticking out of the barn's windows.[23]

Help is sent to keep the enemy from racing through into Bastogne. Forty men from the 501st's A Company rush to set up a line behind the gap between F and G northwest of Marvie before the enemy can get there. Company F mortars, behind me, launch a barrage into the woods to my left. I hear firing to my left and see gun flashes going on behind me and to the right. None of us in the five-man crew can see anything to fire at in front of us. Members of the F Company command post, located directly behind our position, flee for safety through the woods. Twenty-four-year-old Harry Bliss, part of the F Company's heavy weapons platoon, is defending them with machine gun fire in the hedges three hundred yards behind me to my left. Bliss mows down the enemy with the gun and kills another with a grenade. Only one enemy soldier survives. Bliss is wounded and dies the next day.[24]

In Marvie, two German tanks rip into the village and shoot up houses. A bazooka squad led by Niland sets up in a corner house and takes out the trailing Mark IV tank. The lead German tank aims its gun at the house and fires, exploding the house from short range just as the squad and Niland run out the back. Without support, the surviving enemy tank turns around and tries to withdraw, but the roads are so narrow, it can no longer maneuver its gun. The tank backs into a narrow street between two houses across from the church but can't conceal the gun, which sticks out into the cross street. When someone in the tank opens its hatch, Feeney and Panic, still on the second floor of the house, drop a grenade down the hatch and kill the enemy crew.[25]

Team O'Hara moves a couple of Sherman tanks into Marvie after a protest from Colonel Harper to Colonel O'Hara requesting tank support in the town. O'Hara's men already have their hands full with the enemy on the Wiltz and Arlon roads. Niland directs the setup of two US tanks in position to keep the German tanks from breaking clear through Marvie.[26]

German tanks again try to get past the roadblock in Marvie caused by the destroyed half-track. The lead enemy tank is hit by the two Shermans, completely blocking the road. The gun of one of the Shermans jams, and it then withdraws. The enemy tanks behind the blockage can't get into Marvie on that road. One is damaged by the 326th Engineers and can't move. Before they abandon it, its crew shoots up the town with phosphorus shells, burning to the ground houses occupied by US defenders.[27]

Sherman is in a house on the south side of Marvie with G Company command, led by Regenburg. The enemy is all around them, surrounding the house. Heavy German machine guns spray the village. Tanks pummel the houses. Since it is dark, they can't see outside very well; any light comes from burning houses.

"What are we gonna do?" another runner asks Regenburg.

"Damn Krauts have us surrounded," Regenburg replies.

"Damn it, we can't just sit here!" the replacement runner protests.

"What else we going to do? Walk right out the door?" Sherman asks.

"Grenades, they're gonna throw grenades in the window." The runner keeps up. He is terrified. "I can't stand it anymore, damn it!" He bolts out the door, enemy machine gun fire erupts, and he is killed. Later, when fighting in the immediate area quiets down, G Company command escapes in the darkness.[28]

The burning village lights up the snowsuit-clad German infantry, making them easy targets for the beleaguered American defenders. Still, the enemy fights tenaciously for Marvie, house by house, but fails to advance because of lack of successful tank support in the village.

The enemy continues to put intense pressure on the Arlon road just to my west, with F Company fighting off enemy tanks and infantry with support from O'Hara's tanks. Company F falls back six hundred yards. Heavy German artillery again slams 1st Platoon of F Company now well behind my right. American artillery fires back in kind.[29]

In the middle of 2nd Battalion lines, Headquarters Company manages to reorganize thirteen hundred yards behind our original lines. The platoon from A Company of the 501st is on their right flank. The breach in the line between F and G is repaired, with assistance from Hibbard's squad and the platoon of the 501st. Easy Company still manages to hold almost all the north half of Marvie. What is left of the decimated Company G reorganizes on the north side of Marvie at 0300 and holds a line running to the northwest to cover the gap between the north end of Marvie and Headquarters Company's line after being pushed back by five hundred yards.[30]

At 0445 the enemy reorganizes for another push to break into Bastogne, but they make little progress in the waning hours of darkness. By dawn the Germans still hold Hill 500 and several houses within the center of Marvie, but 2nd Battalion defenses have held.[31]

The five of us in our foxholes and the one man in the farmhouse are definitely well behind enemy lines. We continue our diligent lookout to the south. Still, there is no sign of any enemy we can engage.

Company command receives word of possible air strikes, an attempt to encourage the enemy to pull back. Sherman is surveying the situation for Lieutenant Regenburg. Beginning at 1030, P-47s begin making bombing and strafing runs on the enemy positions, including in front of 2nd Battalion, a beautiful scene in the eyes of the exhausted US forces. Our troops set out orange panels to show our pilots the dividing line between US and German forces. At 1350, six P-47s are making strafing and bombing runs on German positions on Hill 500 and south. One of the P-47s, with eight .50 caliber guns blazing, makes a run toward the center of Marvie in spite of the orange panels in plain view under clearing skies.[32]

Sherman and the men around him frantically try to wave the pilot off the attack, but the pilot lets loose a rocket as Sherman and another man dive through the basement door and tumble down the stairs. The rocket hits the base of the house, shaking the foundation violently. The .50 caliber bullets tear the house up, but both men survive.[33] I can hear the explosions, but trees block my view.

The enemy is no longer pressing determined attacks against 2nd Battalion but is still firmly in control of what used to be Screaming Eagles territory after significant gains. The guns that were behind us are no longer there. The roadblock on the Arlon road is two hundred yards further back from where it was at the start of the fight. In the center of 2nd Battalion's line, the Screaming Eagles have been pushed back over fifteen hundred yards. Half of Marvie is still in the hands of the Germans.

An enemy tank is located at the south end of Marvie. Colonel Harper orders the remaining Sherman tank in Marvie to attack a haystack on the south end of town that is concealing a German Mark IV tank with its muzzle sticking out of the hay. The enemy tank is destroyed. O'Hara's tanks outside of Marvie follow suit and pound German infantry hiding in houses around the southern part of the village around Hill 500. In the afternoon, another airdrop brings in more supplies. Enemy artillery falls throughout the day, with lesser but heavily concentrated US artillery firing in return. At 1645 the P-47s attack again in an impressive display of firepower, only this time hitting the enemy.[34]

The enemy has done severe damage to 2nd Battalion at great cost to themselves. Apparently the Germans again have had enough of us. They don't push the attack in the Marvie area, even though we are spread out so thinly. They have broken us and in a desperate fight disengage after suffering tremendous losses.[35]

They ask for and receive permission to remove their dead, and in a steady stream they begin to carry wounded and dead German soldiers into the forest.[36]

Now they concentrate their effort on the west perimeter again. In their way now is the 327th's 3rd Battalion (the 401st). The Germans have had enough of 2nd Battalion and O'Hara's supporting tanks and men. Bastogne is bombed and strafed by enemy planes several times that night.[37]

About midnight, I head over to the barn to warm myself with fresh milk. The Luftwaffe's Bed Check Charlie is doing his thing, bombing Bastogne.

The explosions ripple through the night air, and I can see flashes of fire. I can also easily see the aircraft in the moonlight. Mesmerized by the sight, I leave the foxhole to get a better look. The plane looks like a Junkers fighter bomber. As the plane banks over Bastogne, heading toward my location, I can even make out the gunner in the front of the aircraft, illuminated by lights inside. Closer the enemy aircraft comes. I think about shooting my rifle at the plane: I'll just hit ol' Bed Check Charlie. Then I hear a continuous whipping sound ahead of me. "What the . . . ?" I speak out loud as I glance down into the snowy landscape ahead of me. The snow is jumping up in the air in two columns coming my way. The aircraft gunner is shooting at me.

I am forty or fifty feet or so from the foxhole, so I turn and run as fast as I can in an attempt to save my life. As soon as I am close enough to my foxhole, I jump with all my might. I can feel snow flying from the impact of the bullets. The whirring sound passes over the foxhole and on to the other side. With my face down, I can hear the plane's engines pass overhead. By the time I gather my senses and peek out of the foxhole, the Junkers is gone. My green uniform must have stuck out in the moonlit snow, making me an easy target. My foxhole buddy just looks at me and says nothing. I can imagine his thoughts.

After another cold night, Christmas day arrives without any special implications for me and my squad. I still can't figure out why I am leading a squad without getting promoted, something that is really beginning to bother me. I need something else to think about. In the wee hours of Christmas, the enemy moves hard against the 401st and 502nd to the west.

After another trip to the barn, I get back to my own foxhole. At 0900 I spot a three-man crew of German soldiers wearing white snowsuits and pulling a sled loaded with radio equipment. They come out of the trees and over the ridge in front of us to the west. They trudge along, unaware that anyone is watching them, heading between my squad and F Company at the roadblock on the Arlon road and getting close to the guys in F.

"Don't they see them?" my partner asks.

"I think they're asleep," I reply.

I scurry over to the farthest foxhole, where the BAR man is watching the scene, and order, "Fire over toward those guys to wake them up. Make sure you don't hit our own guys."

The shots of the BAR echo out over the plain. The enemy soldiers instantly hit the snow-covered ground and remain motionless. The guys from F wake up and make quite a bunch of noise, knocking stuff over and shouting at each other. The noise is almost comical. The snow must have improved the ability of sound to travel a long distance. We are probably scaring the Americans and Germans alike. Some more shouting transpires, and the Germans, lying face down, are captured by Lieutenant Hibbard's squad, which is still attached to F Company.[39]

"I wonder why the Krauts didn't see us," my partner says.

An hour after firing over the enemy patrol, we hear gunfire back behind us to our left. Throughout the day there is sporadic small arms fire, tank movement, and enemy artillery shelling in various locations across 2nd Battalion's front.

The five of us settle back into the foxholes. For our squad, Christmas dinner consists of more warm milk in the barn and K rations. In the late morning a messenger drops off a piece of paper with a message from General McAuliffe:

> 24 December, 1944
>
> Merry Christmas!
>
> HEADQUARTERS 101ST AIRBORNE DIVISION
>
> Office of the Division Commander
>
> Merry Christmas! What's Merry about all this you ask? We're fighting—it's cold—we aren't home. All true but what had the proud Eagle Division accomplished with its worthy comrades of the 10th Armored Division, the 705th Tank Destroyer Battalion and all the rest? Just this: We have stopped cold everything that has been thrown at us from the North, East, South and West. We have identifications from four German Panzer Divisions, two German Infantry Divisions and one German Parachute Division. These units, spearheading the last desperate German lunge, were headed straight west for key points when the Eagle Division was hurriedly ordered to stem the advance. How effectively this was done will be written in history; Not alone in our Division's glorious history but World History. The Germans actually did surround us, their radios blared our doom. Their Commander demanded our surrender. In the following impudent arrogance:

[McAuliffe's letter goes on to repeat the German ultimatum message, and then concludes:]

> Troops are counterattacking in force. We continue to hold Bastogne. By holding Bastogne, we assure the success of the Allied Armies.

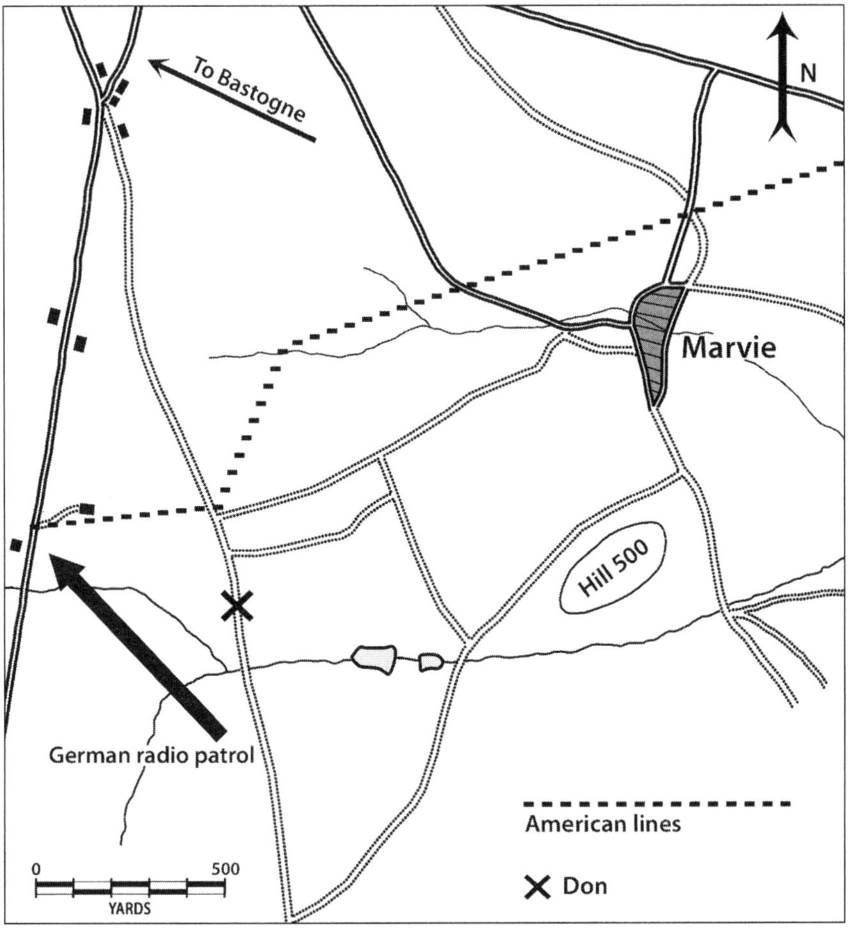

Don's position in the Marvie defense area, December 25, 1944.

> We know that our Division Commander, General Taylor will say: "Well Done"
>
> We are giving our country and our loved ones at home a worthy Christmas present and being privileged to take part in this gallant feat of arms are truly making for ourselves a Merry Christmas.
>
> A. C. McAuliffe
> Commanding[40]

As I look around after we read the letter, I notice that none of the replacements have much expression on their faces. "Hmmm," is all I say as I go back to the foxhole and look out to the south. Late in the evening, small arms fire can be heard on the Arlon road; mortar fire falls on the area, and P-47s drop napalm on the enemy, resulting in astonishing fireballs. Late in the day we can hear tanks moving from west to east.[41]

The small villages of Champs, Longchamps, Senochamps, and Rolle are now the battlefields. Infantry and tank units on both sides slug it out. American forces fall back as the enemy confidently attacks and moves forward with eighteen tanks in support. However, not one of the enemy tanks survives the vicious counterattack of the seemingly overwhelmed Americans. Hitler's army has a cornered wildcat on its hands and can't get that ferocious cat out of the way. In our area, enemy mortar fire goes over our heads and falls well behind us.[42]

Early on December 27, an American jeep coming from the north shows up at out foxhole position.

"Hey there!" the driver greets us.

"What's goin' on?" I reply.

"Some of Patton's tanks got through late yesterday and made contact with the engineers over there," the driver says, pointing west toward F Company. We must look a little dumbfounded, as we haven't noticed the tanks are there, in spite of being on the lookout. This is just another demonstration of how isolated we are at times.

"We've got a guy in the house who can't walk. He froze his feet pretty badly and needs to get to Bastogne," I say, pointing back at the house. "Can you take him to Bastogne?"

"Sure can," the driver says in a Southern accent. We walk over to the house, bring the disabled man out to the jeep, and load him up. No one says much, and the driver quickly takes off. I'm not sure why none of us have frozen to death.

Also on December 27 at about noon, more supplies are dropped on Bastogne from the air through parachutes and gliders. We hear gunfire back toward Marvie as Screaming Eagle patrols attempt to probe enemy positions on Hill 500. Later on that day we receive word that General Taylor is back in command, and the 101st is getting ready for offensive maneuvers against the enemy.[43]

December 28 is a foggy and misty day. To the south of us, around 0930, I can hear a rumbling over the ridge. The replacements and I look at each other and then back out to the south. "Could that be some of Patton's tanks?" someone mutters.

Three US Sherman tanks come into view heading right for us, coming around the curve in the road. Since we are pretty close to the road, I start to

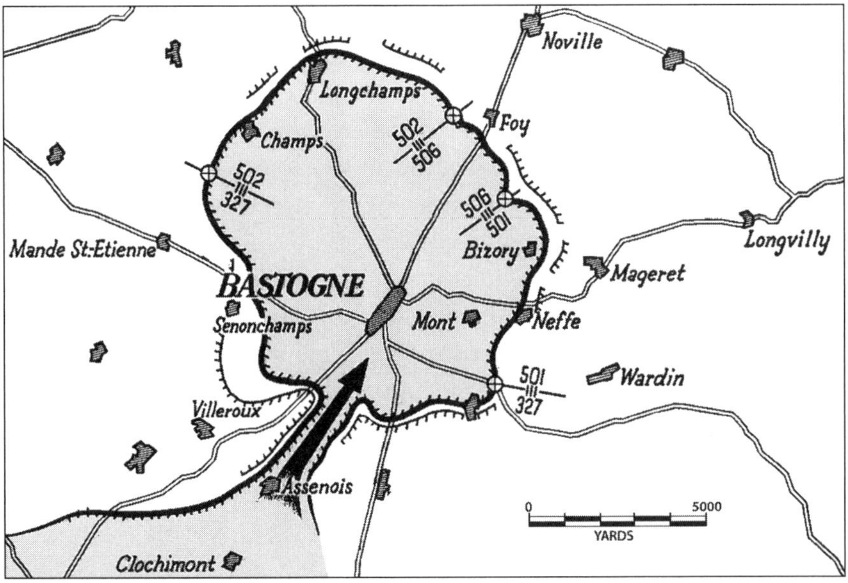

Patton relieves Bastogne, December 26, 1944.

get a little nervous. "Could be Krauts!" I say out loud, not really believing the tanks are in German hands. I am concerned about being fired on by the tanks, whether driven by Americans or Germans; the American tanks could easily mistake us for the enemy if we are not careful. I think of the mines we've set up on the road.

"What are we gonna do?" the guy in the front foxhole shouts.

"Well, you better stop them!" I yell loudly. "Flag 'em down! Let 'em know we're here!"

The lone replacement in the west foxhole stands up and waves his rifle as he points to the mines. One Sherman drives into the yard of the farmhouse. We stay put while a couple of soldiers in the tank get out and go inside. A while later they come out with valuables from the house. They don't seem too friendly and stay in their tanks, keeping watch for the enemy. I don't like them, but I find their presence reassuring.

These tanks, part of the 4th Armored Division, have driven and marched at an almost impossible pace for seven days to get to us. The weather for them has been miserable; the Germans fought them along the way, and they are exhausted. The 4th has lost one thousand men and more than half of their tanks.[44]

I am upset about the tank crew's stealing from the Belgian family—the family that has been risking their lives to help us, giving us food and shelter. I don't go into the farmhouse again out of embarrassment. One of my foxhole mates does go in and finds that the place is torn up.

For the next several days, Patton's 4th Armored continues to expand the corridor that has been opened up to the south of Bastogne. Heavy fighting continues around Bastogne as the perimeter becomes bigger. The enemy still isn't giving up on taking Bastogne. In a change of procedure, on December 28 dead US soldiers are no longer being buried in Bastogne but instead are being taken outside the perimeter as US troops push the enemy farther back.[45] At noon, enemy tanks reported near Marvie fire on Easy Company's positions, but no infantry attack comes. A sizable German concentration of troops is still reported on Hill 500.

On December 29 the weather is better but not great. It is good enough for the Germans to bomb and strafe Bastogne from the air with three Junkers 88s, destroying a tank and several other armored vehicles.[46] Remembering my Bed Check Charlie ordeal, I stay in the foxhole. Considerable numbers of enemy troops are moving across the south but seem not to be interested in engaging us.

On the Offensive

WITH PATTON'S FORCES NOW HEAVILY ENTRENCHED ON THE southern sector of the Bastogne perimeter, the 327th is being relieved late on December 29.[1] The five of us who have spent so much time out in the cold in front of the lines head down the road back toward Marvie. At the intersection seventy-five yards behind us is a well-camouflaged antitank gun manned by three soldiers. I am surprised, because I never knew they had come back after the fighting several days ago. There are no other soldiers around them, which seems strange.

When we get back to Marvie, we hook up with the rest of G. Nobody says much of anything to each other. I see Boz, and he doesn't seem quite right. Later, I am told what happened to him and others on Hill 500. Boz was wounded there, but he is still with the company. He isn't his usual self, and doesn't talk much. Company G lost a number of men killed, wounded, or captured. Lieutenant Morrison is one of the missing. Captain Evans has been evacuated and is recovering from his wounds. I am tired and would be happy to go back to Bastogne. A lot of guys are limping because of frozen feet.

Together, the company heads back to Bastogne. Along the way, the guys and I chat a little and share experiences of our battles. One thing that is said really makes me mad. "Sure was nice for Patton's tankers to bring us the Christmas fixin's. Their turkey was real good!" a guy in the company says, while grinning from ear to ear.

"Turkey?" several of the replacements and I say almost in unison.

"Yeah, five candy bars, seven packs of cigarettes, some turkey, and some other stuff," the guy adds.

"The dirty devils!" I growl. I don't care about the cigarettes, but the idea of the food is hard to take. "First the tankers steal from the Belgian family, and now this! Those dirty devils!."

Some of the guys are being treated for frostbitten feet. The doctors have a pill they give to help them. My feet hurt, but I don't say anything. Lloyd

Gross decides to take the pill. The doc tells him to lie down in a haystack when he takes it. He sleeps the next day away. Denis Parsons's feet are so bad that they ship him to France.

During the afternoon of December 29, Regenburg updates us. "The enemy is making another push on Bastogne," he says. They no longer have us cut off; we're moving north. They still have eight divisions trying to take Bastogne."[2]

We hear from fresh troops that our ordeal of being surrounded has spread to the States and that the story of how we have doggedly faced down the enemy against all odds has made us heroes. I am tired. I can't help but think that I might just survive the war after all. But the battle is not yet over; the enemy is still determined.

Company G bivouacs near where the 969th Field Artillery Regiment is set up. I am disoriented and don't know exactly where we are in the Bastogne area. The 969th, an African American artillery unit, is firing their big 155 mm guns toward German positions—not with any urgency, just a shot once in awhile. The 969th has an elaborate camp of huts made of logs and equipped with makeshift stoves. The smell of coffee is in the air.

The noise coming from cannon blasts is deafening, shaking my inner being. Artillery shells make bright streaks in the clear, cold, late afternoon sky, screaming into the distance toward the south. I am curious and walk over to the artillerymen with a couple of other guys. I soon realize we owe a lot to this skilled artillery unit.

"You guys sure saved us from the Krauts! You tore 'em up pretty good," I say to a couple of men who are readying their gun for more action.

"Just doing our job!" one replies.

"What are you doing now?" I ask.

"We're just sniping," another answers.

"Sniping with a 155?" I reply, chuckling.

"We put 'em where they tell us. Shot some tanks right there'bout on Christmas. Had to lower these guns real low to hit 'em," the older one continues. He points to a spot not even a hundred yards away. They must be talking about the German breakthrough with the 401st, I think to myself.

"Thanks" I say. "Without you we wouldn't still be here." They have saved our lives. The 969th repeatedly held the enemy at bay during attacks on the perimeter lines.

I notice now that my feet are hurting pretty badly, causing me to limp. Up until this point adrenaline has kept me from noticing how badly my feet hurt, but now that the battle is winding down, the pain is becoming more obvious.

Second Battalion heads to camp in the northwest part of Bastogne, where we put down for the night. We find an open building with no heat, where I unroll my sleeping bag. The bag isn't very heavy, so I am still cold, but I manage to get some sleep, finally.

The next morning we are up bright and early, expecting to move out to the perimeter. While we are gathering our equipment, Lieutenant Hibbard speaks to me.

"Rich, are you okay?"

"What do you mean?" I ask. "I guess I'm okay."

"You're limping around. Freeze your feet?"

"It got pretty cold in the foxhole. I couldn't move around much. It's probably just a bit of frostbite."

"Have the medics check it out," Hibbard orders.

"Yes, sir." Reluctantly, I head over to the medic station.

A young medic of about eighteen or nineteen checks me out quickly, saying, "That's a pretty good case of frostbite you've got there. You need to stay warmer for a while." He sticks out a note, which I take reluctantly.

Following Hibbard's orders, I head over to battalion headquarters and give the note to the orderly.

In a few minutes Lieutenant Regenburg comes out of an office. Seeing me, he says, "Rich, you're assigned to company headquarters. You'll be a runner to the front for G command post."

I can't quite understand how I can be a runner with bad feet, but I have to obey orders. Within a few minutes I'm handed an M1 rifle, and I am now a runner. At least I'll stay warmer behind the lines and get to visit with Sherman more. I think about Proppe, who was a runner when he was killed.

The next day, at 0730, we scramble for cover because of a German air raid, and 2nd Battalion's office takes a direct hit. Second Battalion moves a little less than two miles northwest of Bastogne to Hemroule. Except for sporadic artillery firing out in the perimeter area, things are quiet.[3]

For the next couple of days I don't hear or see much in the way of fighting. The 969th continues its "sniping"; we hear the explosions in the distance. They are using artillery shells that burst above ground instead of burrowing into it, thereby hurling shrapnel at the enemy over a large area. We hear reports of fierce tank battles going on between the Germans and Patton's tanks. Hitler is moving his fanatical 9th and 12th SS Panzer Divisions and his personal Führer Grenadier Division into the Bastogne area in an effort to turn the tide again in favor of the Germans in the Ardennes.[4]

More replacements, 408 to be exact, are added to the 327th. We bivouac in the Champs area. Armed with an M1 rifle instead of a bazooka, I still have no snow boots, but I am dressed a lot warmer than I was the last time I left Bastogne. Company strength is listed at 87 men.[5]

Company F of the 2nd Battalion and the 10th Armored take Champs with little resistance on January 2, with G in reserve. The 506th, just to the north of us, on their way to clear Germans from Jacques Woods, is hit by the Luftwaffe .[6]

Later that day, as I am carrying a message out to the perimeter line, I see a group of fifteen German prisoners guarded by a US soldier with his rifle pointed at them. They are jumping up and down, because they are clothed only in their long underwear and socks. They were ordered earlier to take off the American uniforms they were wearing when captured. The guard doesn't look very happy with the formerly disguised enemy. According to the rules of war, it is well within our rights to execute enemy soldiers disguised as our own troops.

"Kind of mean to do that to them," the replacement next to me says.

"No, it sure isn't," I reply shortly. "They should have been shot for breaking the rules of war." The replacement looks wide-eyed at the prisoners as we walk on by. Several German soldiers have been executed by the Americans in Belgium for breaking the rules of war, but I have no idea what will happen to these guys.

More snow falls over the Bastogne area, and in some places it is waist deep. Roads are covered with ice, making walking and driving difficult. Tanks are pretty much limited to advancing along the roads, where they become easy targets. I hear someone say that the temperature is ten degrees below zero. Daylight, which comes at 0800, doesn't make things seem much warmer.

To the north of Bastogne are farm fields, woods, and hills. The forty-foot-tall trees provide the enemy with an excellent opportunity to shell us with tree bursts—shells that explode above the ground when they hit the treetops—designed to kill and maim as many American soldiers as possible. The cold temperatures make water hard to get, as almost everything is frozen. I become thirsty from trudging through the deep snow and ducking under branches. My legs are tired, and my lungs hurt. Mostly my throat is parched. Coming over a hill, I can hear and then see a creek not completely frozen over. I wonder if it is spring-fed. Stumbling through the branches and

North of Bastogne, Don needed to quench his thirst. After drinking, he noticed the dead horse in the water.

the snow, I come to the creek and fill my canteen. The water feels so good on my throat. "Best water I've ever had," I think out loud to myself. Refilling my canteen, I follow the creek upstream for a little while. As I round a bend in the creek, my eyes settle on a dead, bloated horse in the water. I don't know what to do. Maybe I'll get sick. I walk on, keeping the water, as I am so thirsty.

The main part of the US counteroffensive at Bastogne begins in the early afternoon on the January 3. The terrain puts the defending Germans in an advantageous position, giving them the high ground. The battle rages back and forth. The trees in particular create problems for American troops. Low branches, coupled with the deep snow, make movement difficult for those venturing out of foxholes. Fighting on the perimeter is at very close range. More than once, soldiers stopping to take a breather find they are sitting on a snow-covered frozen body that they thought was a tree stump.

Later in the day, Regenburg calls me over to him. "Rich, contact platoon leaders!" he barks. "Second Battalion is moving up!"

"Yes, sir!" I answer.

"The Germans are forming for an attack in the Longchamps and Monaville areas," the lieutenant tells us. "Enemy tanks are on the road between Bertogne and Compogne, out just a couple of miles. We're not sure how many, the fog is too thick to tell, but likely it's a good-sized force, and they might be SS."[7]

At a little after 1300, the 502nd reports hearing tanks moving closer in. Possibly forty enemy tanks, mostly Mark IVs, are coming along with a battalion of infantry, moving down the road from Compogne to Longchamps. From there the enemy forces fan off the road for an attack.[8]

The enemy tanks, leading the way, hit the US lines where the 502nd is positioned. Bazookas firing in return have a chance of stopping the Mark IVs, but rockets hitting the German Royal Tiger tanks bounce right off. The Tigers keep up the pressure, hoping to keep the Americans from hitting the more vulnerable Mark IVs. Enemy tanks stop right on top of American soldiers' foxholes. If the ground is somewhat soft, the enemy tanks' tracks will spin over the foxhole, grinding the soldier to death. If the ground holds, the tank driver will race the engine, filling the foxhole with exhaust fumes, including deadly carbon monoxide. American soldiers who try to run away from the tanks are easily shot by SS infantry. Other GIs stay in their foxholes and shoot at German infantry from under the enemy tanks. After some time the tanks advance deeper into the American lines, leaving the survivors to shoot their way back to our lines.[9]

As a runner, I am now in almost constant motion, which keeps the blood circulating in my feet. In the forested areas, I find it particularly easy to get lost. Getting lost might mean venturing into German positions. Needless to say, the situation is nervewracking.

Upon getting back to G Company, I find that we are moving up to advance on enemy positions. The fog is thick, and we move out blindly into snow that is waist deep in places. Gunfire can be heard in the distance, but with the trees and fog it is hard to figure out directions and identify the sounds. Lieutenant Hibbard, who is never good with maps, leads us away to our positions. After about half an hour, I can see a frustrated look on his face. He doesn't have to say anything: we are lost. He studies the map carefully and is sure of one thing. We've crossed enemy lines somehow without running into the enemy.

Word about our predicament passes among us. If we run into the SS, we are in serious trouble. German companies and squads that ended up behind US lines in the earlier part of the struggle for Bastogne didn't fare very well with the Americans. It is almost assured that the SS will quickly kill us if they find us.

Hibbard leads us through the woods for another hour or so. He and other officers talk things over. Before long, though, we find some troops from the

502nd and breathe a huge sigh of relief as we realize that we have wandered back across the battle lines and are in American territory once again. I know how Hibbard must feel, having led my squad of replacements at Marvie to an outpost much too close to the enemy.

Hibbard orders me to report our position to battalion command post, where it becomes apparent to the commanding officers that losses are heavy. More than forty men from Company D of the 502nd are out of action as a result of the three-hour battle alone. Still, the 502nd has succeeded in holding most of their positions. The enemy has lost two-thirds of their tanks in the fight. The 1st Battalion of the 327th moves in to relieve the 502nd.[10] We are right behind them in the woods, ready to support. Night is falling on January 3.

Being a runner definitely gives me a different perspective, because I am beginning to see how the units work together to counter enemy maneuvers. Sometimes elaborate plans are successful; sometimes success is a result of plain luck. For example, one night a German runner walks right up to an American machine gun squad, mistaking them for his comrades. From him and other prisoners US interrogators discover the enemy's plan to launch a second major attack in just a few hours. Soon after, US artillery back in Bastogne pounds the area where the enemy attack group is forming, thwarting the German plans, at least for a while.[11]

At 0530 on January 4, the delayed enemy attack on Champs finally comes, starting with an intense German artillery barrage spearheaded by several giant Panther tanks. The center of the line of the 1st Battalion of the 327th is overrun by the enemy. Company C is devastated. At regimental headquarters there is a report that the German tanks seem to be able to see US soldiers in the dark.[12] The Germans fight their way into Champs, but 2nd Battalion is ready in reserve to stop them, and we'll soon see action. They must be pushed back.

The Germans have pushed deeply enough into US lines to create a situation in which they are now in a vulnerable position. The 327th and 502nd have cut off the lead elements of the main German thrust. The enemy in the Champs area is basically surrounded by the Screaming Eagles, and an attack is being planned to clear the Germans out of the town.

Simpson comes by and tells me to report to Lieutenant Hibbard.

"Rich, take these replacements and set up five hundred yards north," Hibbard orders. "Don't let anything come down that road out of Champs. Clear?" Hibbard seems more tense than usual.

I look at the three replacements standing about twenty-five feet away. They look pretty green to me. The taller guy with black hair is arrogant, which annoys me because I doubt he's seen combat. The other two look like young kids. Although only twenty-one years old, I don't think or look like a kid anymore. I am a battle-hardened veteran, and I don't like the situation. A surrounded enemy is a ferocious enemy, as the Screaming Eagles have already proven; I know we might be facing the fanatical SS youth troops, who won't give up. They'll either fight to the death or fight their way out like a vicious mad dog. The road I am to block is the only way out to the west for the four enemy tanks that are supporting the surrounded enemy in Champs.[13]

"This is suicide!" I protest.

"What did you say, private?" Hibbard bristles at my insubordination.

"Sir, I said this is suicide! Four of us aren't enough. If they break and run, they're coming down this road, and we can't stop them with four. There is no way we can dig in for protection. It's suicide!"

"Get going, private!" replies Hibbard, letting me know who is boss.

"Sir, no way, this is suicide!" I continued to protest, knowing I will not win the argument. I've never talked this way to an officer before. I am steaming mad.

Hibbard just looks at me, expecting me to go on and do my duty. I turn around and round up the three replacements. Then, with one bazooka, one BAR, and two rifles, we head out through the woods to the north as I explain the mission. They are too green to understand.

As we clear the woods to the north, I glance over my map. At the Bastogne–Givry road we head toward Givry another couple of hundred yards and set up. Behind us is an old dairy barn. I order two of the replacements to set up in it. There is no sense in all four of us getting killed when the Germans come tearing down this road. The other two of us try to dig foxholes, but we can't make much of a dent in the frozen ground, so we pile up some snow to provide camouflage.

The American attack begins with the 502nd Regiment hitting the enemy pocket from the east, while the 327th hits them on all the other sides, including in front of us. The SS is putting up quite a fight.[14] We can hear gunfire as the attack unfolds.

We wait and wait. No enemy troops break through, at least not down our road. Finally, we can see a couple of American trucks heading our way. The Germans are cleared from Champs, and two of the four enemy tanks in the village are destroyed. Having received no orders, we stay put for a long,

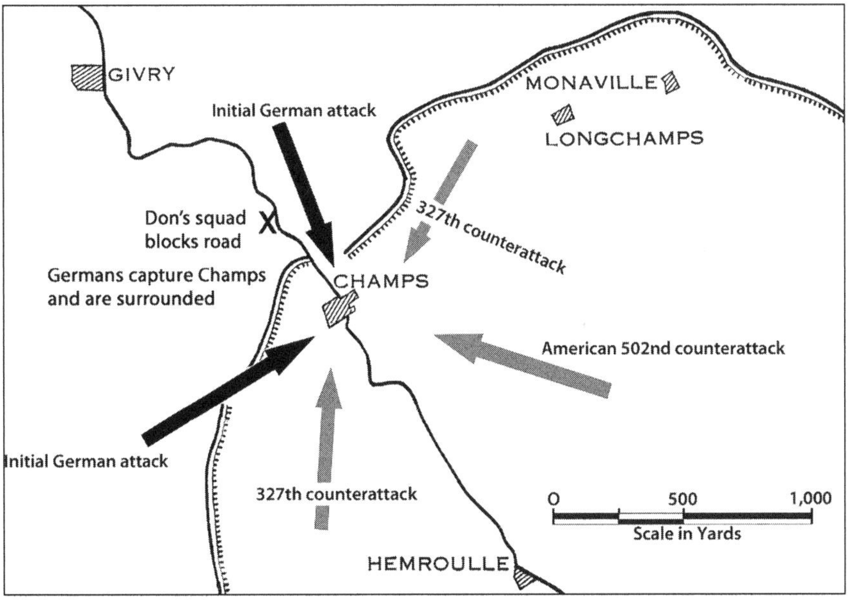

The battle for Champs, January 4, 1945. After breaking through American lines, German armor is subsequently surrounded in Champs.

cold night, alternating every couple of hours between our outside position on the road and the dairy barn.

On the morning of the January 5, movement by American troops and vehicles shows us that the pocket has been cleared of Krauts. The four of us head back to the company command post. Once back, I take a few runs to the front line and back. Late in the afternoon I receive orders to watch over a group of wounded soldiers. There are maybe fifteen or twenty. The seriously wounded already have been taken to Bastogne, and there isn't room in the ambulances for the lesser wounded. Dark has settled in, and I make a round to check the guys over in the dark before finding a foxhole, where I hunker down for the night, keeping a light watch over the group. I am tired, but the weather is too cold to sleep soundly. During the night the medics show up, and they ship the wounded POWs out.

I manage to get a little bit of sleep during the night, just before daylight brings in another bone-chilling day. Crawling out of my foxhole, which is hard to do because I am so stiff from the terrible cold, I notice a soldier from the 502nd heading my way between the trees. Whoever he is, the guy seems to be lost. I really don't know where I am, either. I make my way toward him. His body language shows me that he is glad to see a fellow American, not a German.

Suddenly, the swoosh of incoming shells breaks the silence. Wham! Wham! Wham! Each German shell hits closer and closer to me. I take off running away from the shelling as fast as my feet will take me. Swoosh, Wham! Wham! Wham! The shells explode around me. I come to a bank and jump in while running at full steam. The bank is steep and long. I fly through the air about ten feet or so and then roll the rest of the way down the embankment. On my belly, I look up and am staring into the face of an officer hiding underneath a jeep parked outside of company headquarters. When the shelling stops I brush myself off and head back up the hill. There is no sign of the guy from the 502nd.

Captain Evans, recuperating somewhere, rejects my promotion again, saying they already have too many sergeants. My bitterness towards the captain grows deeper. I know I am a better soldier than many of the sergeants.

To the northeast, near Foy, the 501st and 506th are trying to push the SS out of Jacques Woods.[15] Those German troops are tough and mean. Now, after a few days of attacking each other with little success, both sides are regrouping and licking their wounds.

The Germans finally decide they've suffered enough losses and begin their withdrawal from the Belgian Bulge. They plan to focus on defending their homeland against the Americans, English, and Canadians in the west and the massive Russian army in the east. In order to withdraw, the German army has to protect its defensive flank aggressively in the Ardennes area.[16] If US forces penetrate the flank in a decisive manner, the Allied armies could race on towards Berlin, ending the war in Europe.

Preparation for the next attack is no longer a big deal for those of us left from the original roster of the 327th. We are well past the time on the front lines when the army considers soldiers to be at their peak. We are numb and totally oblivious to living or dying. In many Screaming Eagles squads very few of the original soldiers are left.

Second Battalion moves up to the line in the Champs area again on January 6, without much action. The Germans are regrouping to the northeast to protect their withdrawal from the Foy–Noville area. During the quiet of the next few days, laundry service is started. It feels good to have fresh clothes for the first time since the Battle of the Bulge began.[17]

January 7 is marked by news that General McAuliffe will be leaving the Screaming Eagles for his own command in the south. Division command is moved to the southwest of Bastogne to avoid German artillery. Snowsuits for soldiers finally arrive, giving us some camouflage in the snow and much needed warmth. The 327th provides support for the newly arriving

17th Airborne Division, which is making a sweep in front of our northwest perimeter. The attack bogs down before there is much change in the lines, so other than moving, we see no action. Now attention is being prioritized for the next 101st objective: the retaking of Noville.[18]

This time the 101st, with the 17th Airborne Division on the left flank and the 6th Armored Division on the right, is to spearhead the attack. The village of Recogne, to the south and west of Noville, is to be taken quickly. In order to take Noville we must clear the enemy from wooded areas and from high ground northwest of Noville. The attack gets off at 1100 under heavy snow. Tanks find the going extremely difficult as they struggle to get traction. No air support is possible because of the weather.[19]

On January 10 the Screaming Eagles manage to make some modest gains. The weather is cold and cloudy; the temperature never reaches fifteen degrees Fahrenheit. German tree bursts hammer US forces, and several units need to retreat. The Screaming Eagles spend the day moving forward and backward, with G in reserve.[20] The enemy is still fighting hard.

On January 11, 2nd Battalion is back on the front line south of Foy, but there is no real action. The next day is also very quiet, with very little action for us.[21] Rumors fly that the 101st is about to be relieved from the Bastogne area. Maybe we really are done fighting for a while. Late that afternoon, Sherman and I are talking to each other about home. Another private joins the conversation.

"You guys want a haircut?" the guy asks.

"Sure do, I need one bad," Sherman replies instantly. Before long Sherman has a pretty decent haircut.

"You want one?" the other private asks me.

"Why not," I say, since Sherman's looks okay.

About halfway through my haircut, Lieutenant Regenburg comes up, barking, "New orders! We're moving up to the front lines, now!" My haircut isn't even half done. The barber takes off for his squad, leaving me with a very strange hairdo. Thinking hopefully, I decide that my new look might succeed in scaring any Germans who might capture me into letting me go.

On January 13 the attack on Noville is to begin at 0830 and is to be spearheaded by the 327th. The 506th regiment is to cover our left flank, and the 502nd, along with the 11th Armored Division, is to cover our right. Artillery will pummel the enemy positions in front of us for three minutes ahead of the attack. There is a long open area between the opposing lines. We are ready to attack, although Companies A and C need to be combined into "Ace Company"; because of earlier losses, they are still well below normal strength.[22]

The attack is delayed because of the snow and lack of effective communications between regiments. General Taylor comes to the 327th Regiment command post to find out the reason. Then he gives a message to the runners. My job as a G Company runner is to get the message back to Lieutenant Regenburg, which I do in good order: "Sir, General Taylor has ordered a hundred-dollar fine for any platoon that doesn't reach its objective by 1630."[23]

Ahead of the company are open fields north of the Foy–Mageret road. The enemy is solidly dug in both in front of and behind the woods on the far side of the fields. The enemy also has ample artillery support in the area. Although Regenburg's face is without emotion, I think he isn't too pleased to be leading men across an open field against accurate, heavy enemy artillery.

The attack begins forty-five minutes late, with the men of the 327th, including G, passing through the front lines of the 501st. The glidermen cross the road and then race across the open field, but the attack bogs down when enemy self-propelled guns hit our attack hard. The fighting continues for three hours, without making a further dent in the enemy line.

Bazooka crews eventually knock out the enemy SPs, and with the SPs out of the way, the speed and tenacity of the 327th's advance surprises the Americans as well as the Germans. German tanks and artillery hit back at the 327th hard, but the advance continues. Because of the rapid assault, bazooka gunners are able to get within fifty yards of enemy tanks before the enemy can react, making the monster machines easy targets. As a trained bazooka man, I feel regretful about not having a bazooka at the moment. I've never actually gotten a shot off against enemy armor, and now that there is an opportunity, it's not my job. Lloyd Gross is hit by shrapnel from a German 88 shell. His helmet is torn up, and he is bleeding profusely from his head. Part of his hand is missing.[24] Someone yells for a medic.

I shuttle back and forth between G command post and platoon positions. As the attack continues to unfold, squads drop grenades into the chimneys of German dugouts and capture the enemy soldiers as they run out. It is hard to keep up with the advance.

By 1600 the 327th has reached Jacques Woods thirty minutes ahead of schedule. At regimental command the officers are concerned with several new developments. First, the 327th is advancing so quickly that there is a risk

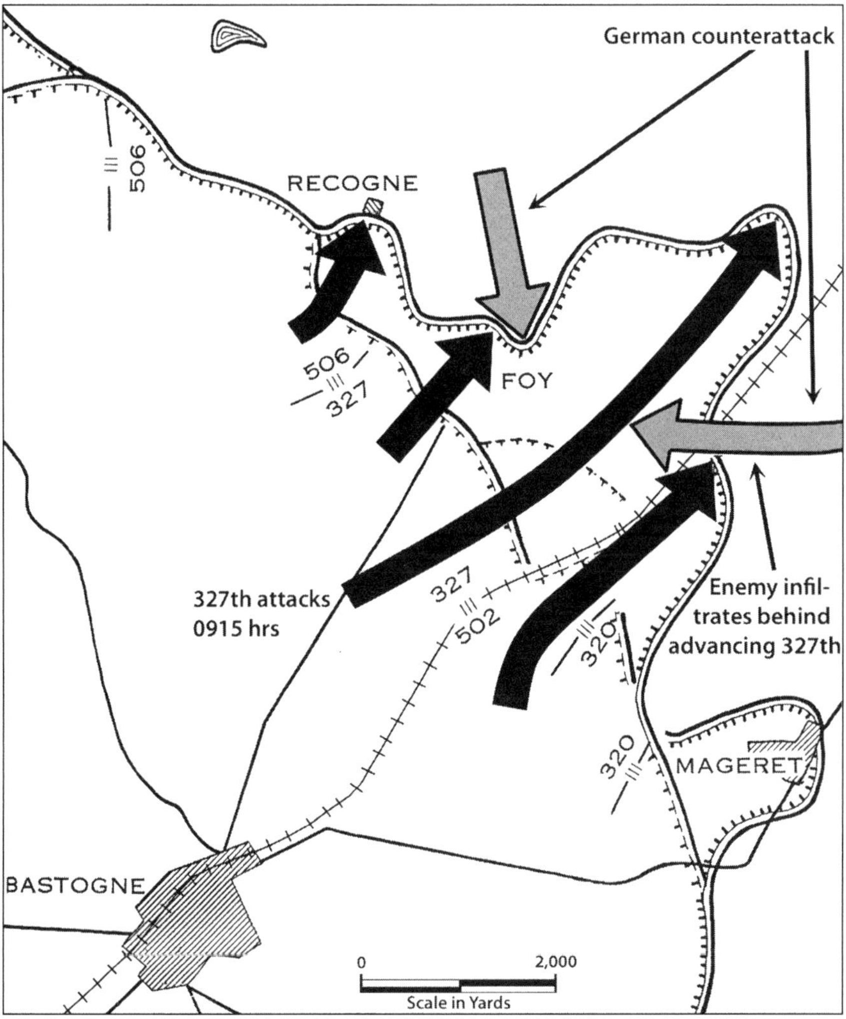

The battle near Foy, January 13, 1945. The 327th pushes into German-held territory in a rapid advance, leaving its flanks vulnerable to enemy attack.

it will be surrounded by the enemy, as the 502nd and 506th cannot keep up and protect our flanks. Second, the depleted Ace Company is surrounded in Jacques Woods. In addition, groups of German soldiers are still behind us, making it even more hazardous to run messages. The advance is halted to allow us to shore up our defenses.[25]

The Germans shell the woods, causing tree bursts. Niland is hit in the arm by shrapnel, which maims his elbow and forearm. The medic mentions,

"The wound looks like a for sure amputation." During the rest of the evening snow falls, and the temperature sinks down to around zero. The 327th has lost seventy-seven men today.[26]

At 0415 on January 14, the enemy counterattacks our flank in the Foy area with six tanks, making our position even more vulnerable. We thwart the first enemy attack, but at 0600 the enemy attack with fourteen tanks succeeds in taking back Foy, to the west. By 0930 the 506th recaptures Foy from the Germans. The 327th spends a good part of the day fighting to relieve the surrounded Ace Company as well as shoring up the flanks. For an army that is in retreat, the enemy certainly is coming at us hard, inflicting fifty-three casualties on the 327th, including eight killed.[27]

By now, American air support has restarted as the weather improves. Seeing P-47s screaming through the sky as I deliver messages is very comforting; they are dropping what seems like thunder on enemy positions. Unfortunately, because the fighting is so chaotic, it is often difficult for the American pilots to tell which side is which. In the afternoon I am delivering a message and see one of the fighter bombers peel off, heading toward an American position. The plane drops a five-hundred-pound bomb on an American squad from the 502nd near the railroad tracks. I am only about a hundred yards away and can feel the intense concussion when the bomb hits. My heart seems to stop and my mind seems to explode. With the explosion the 502nd squad vanishes. The force of the explosion is so great that no trace of the soldiers is ever found where the crater is. When Colonel Harper comes to the site later, he declares that no one was killed, but I know this could not be true, because I clearly saw the bomb drop right on top of the American soldiers.[28]

Regenburg tells us we have lost contact with the 502nd along the railroad tracks on our right flank. The enemy could mount a successful attack in between areas dividing regiments. "Rich, take a squad and find out where the 502nd is," Hibbard orders.

I am fuming mad. I'm tired of being asked to lead squads without being promoted. Squad leaders should be sergeants, not privates. Not only does this deny me a large pay bonus, but it doesn't allow me to receive the respect I deserve. After all, I am one of the few left who have been serving with the unit since D-Day. Why should I have to bear the burden of leading a squad without the benefits of being a sergeant? Hibbard knows that a sergeant should be leading the men, which means that he believes I am capable of being a sergeant, but for some reason I am not promoted.

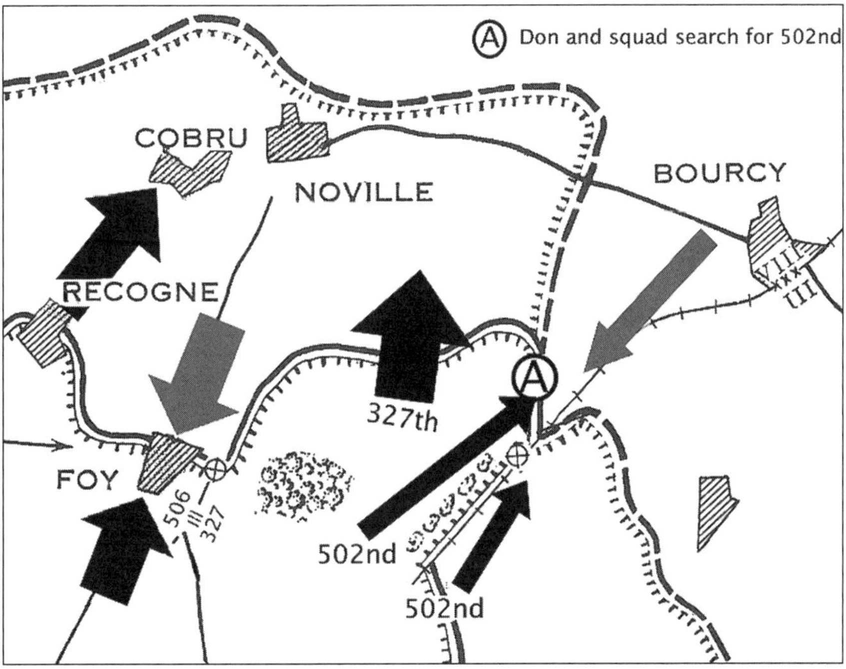

German attempt to cut off the 327th at Noville, January 14, 1945.

"No, sir, I will not lead the squad!" I retort. Hibbard looks at me with a stunned expression on his worn face. "See how I have one stripe on my arm?" I say, while pointing to the rank patch. "By rank I can't lead the squad, sir! I'll go and I'll do my part, but I won't lead. I can't lead. Technically, I'm not qualified, sir." I am right, and Hibbard knows it. He'll have to find someone else to lead the scouting patrol.

I go, and the patrol takes place without any enemy contact, although enemy troops are in the area. A railroad is a natural dividing line between the 327th and the 502nd. The patrol does manage to make contact with the 502nd, which fills in a gap through which the enemy could counterattack. The area between units is always a weak point that can be exploited by the enemy; the Germans try to wedge through this gap but are not successful.

January 15 is a cloudy and cold day. By 1145 the 506th Regiment begins an assault on Noville, and the small village is soon in American hands. After relieving Ace Company of the 327th, G advances to the high ground east of Noville against moderate resistance.[29] Most of my time I spend running orders between company headquarters and the sergeants. There isn't time for conversation. The men are tired and don't communicate well.

During a break in running, Hibbard assigns me to help with a burial detail. A two-wheeled army wagon is pulled in by a jeep. I assist the burial detail in picking up frozen German bodies, which we stack on the wagon. The task is made difficult by the odd positions in which the bodies are contorted and frozen solid. Arms stick up. Legs bend backwards. The stacking is difficult. Some have eyes open, others shut, and some are missing body parts. We work without saying anything.

After we get the fifteen bodies on the wagon, we can see that they won't stay on during transport. But my farm experience and the fence around a nearby pasture give me an idea: "Let's use the barbed wire fence." We jerk the wire off the fence posts and wrap it around the bodies and the wagon. Then we twist the ends together to hold things in place. The rest of the crew drive off with the bodies.

On January 16 the 327th pushes out the right flank uphill to assist the 502nd, and Bourcy is captured. Heavy German artillery again falls in the area. The 327th suffers fifty-four causalities and captures a large number of prisoners.[30] Hibbard finds me again.

"Rich, escort these prisoners to regimental headquarters," he orders. Two of the eight prisoners have wounds and are on stretchers. I place my M1 against a tree, carefully keeping myself between the prisoners and the weapon. I motion for the uninjured prisoners to pick up the wounded men on the stretchers. "Private! Pick up your rifle, now!" Hibbard yells, his voice strongly inflected, startling me.

I turn and look at him in puzzlement and ask, "What for? They just surrendered. If they wanted to run, they wouldn't have surrendered."

"Pick up your rifle, private!" Hibbard is persistent. So picking up the M1, I motion to the prisoners to move. The unwounded prisoners motion and point at their wounded buddies, acting concerned about them. I think they are more concerned that I will shoot if they make a wrong move and want permission to pick them up.

The prisoners and I head down a path through the woods away from the front lines as incoming German 88 mm shells hit, Swoosh, Blam! Blam! Blam! landing too close for comfort. The prisoners and I run as fast as we can to a ditch off to our right. The shells slam the ground and hit a tree to our left. My heart pounds heavily as I survey the situation. Another string of shells swooshes in a little bit closer, shaking the ground and throwing shrapnel. The prisoners are wide-eyed, looking at me, wondering what we should do. They aren't sure whether to be more afraid of me or the shells. Then I notice their buddies on stretchers were left back along the path.

After a period of silence, I motion to them with my rifle to go and get their buddies.

"*Nicht, nicht,*" they say several times, shaking their heads from side to side. They are scared. I motion again. They don't move.

"Go!" I shout at them, trying to be assertive. Still they don't budge one bit. I point my rifle at the first one, put my finger on the trigger, and yell, "Go!"

For several seconds, the Germans just stare at me with terror in their eyes. My heart is pounding. Then, one of the prisoners gets up, and the others follow. Together they retrieve their comrades on the stretchers. I climb out of the ditch myself. We head on toward regimental headquarters, where the prisoners are placed under new guards. The Germans again are acting very concerned about their wounded buddies. I chuckle out loud as I picture them leaving their dear buddies out on the path when the artillery hit. They didn't seem too concerned about them then.

After I release the prisoners at regimental HQ, First Sergeant Hayden has me, since I know my way around the area, accompany him on an inspection of all the 327th's companies. Company G is now down to about 40 able-bodied men out of the 120 we had when we came to Bastogne, including the replacements we added when we left Marvie. We have lost so many good soldiers since D-Day in June that I am beginning to think my time for living is about up. Hayden and I continue the rounds, one company after another. Upon arriving at each company, we find the same thing: troops are just sitting around with their heads down. Few, if any, look up. There is no talking. They are spent.

"The guys aren't bitching," Hayden murmurs as we walk back to regimental HQ. "Not good. If the enemy makes an attack on our positions, I'm not sure they'll even look up."

The Noville area is finally firmly under American control. I am exhausted and numb. The rage inside me is bottled up by the numbness. The Screaming Eagles have given their all and no longer care about anything. They don't have any energy left to care. After Hayden's report on the 327th to Colonel Harper, other reports come in from other regiments. Taylor wants to push forward. Junior officers contact the chaplains, who in turn contact General Taylor. They tell Taylor that if the division isn't pulled off the line, it will be destroyed. Even though Taylor doesn't want to back off, the chaplains win, and orders are given to begin withdrawal of the division from the front. Personally, I think the reluctance of our commanders, such as Taylor, shows that they are thinking of their own glory too much at the expense of regular soldiers on the ground.

Company G is called on to clear up a pocket of enemy soldiers while they are protecting the 401st's left flank. The guys sluggishly answer the call. I am on the front line when a fierce firefight breaks out between the 1st Squad of 2nd Platoon and the Germans. I lead the squad, because of my familiarity with the area. We are advancing from a clearing between trees when machine gun fire rakes our line. The squad breaks off the advance, and we run back away from the Germans to regroup. Sergeant Hanlon motions for us to get behind a fallen tree. One of the replacements covering our retreat goes down, hit by a bullet in his upper back. He is just beyond the tree.

"He's down! He's down!" someone shouts.

Turning to look, we see the Germans advancing toward us. There are a lot more of them than there are of us. We keep firing rifles to keep them from overrunning us, but the situation doesn't look good. They make another charge at us, and we force them back. From behind the tree I can hear the wounded replacement making loud, strange noises as he struggles for his life, rolling back and forth. A couple of us try to go get him, but the enemy fire keeps us pinned down. Again the Germans charge, and again we hold them off, and they back away.

"Medic!" I yell. Sometimes, the Germans allow medics to take care of the wounded, but at other times they shoot at the medics. I start to go over the tree to get the wounded soldier.

"Rich, stay put! That's an order!" Hanlon yells.

"Medic! Medic!" I yell.

Coming over to me, Hanlon says, "I can't risk a medic. We don't have enough if they kill him." The young soldier's agony continues for hours. Through the evening he is gasping for breath. The gasping turns to gurgling sounds, which get softer and softer until there is silence as the sun goes down.

Enemy rifle fire continues to come in. As much as the situation stinks, we know that we can't risk the lives of several other men to save him. We all know that if we were in the same situation as the poor replacement, we wouldn't be saved, either.

After the sun goes down, the medic is called in, and he crawls out to the replacement, who by now is lying motionless. The medic quickly crawls back.

"There's no helping him. He swallowed his tongue and choked to death." The medic seems pretty disgusted with the situation. It probably would have been easy to save the man if we could have gotten a medic to him sooner.

Anger comes over me. I am furious. Why did we have only one medic for the entire company? There simply aren't enough of them. My angry thoughts turn toward my hometown, where there are lots of Mennonite guys who for religious reasons won't fight. They could serve as medics, but most of them stayed home safe from war. Why won't more of them serve? We surely could use them. Our squad straggles back. We are trucked six miles to Sibret, where we are placed in reserve.[31] Hibbard and Hayden put me up for promotion.

Some of the guys are invited to a ceremony in Bastogne, where medals are awarded for bravery and the mayor of Bastogne presents the division with the flag of the city. General Taylor, who accepts the flag from the mayor, is handed a receipt from General Middleton, corps commander. The receipt says:

> 18 JANUARY 1945
>
> RECEIVED FROM THE 101 AIRBORNE DIVISION
> THE TOWN OF BASTOGNE, LUXEMBOURG PROVINCE, BELGIUM.
> CONDITION: USED BUT SERVICEABLE, KRAUT DISINFECTED
>
> TROY H. MIDDLETON
> MAJOR GENERAL USA
> COMMANDING

As the 101st marches past reviewing officers, above the officers' heads is a sign that reads: Bastogne—Bastion of the Battered Bastards of the 101st.[32]

Rumors fly. Many of us hear that we were going back to Mourmelon and then on to the Far East to fight the Japanese. As advance elements leave the area, we are informed that the division is going to Alsace, France, 160 miles to the south. Nobody wants to go fight the Japanese, who are said to be fiercer than the most fanatical German SS soldiers. We load into more than one hundred ten-ton trucks and nearly as many smaller two-and-a-half-ton trucks. The weather is cold and snowy, the roads very slippery. For thirty-six hours we try to keep warm in the trucks as we head to our new destination.[33]

Alsace

Worn out, exhausted, and depleted in supplies, the Screaming Eagles make the long, frigid trip by truck from Bastogne to Alsace by way of Veau Lebere, Belgium, and Schalbach, France. The trucks slip and slide their way in the falling snow.[1] Conditions in the back of the trucks are as miserable as those of a frozen foxhole. The route is far out of the way, compared to how the crow flies. The mood of the soldiers is amazingly quiet, however. They show no emotion at all, and there is little talking. The war never seems to be over, but I am now pretty sure that I'm going to live to the end.

Most of the American army currently in Alsace has fought its way across Sicily and into Italy against stiff enemy resistance. Later, these soldiers, invading southern France, drove into the Alsace region alongside the French army. The Germans counterattacked and pushed into Alsace on New Year's Day under orders from Hitler in an operation called North Wind. But although the German attack pushed the Allies back, it has bogged down by the time the 101st arrives on the scene. We are going into what is believed to be a quiet area to regain our strength.[2]

Alsace is a long, wide valley between the Vosges Mountains of France and the Black Forest of Germany. It became a part of Germany following the Franco-Prussian War of 1870–71 and then went back to the French Republic following Germany's defeat during World War I in 1918. Germany reclaimed Alsace after the fall of France in 1940 upon the onset of the war in Western Europe. The sector where the Screaming Eagles are taking up positions is predominantly German in customs and language, but French language and customs are also very noticeable. We are warned by command that even though this is deemed to be friendly territory, there are known to be many ardent German supporters who might cause problems. In Shalbach, Company G receives fifty-five replacements to go with the fifty-nine of us who made it through the hell of Bastogne. Some of the fifty-nine include replacements received in early January after the encirclement was broken.[3]

On January 25, Company G entrucks and moves to Bossendorf, where we spend the night. The next day we arrive at Uhlwiller, France, where we march three miles and set up defensive positions along the Moder River to the west of Haguenau.[4] Hibbard and Hayden inform me my promotion to sergeant has been turned down by Captain Evans, who will be rejoining the company soon.

Parts of eight worn-out German divisions directly face our four American divisions. American commanders not with the 101st in the area are concerned about our being outnumbered by the enemy. The commanders are surprised that the Screaming Eagles do not seem to be too concerned about facing a lot of Germans. The 101st's Major Leo Schweiter, referring to our exploits in the defense of Bastogne, sums up our feelings: "What the hell are you so worried about? The 101st alone can lick five German divisions simultaneously. We just did."[5]

Just before our arrival near the front, the enemy began to make noise by crossing the Moder River at Haguenau and Kaltenhausen, but they were pushed back after inflicting heavy casualties on the Americans. This fighting is dying out as we arrive. After dark on January 26, through the early hours of the next morning, with the 327th on the right and the 501st on the left, we take up positions along the south bank of the Moder River about half a mile to the west of the city of Haguenau. The 502nd and 506th are behind in reserve.[6] Former Screaming Eagles commander General McAuliffe, now commanding the 103rd Division, is to the left of the 501st, which is a comforting thought, as we know he is a good commander. Command posts are set up in houses and cellars, so I get to sleep indoors as a runner.

Across the river is the Haguenau Woods, consisting mainly of tall evergreen trees. The enemy is hidden in the thick woods, which measures about fifteen miles long and five miles deep. Cleared land extends about a mile from the river to the woods on the German-held side. On our side of the river the evergreens are not nearly as thick, leaving the ground almost bare in places. The ground is currently covered with snow, which is good camouflage; our snow capes keep us well hidden. Pointing to the sky several miles to the rear are large searchlights, which reflect off of low clouds to illuminate the enemy's positions.[7]

On the first night the enemy launches an eight-man patrol right out in front of the 327th to see what we are made of. Dressed in white capes, the riflemen of G hold their fire until the Germans are very close. Half of the Germans are killed right away when we fire. The Germans show their appreciation of our combat skills by letting loose mortar rounds on 1st Battalion, which is roughed up by the barrage but suffers few casualties.[8]

Evans is back with Company G on January 29. We move into reserve in Schweighouse. The 327th receives 487 high-quality replacements and these new men are very successful at integrating into the regiment,[9] although there are a couple of dramatic exceptions. One of the replacements accidentally sets off a grenade in his pocket, killing himself and a couple of other replacements. The new troops are assigned to old-timers to teach them the best methods for staying alive within gun range of the enemy, greatly helping the situation. It seems that the army is finally learning from earlier mistakes on how to integrate replacement soldiers.

The 327th and Company G command posts are located in a comfortable house with a cellar. Even though I am outside a lot running messages, I now have a comfortable house to sleep in, and this is a luxury compared to what I had in Bastogne. The house is especially nice because the weather is even colder than when we were in Bastogne. Men out on the front lines also stay in schools, in buildings of different kinds, and even in the bedrooms of local villagers' homes.

Several miles down the Moder River to the right, the enemy still holds some ground on the south side of the river. To encourage the Germans to pull back entirely to the other side, and to capture enemy soldiers for interrogation purposes, command plans Operation Oscar for January 31. The raid, to be led by Company E of the 327th and Companies A and B of the 501st, is to occur across the river from us. German tanks are in the area, and our troops are to avoid them. Ahead of the attack, artillery support for us is to be fast and furious. Those of us in G Company are brought out of reserve to fake a crossing of the river in an attempt to keep German eyes off Company E. Basically, all we are to do is make a lot of smoke and pour gunfire into German positions across the river and then stay put.

Footbridges are quickly built by army engineers and finished by 0230. Several engineers are wounded during the construction. The Screaming Eagles cross the bridges during the middle of the night, and the attack begins as planned, with the Americans rapidly advancing from house to house. A German soldier, not knowing what is happening, walks right out of some woods and begins marching with the Americans. I'll bet he was shocked when he realized that he had "voluntarily" joined an American squad. Several prisoners are captured by the quick-moving Americans. Well before daylight at 0500, the withdrawal back to the US side begins. Getting back is harder for the raiders, because they have suffered several casualties and don't want to leave the wounded men behind. Six Screaming Eagles are killed, plus a medic. Several soldiers are missing. Thirty-seven enemy soldiers, including two officers, are captured.[10]

For the next several days we live in relative comfort, watching movies, living in homes, getting our clothes laundered, and using portable showers. Boy, it feels good finally to be clean for days at a time. I honestly can't remember the last time I've taken a shower. I'm sure it has been months. Some guys get furloughs, and a few of them even make it back to the States.[11]

Other than that patrol, our area is quiet from then until February 5, when the enemy fires rounds of 88 mm artillery at the 327th. Payday is February 1. Most of the guys by now have learned to handle their money better and decide it is best to save it rather than getting it converted into cash and spending it or gambling it away. The 502nd gets a band together, and we are treated to several concerts.[12]

The weather warms, and melting snow floods the Moder River. Getting across is determined to be too dangerous after a couple of failed patrol crossings.

About this time we are introduced to a girl named Alsace Annie. Unfortunately, Annie isn't too fond of us Americans, and we don't like her very much, either. Annie is a mobile fifteen-inch gun, mounted on a railroad car, that the Germans use occasionally to fire at our side of the Moder, causing no real damage except to our nerves. Other girls, real American Red Cross girls, operate clubs for dancing and handing out donuts. We like these girls much more than Annie. Winter supplies reach us and make our lives even more "comfortable."[13]

On February 3, G comes out of reserve and are on the front line near the Moder. There is little activity. Things are very quiet until the Germans hit us with artillery on February 10. On February 12, Company C of the 327th crosses the flooded river, captures a German prisoner, and kills about eight enemy soldiers.[14] Regiments and companies rotate back and forth between reserve and support on the line. For a couple of days patrols continue to check out the enemy, and more often than not they do not make contact. Both combatant sides seem to want just to survive until the end of the war—a proposition that works better by not taking unnecessary action.

On February 14 the enemy finally retaliates. A large German patrol comes across the Moder in the 327th's sector following a heavy artillery attack.[15]

The GIs on the line begin firing furiously at the enemy, driving them back. The battery in the company radio begins to go bad, so I am called to run and get another battery from regimental command during the attack. I can see fairly well in the dark, but I feel a bit uneasy, as the fighting is still intense. As I make my way out of a clump of trees into a clearing, I hear something moving among the trees. I swing my M1 rifle around to shoot, and a deer jumps into the clearing and speeds away from the fighting.

My heart is pounding as I try to gather my breath, and my legs are a little soft from the fright. After taking a couple of steps, I trip over what I think is a log. Still lying on the ground, I look back toward the log. In the dark I can just make out a German uniform. My heart skips several beats as I realize I have just tripped over a dead German soldier, who likely had been alive just a few minutes before. If I had passed by just a little earlier, I might have been killed.

I gather myself together and race on toward command. I'm still too shaken to say much of anything to anyone, so I get the battery and immediately leave. On my way back, German shells scream in toward where I am, but not too close. Then I run into Sherman with several replacements. He seems to be looking for something.

"What's up?" I ask.

Sherman is half laughing when he answers. "I was taking these green replacements up to the line when the shells came in. Earlier I told 'em, 'stay with me and do as I do in case something happens.' When the shells came in, I wasn't too concerned, so I didn't stop. But when I turned around, the new guys were gone. Now, I can't find 'em all. Want to help find 'em?" The guys with him didn't see the humor that Sherman did. Sherman had been around long enough to know how close shells would land. The replacements hadn't.

"No, you go ahead," I reply. "Hope you find them. I'd better get back."

During the enemy patrol and in the hours afterwards, five hundred to six hundred heavy German shells fall in the sector of the 327th and 501st, shaking things up good. The enemy pulls back across the river after intense fire from our riflemen. Four days later, they try the same thing against the 3rd Battalion (the 401st). A German prisoner who is captured says that the raid was designed to capture Americans in order to find out exactly what division the Germans are fighting against.[16] I would think they should know that by now; however, I suppose it is probably best for the Germans not to know who they are facing. If they had found out they were facing the 101st, they might have fled.

Jack Sherman, leading replacements, came upon Don in the forest near Schweighouse.

American patrols continue across the river with no real results. Eventually, after several more casualties on the worthless patrols, the battalion commander puts an end to them. There is no reason to take pointless casualties, especially because it seems like the war is winding down. Giant speakers are pointed across the river offering the enemy opportunities to surrender. A few Germans take up the offer. We move to reserve at Wittersheim, located four and a half miles to the rear, and then back to the line at Schweighouse.[17]

With the situation becoming more relaxed, the locals become friendlier, although we can never be sure of their loyalty. For shelter, some of us runners are able to move into the basement of a house. It feels good to stay warm. I notice a couple of local businesses have the name *Rich* on their signs. I intend to stop by and talk to them, wondering if they are related to me, but never do. Personally, I can never tell which half of the locals support us and which half hate us.

One day I round a corner and come face-to-face with a young French girl. She is very pretty, with long black hair, but obviously afraid of me, and she takes a couple of steps back. I'd guess she is two or three years younger than me. "Hi there," I say to her. She looks away but doesn't run, so I give her a big grin, which causes her to relax some.

"What's your name?" I ask.

The girl looks around and then down at the ground. Then, hesitantly, she says in somewhat broken English, "My name is Ma . . . Marie."

"Hi, Marie, my name is Don."

Although still frightened, Marie seems a little curious about meeting an American soldier. We continue with a bit of boy-meets-girl small talk, then I realize I am feeling hungry. "Marie, can you cook?" I ask rather quickly. "I mean, could you cook for us, the guys in my squad on a regular basis? The army food, it's pretty bad."

"No, I cannot," Marie replies somewhat reluctantly, before adding, "I need go home now."

I didn't give up that easily. "Marie, we really could use some better cooking. Please could you cook for us?"

Another soldier walks by and makes some rather inappropriate remarks about Marie's appearance. I can see her face tense up. So many young soldiers in town must be intimidating to a young girl.

"Leave her be!" I yell at the other soldier, who laughs and keeps on walking. Turning back to Marie, I continue.

"Please, could you please cook for us?"

By now I am joined by another runner, and the two of us are really working on her. Maybe she realizes that I am harmless, so finally she agrees to cook for us.

There is a kitchen in the house we are staying in, and Marie goes to work right away. She looks over our rations and asks if we can find some potatoes, onions, and lard. The lard is hard to find, but we locate some during a raid on the mess hall. The girl does what she can with the rations, and when done, the meal tastes very good.

"Marie, come and sit with us," says one of the other runners. Marie looks away and won't sit down. She is still somewhat scared.

"Marie, can you cook for us every day?" I ask her. She isn't sure about every day, but she will do what she can. After she leaves for the day, I call a meeting of the runners.

"Okay, guys, I know she's pretty, but no one messes with the cook! Agreed?" I speak seriously. We look around at each other, and everyone grins. The food is good, so all agree. That night, several of us form a raiding patrol and raid the mess hall kitchen again for more lard and whatever else we can carry.

The next day and the days after that, Marie comes back to cook. She is a marvelous cook and even makes us some pastries. What she can do with the ten-in-ones is incredible. But Marie never will sit down and eat with us, although she soon converses with us more freely.

Life at Schweighouse continues on. Even though we still aren't officially inside Germany, there is a sense that the end of the war is near. During this time I have time to think about buddies lying in graves in France, the Netherlands, and Belgium. A new thought grips the soldiers: getting killed so close to the end of the war seems senseless.

After making a run one night, Sherman and I are walking down the street in Schweighouse, coming back from company headquarters. Behind us a German machine gun opens up, and bullets hit all around us. We take off running and hit the first door we come to, hitting it hard. It doesn't open; it is locked. Brap, braaaaaap, we hear bullets bouncing off the road and buildings. We try three or four more doors, throwing our weight into them, but all are locked.

Down the street we continue running, and simultaneously we hit a door with full force, slinging it wide open. I can feel my body falling in the dark. What we don't know is that the door is the entrance to a cellar. The stairs down are steep, and there is no platform at the top. We don't hit many stairs on the way down to the cellar floor, and the impact sure does hurt. In the dark we don't say anything for about ten minutes. "Whew, that was close," I finally say.

"Close, I don't know how whoever it was missed us," Sherman adds, seemingly still out of breath. After a while we make our way up the stairs. No one else is around.

The next day I awake to one of the runners hollering, "Hey, the food's gone!"

"What? What's going on?" someone asks sleepily.

"Who would have done that?" we wonder. During the night the soldier on guard duty fell asleep, and someone has stolen our rations. That means Marie doesn't have anything to cook for us.

"This is serious!" I shout. I look around and see a local kid watching from across the street. "Hey kid! Where're our rations?" The little guy is wearing a short-brimmed hat and a big grin.

"That house over there!" the boy says while pointing at the street behind us. "They took it during the night." I think he is a French kid tattling on a German family.

"How do you know that?" I ask, humored by his demeanor and good English.

"I saw them myself!" he replies, obviously proud of himself.

Food was important to young soldiers. Don wanted his meal back at Schweighouse.

"Come on, let's go. Them damn Krauts!" I holler at the rest. Grabbing my M1, I head to the house with the others following, mostly out of curiosity. Humored as I was at the boy, I was steaming mad about the possibility that we would get no more meals cooked by Marie.

"Go find someone who can speak German!" Sergeant Hayden orders.

"German? We don't need German!" I say and then bang the door hard with the butt of my rifle. An older man quickly opens the door and sticks his head out. He is concerned the door will break. I stick my rifle barrel into the guy's stomach and hold it there as he stands motionless. Seemingly out of nowhere, the rations and lots of other stuff appear, frantically thrown and pushed out of the house by other family members.

"I've never seen Krauts move so fast!" Hayden laughs hysterically at the response to my bold maneuver. We get it all back for sure and probably some extra. We leave everything except the food. The food is the important stuff.

On February 21, gunfire and shouting wake us out of what has been a good night's sleep. A German soldier is shot trying to come back across the river to our side. Apparently he is by himself. The soldier was coming home on furlough, wanting to see his family in the Haguenau area. I'm not sure whether he thought he'd get in and out without being caught. He isn't wounded seriously, so we let him see his family and then send him on to prison camp. Half of the townspeople want to shoot him; the other half come out to welcome him home like a hero.

On February 26 the 327th is relieved from the area.[18] We say goodbye to our cook, Marie, and leave her all the ten-in-one rations we can find. Food is in short supply for the locals, and this will feed her family for quite some time. Company G pulls out at night, led by Captain Evans.

We leave at night to avoid artillery attacks from the Germans; we'll march to Ohlungen, where we'll load into trucks. I know the area well as a result of all the runs I've made from the line to the company outpost, but the night is so dark from heavy clouds that I can't see the guys around me. We place a hand on the person in front so we can stay in a column and not get separated. Something seems wrong, though, and the thought comes to me that we are lost. Then we find out that Evans has made a wrong turn at one of the firebreaks in the forest, and we have walked in the wrong direction for about half an hour. I hear my name being whispered. I don't answer. Finally, First Sergeant Hayden comes up next to me asking, "Why in the hell didn't you answer?" He chews me out in a whisper; we don't dare make any noise.

"Why didn't Evans ask me to help when we started out?" I whisper back. "If he had, we wouldn't be in this mess." Without waiting for an answer, I continue: "Bring the front of the column back to the last firebreak, about a half-mile back. I can get us going from there."

After a lot of confusion and much whispered profanity, we get back on the right firebreak. Captain Evans doesn't speak to me when he goes by. After a while, I have a change of heart and feel a little foolish. If we had been hit by artillery fire while wandering around like this, I'd have felt pretty bad.

Eventually we make our way out of the forest and to the trucks, where we load and travel to Lorquin. We leave the next day for Strasburg, where we load onto a train, piling into boxcars loaded with hay for our comfort. Eighteen hours later the train rolls into Mourmelon to marching music from the 502nd band. The 327th has had the greatest number of casualties of any unit in the 101st during the Alsace action.[19]

When we arrive, we find that the barracks we stayed in during our first stop at Mourmelon have been turned into a hospital. Pyramid tents, housing six to twelve men each, are already set up for us. Latrines are dug. Helmets become washbasins. Shower units arrive. The food isn't too bad.

On March 15 the 101st Airborne Division becomes the first entire division to be awarded the Distinguished Unit Citation for gallantry in action.

Everything has to be immaculate for the ceremony. We practice the parade march for the ceremony over and over until the division is perfectly drilled and ready. General Eisenhower then speaks to us as everyone stands at attention:

> It is a great personal honor for me to be here today to take part in a ceremony that is unique in American history. Never before has a full division been cited by the War Department in the name of the President for gallantry in action. This day marks the beginning of a new tradition in the American army. With that tradition, therefore, will always be associated the name of the 101st Airborne Division and of Bastogne.
>
> Yet you men, because you are soldiers of proved valor and of experience, would be the last to claim that you are the bravest and the best. All the way from where the Marines are fighting on Iwo Jima, through the Philippines and southeast Asia, on through the Mediterranean and along this great front, and on the Russian frontiers, are going forward day by day those battles sustained by the valor of you and the other Allied units that are beating this enemy to his knees. They are proving once and for all that dictatorship cannot produce better soldiers than can aroused democracy. In many of those actions are units that have performed with unexcelled brilliance.
>
> So far as I know there may be many among you that would not rate Bastogne as your bitterest battle. Yet it is entirely fitting and appropriate that you should be cited for that particular battle. It happened to be one of those occasions when the position itself was of the utmost importance to the Allied forces. You, in reserve, were hurried forward and told to hold that position. All the elements of drama, of battle drama, were there. You were cut off, you were surrounded. Only valor, complete self-confidence in yourselves and in your leaders, a knowledge that you were well trained, only the determination to win could sustain soldiers under those conditions. You were given a marvelous opportunity, and you met every test.
>
> Therefore, you become a fitting symbol on which the United Nations, all the citizens of the United Nations, can say to their soldiers today, "We are proud of you," as it is my great privilege to say to you here today, to the 101st Division and all its attached units, "I am awfully proud of you."

> With this great honor goes also a certain responsibility. Just as you are the beginning of a new tradition, you must realize, each of you, that from now on, the spotlight will beat on you with particular brilliance. Whenever you say you are a soldier of the 101st Division, everybody, whether it's on the street in the city or in the front line, will expect unusual conduct of you. I know that you will meet every test of the future like you met at Bastogne.
>
> Good luck and God be with each of you.[20]

Ike's last line, "I know that you will meet every test of the future like you met at Bastogne," hits me hard. I might have a future. I have been living my life the past two years on overdrive. "Every test of the future. . . ."

Over the next month the Screaming Eagles train for their next battle assignment, Operation Eclipse. During Eclipse, the 101st, along with the 82nd Airborne and a British airborne division, is to drop on Berlin, contact the Russian army, and wipe out German resistance in the capital. Hikes, weapons practice, and mock-up glider training take place at a fast pace. The only reason real flights take place is to get the replacements their official standing as glider troops, and the same type of activities take place for the parachute guys. The new guys can't get full airborne pay like the rest of us without qualifying, which means we have to make the practice flights. Live-fire training is started again and results in several accidental deaths. On March 17 we all cheer the 17th Airborne Division as they take off for a jump into Germany.[21] The war is turning into a race for Berlin.

Marlene Dietrich makes another appearance at a USO show. Movies are shown, and the lines are long. A court is formed to fine soldiers for such infractions as improper uniform, speeding in a jeep or truck, and disorderly conduct. After only two weeks, 139 men have been jailed for various reasons.[22]

Germany

Back in December I was excited when it appeared that I was going to get the opportunity to attend a Christmas service at a very large cathedral. Then the Germans' counteroffensive in the Ardennes occurred, so I didn't get to go. Easter is now approaching, and again I think it would be nice to attend services at that big cathedral. Unfortunately, the army has other plans. On Good Friday, March 30, the following message is read to us by Captain Evans:

"All units of this Division, with the exception of the 501st Parachute Infantry, are hereby alerted to be in readiness to depart from this station on a combat mission at 0800, April 1, 1945."[1]

The enemy is giving its best effort in an attempt to keep the Allies on the west side of the Rhine River. Fighting is now very personal for German troops. We are invading their fatherland. The Rhine had first been crossed on March 7 by the 9th Armored Division. On March 22 and 23, Patton's Third Army crossed near Oppenheim.[2] On March 24, a combined British, Canadian, and American crossing is made toward the north. With these advances, and with the Russians steamrolling in from the east, the German military is crumbling, causing the Allied advance to look like a race to Berlin.

The German army has shown in the past a propensity to hold on to areas stubbornly when common sense makes it plain that they should retreat. The present situation looks like the Germans have not learned their lesson, and this is causing the 101st to be sent back into a combat zone. Thousands of enemy troops are surrounded in the Ruhr area of Germany, in and around the city of Düsseldorf. The Ruhr is the heartland of German industrial might and is the most densely populated area of Germany. Most of the German military weapons are made in this region—a major reason for the Germans' stubborn defense.

We depart April 2 from Camp Mourmelon and move by truck to Büttgen, Germany, arriving on April 5. Büttgen is five miles west of Düsseldorf. The Ruhr pocket is an area of almost four thousand square miles, measuring fifty-five miles from north to south and seventy miles from east to west. In this area the Germans have a large number of 88 mm artillery and antiaircraft guns that were originally designed to protect factories from Allied bombing raids but are now aimed at US troops. The Rhine River separates the Screaming Eagles from about five thousand enemy troops in and around the city of Düsseldorf.[3]

The 101st's divisional front is divided between the 327th to the north and the 506th to the south. Second Battalion holds the north end of the 327th's zone. The city of Niederkassel is Company G's assignment.[4] We stay in nice houses undamaged by the war. I am amazed by the household luxuries the German people have and wonder whether the ordinary people might actually not be evil, as many of us think. The German standard of living is much higher than what I've seen in England, France, and the Netherlands, and certainly much better than that of Wayland. I begin to wonder why there is even a war; the people I've considered to be the enemy for so long seem so civilized.

Theaters are set up so that US soldiers can watch movies during their spare time. Many of these movies have already been shown to us time and time again, but they are still enjoyable. USO shows are frequent. We have never had it so good before. Beer and Coca Cola are widely available for the guys, but the army makes sure we return the bottles after we empty them. Sports such as boxing, baseball, softball, and volleyball are common.

Payday comes, and the guys are still smart about not spending all of it. I guess many of us realize by now that we might stand a chance of returning to the United States in one piece. The prospect of having a nice chunk of money saved upon our return is an attractive proposition. American dollars have to be converted into German marks before we can buy anything anyway. About four hundred glidermen, not yet qualified for hazardous duty pay, go back to Mourmelon for training. A few guys get a plane ride to the French Riviera and England.[5] Our food is awful.

Not all is fun and games. The Germans shoot artillery in our direction now and again. Colonel Allen of the 401st loses his leg during one artillery attack. Patrols across the river occur on a regular basis at night. Company A of the 327th goes out on patrol during the night of April 8 and returns with only half of the original 140 soldiers. On April 11, the 506th launches a patrol with 130 men, and 11 are lost, including several that drown crossing the Rhine.[6]

As the days go by in April of 1945, the Screaming Eagles are confronted with an ever-increasing problem: displaced persons (DPs). The DPs are from

Mate, a displaced person from Croatia who was "adopted" by Don's squad. Courtesy John Sherman collection.

throughout Europe; they were brought to Germany by the Nazis to work as slaves in factories. Camps are formed by us to hold DPs until they can be sent back to their homelands. Food, shelter, and sanitary conditions are a major problem for these people. They are processed out of the front area to the rear as soon as possible.[7]

The DPs are glad their years of work for Germany are over, and for the most part the only trouble they cause is stealing alcohol and other items from German citizens. They are happy and willing to do favors for soldiers, such as cleaning and cooking. Orders are given that soldiers are not to bring DPs along as they move, but many come along anyway.

My buddies and I are particularly fond of a DP by the name of Mate, who is from a small village in Croatia and about my age. He was captured by the Germans in 1941 and given two choices: join the German army or work in a factory. He chose the latter. Mate is handy at sewing, which is particularly nice, because he doesn't charge us much for the work he does. Somehow he got hold of a sewing machine and made himself an American uniform and cap, complete with a Screaming Eagles patch. He looks just like the rest of us. Standing about five feet seven inches tall and weighing 130 pounds, he is a pretty average guy. Mate stays with us throughout the rest of our stay in Europe, and we all plan on taking him with us.

Displaced persons camps are supplied by German village officials, although the army has to provide some food. Nazi officials are replaced by non-Nazis. The locals cause little trouble, although some of the hard-line Nazis are turned in by other locals for various rule violations. A group of Hitler Youth does blow up a school building being used by the Screaming Eagles. Fortunately, there are few casualties, because the building had just been evacuated for a different reason.[8]

Increasingly, the Ruhr Pocket is decreasing in size. Many of the enemy troops are in no mood to fight. A number of them are older policemen, firemen, and others pressed into service late in the war.

With the decrease in action, we have more time on our hands. The army imposes a seventy-two-dollar fine for being friendly with the enemy, which means that it is hard to fraternize with young German women, who are eager to meet American men, having lost so many young men in the war. Even though some fines are imposed, little can be done to stop the fraternization between German girls and lonely young American boys.

With a decrease in tensions, we are allowed to get closer to the locals, but I avoid the girls, because seventy-two dollars is a lot of money for me. Besides, it is important to be alert. Even now, an occasional German artillery shell comes our way. The locals laugh at us when we scatter for cover at the sound of an incoming shell. Once in a while a barrage follows. We laugh at the locals for scattering for cover long after we are already safe.

Payday comes around again. By now I have a big chip on my shoulder over not being promoted. Not that I really want a promotion, but I know I am a better soldier than some of the sergeants, especially some of the new ones. Lt. John Erb is new to the company, and he is in charge of giving pay. Needless to say, I don't respect him. One day, Sergeant Hayden is there with him. I salute Erb when I come in. Taking my money I look at Erb and turn, walking toward the door, without saluting him again as I am supposed to do.

"Dammit, Rich, you know better than that," Hayden says. "Okay, two six by sixes." I promptly start digging two six-foot-long, -wide, and -deep holes as my punishment.

On April 13 we receive news from regimental headquarters that President Franklin Roosevelt is dead.[9] I was only nine years old when FDR first became president, and it is hard to imagine a world without him. Some guys shed tears when a memorial service is held the next day. I don't cry, but I have an empty feeling inside.

Reports come in that the enemy is getting short on supplies and that their weapons factories are shutting down. On April 14, the Ruhr Pocket is cut in half by US troops. In four days' time, all enemy resistance ends, and the army now has to deal with more than three hundred thousand enemy prisoners.[10]

By this time the Allies are pushing the front lines another one hundred miles closer to the German capital of Berlin. The German war effort has pretty much collapsed. Some US forces have already met up with the Russians, and the US Third Army has advanced all the way into Czechoslovakia. Allied command believes the enemy might make a last-gasp stand in the mountainous area of western Austria and southern Germany. Some thirty armored divisions and even more infantry divisions could be there, hiding in the mountainous landscape. This area, 240 miles wide and 80 miles deep, is home to Eagle's Nest, Hitler's vacation spot near Berchtesgaden. The 101st Airborne is given the job of making sure that the area is secure.[11]

The Screaming Eagles begin pulling out, destined for Berchtesgaden, on April 20 in trucks and railroad boxcars. Before leaving, the rail cars are sprayed with insecticide to kill lice and fleas and filled with straw. For the trip I receive five K rations, which are not enough to keep my stomach satisfied, so I guard them with diligence.[12]

The rail lines have been badly damaged by Allied bombings. To get to this area of Germany, the trains need to backtrack through France, Belgium, the Netherlands, and Luxembourg. I notice the landscape is beginning to green nicely with the onset of spring. At Ludwigshafen I board a DUKW, a large, boatlike vehicle that can travel across land and water. These are fairly comfortable to ride in, at least compared to rail cars and the back of trucks.[13]

Somewhere along the route, we are switched back to trucks and arrive in Hausheim, Germany, where enemy soldiers are surrendering in droves—thousands of them, actually.[14] As we speed by, we can see masses of enemy troops marching to the rear, sometimes still armed. Others are sitting along the roadside as we speed past. Behind fighting lines, US forces destroy or confiscate stockpiles of weapons to keep them from being used on us by the German soldiers in our rear. After all the hard fighting, seeing armed enemies is unnerving, even if they have surrendered.

Areas of resistance still exist in Germany to our rear and as far away as the Netherlands, where German troops still hold port facilities. Occasionally we see German soldiers surrendering after being holed up in barns and other buildings. Most of the surrenders are peaceful, although some French soldiers take revenge on their former conquerors, killing some of them mercilessly, even young boys who were mustered into the army in the closing days of the war. It does not appear that there are any German forces fighting us in the area, at least for the time being, for which we are thankful. Because of the colder temperatures at the higher elevations where we are headed, we are supplied with winter clothing.[15]

The house I am staying in is equipped with hot showers. Almost all the houses have white sheets hanging out their windows, showing us that they have surrendered.[16]

The little fighting that is going on is happening ahead of us. On April 28, the 10th Armored Division captures the city of Landsberg, which is famous partly because Hitler was imprisoned there in 1923 after launching a failed rebellion. While in prison there for more than a year, he wrote a book outlining the National Socialist Revolution called *Mein Kampf* (My Struggle). I see a sign marking the building where he was held.[17]

Company G moves to Landsberg. As we approach the city, we begin to see people in dirty and tattered prison garb walking down the road. Many look like walking skeletons. These are survivors of the concentration camps, where domestic "enemies" of the German state were "concentrated." The German guards have fled in the morning in advance of our arrival. The prisoners are mostly Jewish. We see bodies piled up like garbage and many aren't recognizable as human beings.

Driving slowly up to the fence in the DUKW, but not stopping, having to dodge human bodies, Sherman and I throw the live victims our K rations and cigarettes as they lie along the road. The DUKW keeps moving, and we drive away. No one says a word for several miles. We drive alongside several more victims, these walking. They ask for cigarettes, which we no longer have. I glance over and see some German locals. I want to kill them. Why didn't they stop this?

The smells and sights are utterly revolting. Later, we are ordered not to give the victims any more of our food, because it is determined that the shock to their bodies can kill them: they are not used to eating. This makes me feel absolutely awful; trying to help someone could actually kill them.

In Landsberg the Screaming Eagles round up all the townspeople between fourteen and eighty years of age. The local population has to know what has been going on, because the prisoners have worked on local projects, where anyone could see them. Among their many jobs, the prisoners at this concentration camp rebuilt railroads and highways. Basically, they were brutalized and starved, oftentimes to the point of death. In order to enact some revenge on the Germans, the US Army forces the local citizens to dig graves and bury the many dead. Most of them deny having any knowledge of what has been happening at the prison camp, but we know this is untrue. The rotten, awful stench from one of the camps can be smelled even in a town more than a mile away. The surviving prisoners are shipped out and taken to better facilities for medical treatment. However, some of the victims who left the camp before the transfer are still roaming the area, often in search of food.

I tour the camp closest to Landsberg. The sickening smell is still in the air, causing some guys to gag and vomit. The camp is rigged with barbed wire and guard towers; the stockade is about half a mile square. After touring the concentration camp, I know without a shadow of a doubt why my fellow comrades and I have been fighting in this war: Hitler is why. I am serving in the army because he and his plans have needed to be destroyed. Up until now, I have often felt compassion for my enemy. If I had seen the concentration camps early in the war, I probably would have been a lot more brutal in my dealings with German soldiers. When our troops capture the German commander of the camp, General Taylor breaks the rules of war and turns him over to the former camp prisoners, who promptly hang him.

The army is able to get us a hot meal during this time. Concentration camp survivors roaming the area find out and come looking for food. Some of the guys try to save food for them, but I don't know what to do, as we are told it could harm them. They can't carry the food with them, and since many of us aren't feeding them now, they make for the trash cans, scooping out the leftovers with their hands. Sherman and I are upset about the situation, but there is nothing we can do. "They look totally dazed," I quietly say to him.

"Yeah, like they're right here, but in their eyes they are a thousand miles away," Sherman replies.

On April 30 a surprising announcement is made over the radio. "Hey, listen to this!" yells a soldier who has tuned in a military radio station.

"Adolph Hitler is dead," the announcer repeats several times. Soldiers look around at each other, not knowing exactly how to act. We've been through too much to get excited, but the prospect of returning home sends a warm feeling through every soldier's body. Yes, it is a happy occasion, but also very solemn. So many friends and comrades have lost their lives. So many. . . .

We head back to Hausheim and round up equipment and prisoners. Streams of enemy soldiers surrender. Sometimes the only guards for the German POWs are DPs, because there are not enough soldiers available to guard all of the surrendering Germans. Some of the DPs wear the uniforms of other countries, including uniforms of the Soviet Union.[18]

Several days later, on May 1, we get new orders. The 327th heads twelve miles south of Landsberg to Schongau. Then on May 5 the 101st begins arriving in Berchtesgaden. On the way, two Screaming Eagles troopers are killed by enemy fire, the last KIAs of the war in our division. Several German 88 mm artillery guns are fired at us but do not cause any casualties. On May 6 orders come from army command: "Effective immediately all troops will stand fast on recent positions. German Army Group G in this sector has surrendered. No firing on Germans unless fired upon. Notify French units in vicinity. Full details, to be broadcast, will be issued by SHAEFF."[19]

On May 7, German radio announces that an armistice is signed. Colonel Harper receives orders for the 327th to proceed to Berchtesgaden and take over military functions in the vicinity. On May 8, Allied command announces that the war in Europe is over.[20]

On May 9 the 327th leaves Hausheim and heads to Berchtesgaden, arriving the same day.[21] We are warned that there could be pockets of resistance. I certainly don't want to be killed now, right as the war is about to end, and am very happy to find that the Germans offer only token resistance. The scenery along the way is spectacular.

We arrive in Berchtesgaden to relieve the 506th from occupation of the vicinity. Colonel Harper, after speaking to Colonel Sink of the 506th, enters Hermann Göring's hunting lodge. The two colonels gather several souvenirs and are given a tour by a housekeeper. Harper, entering one of the guest rooms, finds a German lieutenant general seated on a bed. The German general shoots himself in the head. Sink orders a shallow grave dug to bury the general, whose helmet is put on a small wooden cross. Both colonels then help themselves to a very large supply of wine. At this point the lodge becomes the command post of the 327th.[22]

After we arrive in the town, I am involved in the capture of a German officer's car. The four-door convertible is beautiful. The officer argues with us repeatedly, begging us not to take it, but he finally surrenders it to us, thinking the car isn't worth his life.

Göring's private train is discovered by soldiers. French soldiers were in Berchtesgaden before the arrival of the 101st, and they shot up the train, damaging priceless paintings that the Germans stole from throughout Europe.[23]

We are ordered to build a high barbed wire fence around the area of what had been a slave-labor prison camp barracks. Six hundred German officers and twelve hundred German troops are then held prisoner under the watchful eye of machine gun–carrying 3rd Battalion glidermen. In the barracks we find seven large drums of cognac, each about the size of a fifty-five-gallon barrel. Harper orders the cognac to be rationed to the glidermen of the 327th, and the liquor is removed under armed guard via trucks.[24]

Glidermen also find an underground shelter under Hitler's home. In it are a sitting room and a bedroom for Hitler and another bedroom for Hitler's mistress. Harper helps himself to several of Hitler's personal books. Also in the shelter are a medical operating room and dental facilities.[25]

Over the next few weeks Berchtesgaden becomes a tourist center for American troops. Troops from all over the area want to see the Eagle's Nest (Hitler's hideout). Looting by soldiers is commonplace, and the stolen artifacts and treasures from throughout Europe begin to disappear—as well as light switch covers and pieces of carpet. Guards are quickly set up to prevent any more looting, but more need to be added. Harper posts two large signs that say that anyone caught removing souvenirs will be prosecuted. Dignitaries such as congressmen begin to show up to see the place. On some Sundays there are more than ten thousand visitors.[26]

Within a few hundred feet of the Eagle's Nest is an elevator shaft in which passengers are lifted directly in. Harper has a German repairman fix the elevator, then requires the repairman to ride up and down several times to guarantee its safety.[27]

The accommodations are extremely nice. The area was a major tourist destination before the war and is filled with nice hotels. I am particularly lucky and get to stay in a hotel alongside Lake Königssee. The lake is beautiful, with steep cliffs leading down to the water on all sides. I have to walk quite a ways from Berchtesgaden, but the scenery is worth the walk. Locals are hired to do most of the cooking and washing, but we still have our DP, Mate, who takes good care of us. Plans are still being made to get him to the States.

Some of the artifacts are moved to Königssee and placed in a large building. The treasures are put out on large tables.[28] Sherman and I are assigned to guard duty. "Look at all this stuff," I mutter to Sherman. "Incredible!"

"Looks like a giant swap meet to me," he says.

One attractive young German woman makes it plain to us that she does not like our presence in the city. She yells at us as we stroll along the lake's edge. Even though we can't understand what she is yelling, we know she isn't happy with how the war has gone. Based on how she is acting, I presume she is from an important family in Berlin. There are quite a few Berliners around the area who came to avoid the bombing in Berlin as well as the rapidly advancing Russian army.

"Hey Sherman, what do you think?" I ask with deliberate mischief in mind. Sherman grins and nods. Then we pick up the young woman and throw her off the bank and into the lake. She is upset with us, but we ignore her; we don't care. She appears to be the high-society type and very arrogant. What we don't realize, though, is that her father is close by. Running up, he hollers in German at us and his daughter (who is thrashing around in the water but able to stand). We don't know exactly what he is saying, but it is apparent that he isn't too happy with us either, so we throw him in, too. Applause and cheering erupt behind us. A small crowd of locals has gathered around to watch the show. They don't care much for the "High Dutch," as they call the Berliners.

Almost every one of us is able to obtain a vehicle from the German families. Fisher rides a general's motorcycle.[29] For the most part the local young women are very friendly, and most soldiers ignore the rules against fraternizing with the "enemy." We take hot baths, eat off of fine china, and enjoy indoor plumbing, and although I don't drink, plenty of fine wine is available. Cows are "accidentally" killed for steaks, and we live pretty well. Most of us figure we deserved it, considering what we've been through. This high life-style continues for weeks.

Berchtesgaden is also a good hunting place for top German officers and government officials. We capture large numbers of them.

On July 12 the 327th moves from Berchtesgaden to Hofgastein, Austria. Some of us are quartered in Goldegg, a little north of Hofgastein.[30] The area is also very beautiful, with waterfalls and plenty of lakes. Some soldiers even get to stay in some local castles. We are there to keep the Soviet army from moving in.

One bad thing is that we are literally at the end of the food supply chain and need to find a lot of our own food. We live by late-night scavenger hunts, which headquarters allows. I find a jar of home-canned mushrooms in a house that has apparently been abandoned. From the looks of things, the man of the house was probably a high-ranking officer in the German military. I can't find any lard or flour in the house to cook the mushrooms in, so I make a midnight run to the unguarded army kitchen, where I find some lard. On the way back to the house, I find some wood shingles in a shed, which I use to build a fire for cooking.

The next day, the homeowner comes around looking for his shingles, but no one says anything about them. After seeing conditions at the Landsberg concentration camp, I am not feeling overly friendly toward the enemy, especially high ranks. The war is over, but there are still dangers. There are too many young men with too much time and way too much alcohol. One night, while I am on guard duty, every two men are given a fifth of 120-proof alcohol. I open it to taste it, then pour some in a lid and put a match to it. It burns the prettiest blue flame I have ever seen.

That night proves to be a terrible one. I spend the entire time trying to keep drunken American soldiers from stealing the locals' horses and bicycles, going from one end of the village to the other to recover stolen property. Some of the intoxicated GIs jump out of the castle through a window and are badly hurt. Others are blinded by alcohol poisoning. From other areas there are a few reports of accidental shootings. Our chaplain calls a meeting with the top officers, and thereafter alcohol is forbidden for US soldiers.

Over the course of several weeks I notice a woman who lives across the street from me. Her husband is a German officer who has been severely wounded: he is missing both arms below the elbow. One day I start a conversation with her, and I immediately discover that she is fluent in English. She is also very obviously arrogant about her standing in society and bitter about the Allied victory.

"Where did you learn to speak English so well?" I ask her.

"I taught in England before the war," she mentions, in between her complaints about American soldiers. "If you Americans would talk slower, I could understand you. What are those guys saying?" She points at a group of US soldiers standing near a jeep.

"I really don't think you want to know," I say calmly. I am tired of her complaining, so I add, "Maybe you want us to leave and let the Russians take over this place?" She doesn't like that thought.

From then in June to mid-July, thirteen Screaming Eagles are killed by vehicle and gun accidents.[31] There is too much alcohol available, and the combination with weapons is deadly. Germans, Austrians, and DPs can't be hired to do guard duty, so this has to be worked into our "busy" schedules and therefore means we still have guns. Captured German soldiers are gradually shipped out of our detention camps to POW camps elsewhere. Many of the POWs are taking their girlfriends with them.

One weekend, Sherman is out exploring the countryside when he discovers some German army equipment hidden away in a cave under a bridge. He comes back to the hotel to get me, and we go to back to the cave to look for souvenirs. Among many other things I find another Luger to replace the one I sold while in the hospital in England.

With the war over in Europe, the army has established a system to decide who will get to go home and who has to stay. We are given points for various things, including the amount of time we have served in the army. Some men in our company have enough points to get a discharge, but in spite of all the action we in G Company have seen, most of us, including me, do not have the required eighty-five points to get the ticket home. The system doesn't make sense to me. This means that we will be headed to the war in Japan, a proposition that does not go over very well with me. I want to go home.

Training soon starts again. Instead of regular hikes, we begin to run up mountains to get in shape for fighting in the mountainous areas of Japan. Brass says that we will soon be shipped back to the States for more training and also to be closer to Japan. However, this idea is soon scrapped, and we are told that we will instead be going to France.

In order to keep our flight pay, we have to continue our glider training, and to get our flights in, we travel in groups to Salzburg, about fifty miles away. Sherman's older brother Ken has been transferred to Salzburg to dispose of poison gas, and Sherman is glad to get to see him. Ken manages to sneak a few rides on the trucks that take the glidermen to the airfield at Salzburg, and he "borrows" a jeep from the chaplain to show Sherman around the area.

Passes are not being issued to leave Goldegg, but Sherman wants to spend more time with Ken, so he asks Hayden for permission to go to Salzburg. Hayden responds sternly as he also glances at me, "You know the restrictions, no passes out of Goldegg, but you probably won't be missed much if you go. Remember, this is an unauthorized leave. It will be bad for the whole company if you get caught." We walk out of Hayden's office.

"I'm going," Sherman decides.

"I'd better keep you from getting hurt, so I'm going, too," I reply. We hitch a ride in a passing GI truck.

During the trip Sherman begins experiencing terrific pain in his lower stomach, and by the time the driver drops us off at Ken's barracks, Sherman is doubled over with severe pain. Ken, comes out to see us. "Jack, hi . . . ," he begins, then he notices the pain his brother is in and says, "This doesn't look good." Ken checks his brother over, then goes to get the unit medic. When they return after about five minutes, Sherman is really suffering.

The medic checks him over. "Don't know what the problem is. He should report to the army hospital in Salzburg," the medic advises.

"No, I'm not going," Sherman protests. "That'll mess things up for the whole company."

Seeing his brother's obstinacy, Ken says, "No changing his mind, the stubborn kid. Be right back. I need to 'borrow' the chaplain's jeep."

Ken drives us back to Goldegg and right to our aid station. Sherman is still in terrific pain, and after the medical staff examine him they put him in an ambulance and rush him straight to the army hospital in Salzburg. Brother Ken follows behind in the jeep.

Later, I get word of Sherman's ordeal. In the hospital they suspect that it is a gall bladder attack, and he is scheduled for an operation the next morning. He is scared stiff. The next morning, two orderlies come into the room and say they are there to prepare him for the operation. "The pain is gone and I don't need a damn operation," Sherman says. The commotion gets the attention of an army doctor, who reluctantly listens to Sherman's objection to undergoing an operation. He reexamines Sherman and determines that the operation will not be necessary. "Saved!" Sherman shouts.

Sherman is then loaded into an army ambulance for transfer to the main hospital in Munich. In the ambulance are four stretchers, upper and lower, two on each side. He is placed on the lower side, and across from him is a beautiful young American woman who became ill while on tour with a USO group. The other two people in the back of the ambulance are officers; the one next to Sherman on the bottom is a captain. The two officers are making conversation with the woman, and, typical of an enlisted man, Sherman is just lying there listening. The officers are doing their best to impress the girl.

"I couldn't believe my eyes," Sherman tells me later. "It was almost like a dream after such a long time to see and be near a pretty girl who spoke a language I could understand. She leaned over and looked at me and asked me something about the 101st and the action that I had seen. The two officers didn't approve and tried to cut into the conversation, but she politely shut them up by saying that I reminded her of her brother, and she was interested in what I had to say. It was awkward the whole ninety-mile trip.

After we were admitted to the general hospital in Munich for processing and release, she looked me up, and we talked quite a bit. What a thrill."

As luck would have it, the young woman's troop was in Munich doing a musical variety show, and she was able to rejoin them there. At the hospital, Sherman, who was now feeling much better, spent his time talking with and helping some of the guys who were confined to beds. The young woman stopped at the hospital to invite him to come by the stage door of the theater, telling him to ask for her so he could see the show. That night, after he showed up at the stage door, she escorted him in to a front-row center seat. It was a great show, and for the last number of the program, a jitterbug dance number, she came off the stage, took his hand, and led him up on stage. Some of the other girls in the troop escorted other members of the audience on stage as well. Jitterbugging was Sherman's specialty, and as he put it, he really cut a rug. She was a terrific dancer. Sherman never saw or heard from her again, and he never learned who she was. All he knew is that he reminded her of her brother, and she reminded him of his only sister, who had taught him how to dance.[32]

With Sherman away, I don't go off base. Athletic events help to pass the time. We set up roadblocks, in part to keep soldiers from stealing cars and driving to Paris for unauthorized rest and relaxation.

Most of the DPs go home, but Mate stays with us, still hoping to get to the States. Simpson and I begin to plot how we can get him back with us. Classes are set up to help us train for civilian life as well as to keep us out of trouble.

Some of the guys come up with a plan to go to Monaco. US soldiers aren't supposed to go there, but some do anyway. I decide not to, because I don't want to risk losing any of my seventy-nine points, vividly remembering what happened to Sherman. I really want to get home.

Long Journey

On July 28, 1945, G Company is packed into forty-and-eight railroad boxcars and taken to Auxerre, France.[1] Sherman is still in the hospital, so he doesn't come with us. The trip is long and slow, especially after we get out of Austria. Because we don't have any seats, the army puts old, musty straw down for us to sit on. We get a few meals along the way, ironically served by German POWs, but hunger sets in. The trip takes a long, long time. Mate stows away on the train, too, wearing his put-together uniform.

The railroad track is very windy because of the mountains. We are often rerouted around tracks that have been damaged by the Allied bombing campaign, and I think we could march faster than we are moving. I do get to see a lot of pretty countryside, though. On the way west we stop next to a supply train. The army doesn't have enough MPs to guard the trains adequately, so a bunch of us jump out and raid whatever we can find from the supply train. Our loot ranges from five-gallon cans of chocolate to gallon cans of peaches.

"Halt!" a military policeman shouts while raising his rifle. "Stop or I'll shoot!" He does fire his gun into the air, but nobody pays any attention. "Stop!" He shouts again, firing several more rounds. Then his voice trails away as he gives up. We don't take him seriously, although maybe we should. I feel kind of bad for him. Getting myself killed by "friendly fire" now would be stupid. Four days later, the train arrives in Auxerre minus a few guys who have fallen from the train while drunk.

France is a big change for us. We have gotten used to the good life in the Alps. France is obviously a lot poorer than where we have come from, which isn't a surprise, considering that France has undergone years of German occupation and has served as the setting for hundreds of battles. The luxuries we've become accustomed to in the Alps are gone; instead of a comfortable bed and indoor plumbing, I have a straw mattress and a dug-out pit for a latrine.

While in Sens, France, Sergeant Hayden again puts me up for promotion. Again, I am turned down by Captain Evans. I don't understand. I decide to enjoy my time anyway. Sens, on the winding Yonne River, has fewer than twenty thousand people. Its ancient streets are made of cobblestones and are incredibly narrow. Command is reluctant to give us passes, because they know that we could get into trouble. The local girls aren't very friendly, either—not like the German and Austrian girls. I want to go home.

In one issue of the army newspaper we see a photograph of General Eisenhower sporting a jacket that gets our attention. The jacket looks like a standard-issue coat but is shorter, giving it a sporty look.

"Think you could make me one like Ike's?" I ask Mate.

"Mate thinks so. Let me see your jacket." Mate inspects my standard-issue jacket. "Ya, ya, I can do this, special friend."

Sherman makes it back. It is good to see him. I am closer now to him than I could ever imagine being to a brother.

In a couple of days I have my new Eisenhower jacket. Other guys think it looks pretty good, so Mate makes a small fortune converting standard-issue jackets into Eisenhowers. I sure hope we can get Mate back to the States.

In the meantime, I get a pass to the French Riviera, flying down in a C-47 transport with the seats removed. A big gas tank is in the passenger compartment, so if we crash, we'll make quite an impression for sure. Turbulence causes the aircraft to make sudden drops every once in a while. Without anything strapping us in, we passengers drop a split second later, hitting the floor hard.

The French Riviera is absolutely beautiful, but we can't get in the water, because sewage is being dumped into it. Most of the soldiers we see are on their way home, taking a last-minute vacation.

"Going home? I ask one of the guys.

"Got my sixty-five in and I'm on my way!" he replies. I am mad. I have seventy-nine points and can't leave. The airborne is too valuable to let us leave with only sixty-five points.

Having saved some of my money, I decide to spend it on some souvenirs to take home. First, I need to exchange my currency for French money. I make some money on the exchange, enough money that after my return to camp I am able to go to Brussels, Belgium, on another leave, to visit my uncle Urban TeBockhorst, who is a soldier at a base in Belgium.

The days march by. On August 7 we learn that an atomic bomb has been dropped on Hiroshima, Japan. We don't know exactly what this means, but we are told the damage is horrific. Nagasaki is A-bombed three days after

Hiroshima. On August 15 we are all overjoyed when the announcement is made that the Japanese have unconditionally surrendered. We'll be going home.

Simpson is assigned to the base mail office as a clerk. Occasionally, Sherman and I also work at the post office sorting mail. Guys get pretty grouchy with us if they don't receive the letters they think they should get and accuse us of throwing their mail away.

Neither Sherman nor I have received mail for a while. We bug Simpson about it.

"Simpson, what are you doing with our mail?" I tease. "You get lazy and throw it away?"

"Probably did," Sherman adds. "He has no shame at all!"

"Get out of here and quit causing trouble," Simpson snaps.

"Let's go look ourselves!" I add and make a move around Simpson to the mailroom door. Simpson blocks me.

Sherman and I playfully take him to the ground and wrestle with him. Simpson is mad and hollers loudly, "Get off me!" We keep it up and half-heartedly rib punch him a bit. Simpson hollers even more loudly, like we are killing him.

"Okay, okay, enough," Sherman says as he stands up. We are all out of breath. Simpson doesn't seem too happy.

Glider training begins again. We have to take three flights to keep the airborne pay. Some of the guys manage to get others to stand in for them and not get caught. I certainly don't want to get killed now, but I take my turn, nevertheless. Safety is emphasized more than ever.

On the way to the airfield I run into some guys from the 42nd Rainbow Division with their colorful shoulder patches. That is the division the 101st replaced at Haguenau in Alsace, and they'd been pushed around by the Germans before we got there. Naturally, the 42nd soldiers are bitter about what happened and think the 101st troops are arrogant.

"You guys get all that extra pay for ridin' around in a little ol' airplane?" one of them taunts. "Why'd the army do that?"

"Maybe you'd like to try?" I retort.

"Sure, we'll ride around in that little ol' airplane," another chimes in. "How hard can it be? Maybe the army will pay us for sitting down on the job!"

I walk up to a pilot and speak to him. "These guys are poking fun at us. Could you take 'em up with us and give 'em a bit of a scare to shut them up?"

"Sure, load up!" the pilot replies. "I can take care of these guys."

The three soldiers from the Rainbow Division watch us buckle in and then do the same. I try not to smile as the rope connecting our glider and the towplane tightens. The Rainbow guys are grinning from ear to ear and chattering like a bunch of kids. But when the towplane flings us into the air, a sick look appears on their faces, and a couple of jostles from turbulence as we climb higher bring frowns.

With a jolt, the tow rope is released, and we are free. For the first few minutes the flight is as smooth as can be. We make easy banks and turns.

"Nothin' to it!" the Rainbow guys shout and laugh. One is starting to look a little sick, though.

Suddenly the pilot takes the glider into a steep climb, which surprises me, as up to now I've only seen gliders begin a fall to the ground when released by the towplane. Never have I felt them, at least seemingly, go up much. Our airspeed slowing quickly brings the glider to a stall; its nose turns toward the ground. Faster and faster the glider drops, with its nose almost straight down. As I look out the front, objects on the ground are getting larger and larger. I can make out a truck through the front window. I am starting to get a little worried myself. The Rainbow guys are terrified.

"We're gonna crash!" someone screams. At the last possible moment, the pilot pulls the glider out of the dive, and we barely clear the truck. The ground races by. The pilot takes us through a couple more sharp turns and climbs and then we level out for approach to the airport. My stomach seems to be in my head. No one says anything until the glider rolls to a stop and we all get out.

"Got two more rides to go!" I say to the Rainbows.

"You can have your hazardous duty pay," they respond sheepishly. As they walk away they look back a couple of times but don't say anything more. We don't get any more flack from the Rainbow Division.

"I wish you wouldn't do that again," I say to the pilot. He chuckles. I don't want to die in a useless glider training incident after the war has ended.

Athletic events are again organized to help pass the time. I join a softball team and hear that G Company is putting together a baseball team to compete in a divisional tournament. I consider checking it out, thinking about my success on Niland's basketball team, and watch a practice. The players seem good, really good, so I decide that maybe my joining is not such a good idea. Instead, I continue with softball and take some classes being taught by French civilians and US soldiers.

I manage to get a pass to Paris, and the eighty-mile train ride west through rolling plains and farm fields goes by quickly. Paris is an incredible sight for a small-town boy from the Midwest, and I'm sure I am wide-eyed as I make my way down the streets. I stay perfectly sober, unlike many others, but when I write my parents I don't tell them about seeing purple-haired Parisian girls, knowing they'd think I had been drinking.

Captain Evans approaches me one day out of the blue. I don't understand why he is suddenly nice to me, although he has had to notice that I am a pretty darn good soldier and leader. "Rich, are you interested in becoming an officer in the United States Army?" he asks. "I'll put you up for promotion."

I must have looked at him rather strangely. Why ask me now? I think to myself with bewilderment. "No, sir, I just want to go home," I answer. End of conversation. After all the trouble he's given me about promotion, he has some nerve to ask me now.

Simpson gets promoted, and I become the mail clerk. I hope someone doesn't think I'll steal mail. The days pass by monotonously. Mail sorting helps to break the tedium, but all of us are bored out of our minds. The soldiers of the 101st are still not allowed to be discharged early, because we are still too valuable. Valuable for what, I don't know. There are some rumors about the Soviets causing problems and Patton wanting to take them on. Finally, the army lowers point totals required for discharge from the 101st to eighty points, which I have by now accumulated. I am qualified for discharge and soon will be going home.

Immediately upon being notified that I am being discharged, I am ordered to report to a camp at the port of Le Havre, France. The train is leaving immediately, and I don't even get a chance to say goodbye to Sherman, Boz, Simpson, Mate, or anyone else. I am disappointed that I cannot say goodbye to my buddies, but orders are orders, so I pack up and leave. I am able to register my Luger with the FBI before leaving.

Leaving is harder than I expected. Although many of the originals in G Company are dead, missing, or wounded and at home, I have trained, fought, laughed, killed, and faced death with these men. I have an empty feeling, yet I can't wait to get home.

The passenger train car is in very poor condition, but I don't care as long as the railroad is pointed towards home. We arrive in Le Havre in the early evening, and I go to my assigned tent barracks. Waking up the next morning, I anxiously await orders telling me what ship I should board for home. But no orders come that day. The next day is no different. We learn that there are

By 1945, Don was a very different young man from the one who left home in 1943.

not enough ships available to take us back. The wait is extraordinarily boring. The only person I know there is Lieutenant Morrison, which doesn't do any good, since he is an officer and I am not. I've always respected Morrison and don't want to be insubordinate. Not now, anyway. I haven't seen him since Marvie, when he became a prisoner of war the second time.

Finally, on November 7, after nine long days of waiting, orders come, and we are leaving in the afternoon on a landing ship, tank (LST). The ship is designed to operate in very shallow water so it can move heavy equipment such as tanks to shore during an invasion or to resupply such equipment without a loading dock. The smell of human sweat inside it is dreadfully bad and pungent enough to knock me down. Bunks are stacked nine high. I can't stand being in the bunk area, so I spend most of my time topside. There isn't any place comfortable to sleep, but at least the air is fresh. Below deck is a large map that shows our position in the ocean. The map gives me the courage to withstand the terrible conditions, because it appears that we are making good progress.

A couple of days out, storm clouds appear on the horizon. The sea is beginning to get rough. The captain orders us all below deck. Boy does it stink down there, and the heat is unbearable. Hundreds of soldiers become seasick, adding to the smell. I think the waves surely are going to capsize us.

Because of the motion, it is impossible to move around, meaning that we can't leave our bunks. Soon it is difficult even to stay in my bunk. In order to avoid falling out, I have to shove my legs into the bunk above me, and then my muscles begin to cramp and ache from the stress of trying to hold myself in. At least when I am lying down, cramped as I am, seasickness doesn't bother me as much. I try to eat, but the eggs in the galley smell spoiled.

The storm howls on. We get word that another LST is in serious trouble and might sink. Our ship heads back toward France to help, but later we turn around before reaching the distressed vessel. The worst part of the storm lasts more than three days. When it eventually dissipates, we are finally able to go above deck and breathe the fresh air. Other groups of men gather to gamble away money in card games.

After eleven days, the east coast of the United States appears. I can make out New York and eventually the Statue of Liberty, just as the sun is beginning to set. My heart is pounding. "Home, I'm almost home," I think to myself. As the LST goes by the Statue of Liberty, a tugboat near us is playing "It's Been a Long, Long Time." That is a pretty nice thing to do. It *has* been a long time.

The LST docks in the harbor right next to another LST with cables wrapped around the hull. "That's the ship we tried to rescue," one of our deckhands tells a group of us. "The captain was afraid she would split in two during the storm, so he had cables wrapped around her. Funny thing, she beat us back!"

Soon we are loading onto a train, and in a short time we arrive at Camp Shanks. I am processed and assigned to a barracks, where I spend the night before boarding another train. That evening I leave the base and walk around New York for a while. I buy a camera but soon realize that it is useless, because it is impossible to purchase film. However, the camera soon allows me to meet many girls who are eager to have their picture taken with a soldier. Of course I never tell them that I don't have any film.

The next afternoon I board a train for Chicago. It is a standard passenger train, loaded mostly with civilians. The New York countryside looks nice. During the night I can't sleep because I am so excited finally to be going home, but I also feel numb. I keep to myself and think about the past couple of years. Everything seems so peaceful here.

At 1945 on November 21 the train arrives in Chicago. The station is very close to the naval base where I am to report for discharge. I am so excited that I feel numb. Soldiers file out of the passenger car quietly. Grabbing my bag, I walk through the gates and join a line that winds into a long, gray building. No one says much. Despite the excitement, the lack of sleep is beginning to catch up with me. The line moves quickly. Once I get inside, I can see desks with men who are taking things away from the bags every soldier has. Behind the bags, close to the wall, are piles of gear. Helmets, clothes, boots, and all kinds of other stuff are in a pile. There is some bickering over what is being taken, but it looks like the army is getting almost everything from the guys. My turn is coming soon, so I take my baseball glove out of my bag and drop it on the floor. As I move closer to the desk, I scoot the glove with my feet; I want to be sure that the army won't take that, too.

"Next," the soldier behind the desk says, without any inflection in his voice. He has reddish brown hair and glasses and isn't much older than me. All the desk workers are sure in a hurry. I hand him my papers and my bag. Quickly, he dumps out the bag and rummages through my stuff, taking a good look at my Luger. Then he asks me for the proper paperwork that verifies that I can keep the gun. I pull the paper out of my front pocket and hand it to him. He grunts and hands it back. Picking up some of my stuff, he begins tossing things into the pile. He let me keep my overcoat, dress uniform, and Luger. Everything else is gone: my underwear, helmet, canteen, and combat uniforms—all gone. I feel quite disgusted and violated. I have given so much the past two years, and now the military is keeping petty stuff that has no real value to them. This is personal stuff that has been with me through everything. In particular, my helmet is hard to separate with, because it has been my protector, toilet, cooking pot, and shovel. I have a smaller bag in which I put the Luger, the baseball glove, and my other belongings; everything easily fits into it. The whole process takes only a couple of minutes.

"We can put you up for the night in the barracks, if you want a place to sleep," the desk clerk says with a friendly tone. "You can eat at the mess hall, too, if you want," he adds.

I nod and head out the door, turning to the right. I find the mess hall just a couple of minutes away. One last army meal isn't going to hurt me. I am getting hungry, anyway.

After a quick meal, I head toward the main gate and to the station right next door. I am a free man, with no one to tell me what to do. I want to get home. Approaching the station ticket counter, I ask, "Can I get to Mount Pleasant, Iowa, yet today?"

"Sure can! Train leaves within the hour," the clerk replies.

"Great! Give me a ticket." I give him the money and he holds out a ticket. The time flies by quickly as I wait on a hard seat along with soldiers and civilians.

The diesel-powered train heads out of the station. We make several stops before getting out of the city. A couple of teenage girls come on board, talking rapidly and giggling at almost anything either one says. The girls are totally oblivious to anyone around them, and it is the first time I have seen girls act like this in a long time. I don't know if it is the stress of war or personality differences, but girls in Europe did not act like this. I know I am home.

The girls get off a couple of stops later, before we are completely out of the Chicago area. After that, the trip is quiet. The hours go by as the train passes small towns and train stations. I lose track of time and our location after a while. I never actually sleep but sit quietly, thinking mostly about nothing. Sometime after eleven p.m. I hear the conductor call out, "Mount Pleasant!" It is time for me to get off. I didn't even realize we had crossed the Mississippi and were in Iowa.

As the train slows down, I contemplate what to do next. It's fun to make my own decisions for a change. I had never really had the chance to do whatever I wanted, because I went from living at home with my parents directly into the army.

As the train slows, the thought crosses my mind about calling Mom and Dad. I decide not to call, as it is after midnight. Their old car isn't very reliable, anyway. Rubber for tires is in short supply, and I know when I left for the army their tires weren't in good shape. Flat tires are fixed by a large patch called a boot, and the boot can make the tire uneven, causing the car to shake. The patches don't hold up well, either. I decide to call my dad's brother Nick and his wife, Oleta; they live in Mount Pleasant, and Uncle Nick will be glad to see me.

The train stops, and I easily make my way out of the train car and down the steps. I am much better at walking down aisles now than I was during my first bus trip to Camp Dodge on my way to basic training.

The train station is empty and poorly lit, but I find the pay phone and dial the local operator. "I need Nick Rich, please."

"Nick Rich of Mount Pleasant? Here it is. Kind of late. Are you sure?"

"That's OK. He won't mind," is my reply. The phone rings quite a few times. I figure they are already asleep.

"Hello? Who is this?" Uncle Nick asks.

"This is your nephew, Donald."

"Donald! Well I'll be! Everything okay?" Uncle Nick asks.

"I just got into town. I'm at the train station," I answer.

"I'll come and get you. It will take me a bit to get dressed. Oleta! Donald is over at the train station!" The excitement in my uncle's voice made me feel good.

"No, that's okay. I'll get a taxi and be there in a few minutes. Mind if I stay for the night so Mom and Dad don't have to pick me up yet tonight?"

"Of course, you're always welcome. Are you hungry? Oleta, get some food together for Don," I hear Uncle Nick say.

"Don't go to too much trouble. I'll probably be there in twenty minutes or so." I am feeling hungry again.

"Okay, we'll see you in a bit," and with that Uncle Nick hangs up. I am feeling good about things.

I get the operator back on the line and have her hook me up to the local taxi. The taxi arrives after a short wait; there isn't too much business in town. The driver asks if I am just getting back from the war. I tell him that I am but don't offer any information. Less than ten minutes later I am at Uncle Nick's home. The lights are on. I pay the driver three dollars and gather my stuff. Uncle Nick and Aunt Oleta are already at the door before I get up the steps.

"Don, so good to see you!" Uncle Nick says, giving me a hug.

"You've changed so much! Just look at you!" Aunt Oleta adds with another hug.

"Come on in and relax," Uncle Nick continues. "No hurry to get to bed. Tell us about yourself. How ya been?"

"You want to call your mom and dad?" Aunt Oleta asks. "Your mom would sure love to hear from you!"

"There's no reason to wake them up. I'll call first thing in the morning," I answer.

We talk and talk for a couple of hours, finally heading to bed around two in the morning. It feels good to be back with family and in a nice, comfortable bed.

Tired as I am, I get up and call home at eight in the morning. I realize that it is Thanksgiving Day as the telephone rings.

"Hello, Mom?"

Afterword

To the friends who read this book:

I have been compelled to have my story finished and published before I die, as it is a part of history that I want to leave for my family and the next generation. I sincerely hope that after reading it you have a better understanding of World War II and the soldiers who fought it. Relating the story hasn't always been easy for me, because the memories are sometimes emotionally painful. As you have read, one of my best friends was killed suddenly by a sniper's bullet. I still have a difficult time dealing with such things as the terrified feeling I had during the shelling at Veghel and the helpless feeling I had with the replacement soldier who died a slow death near Foy.

Depression and bitterness from posttraumatic stress disorder can ruin the lives of soldiers more than the physical wounds from combat. The actual battles for me have been over since 1945, but the emotional battles from the memories have been with me for more than sixty-five years.

In my story you read how I first accepted Christ as my savior in Reading, England, in the spring of 1943. You also read that I promised God that if I lived through the war I would come home and serve Him. I have tried to do this to the best of my abilities, and though I have failed many times, He has never failed me.

I returned home from the war and started going to church but became disillusioned and slipped away from church life. I married my wife, Mary, in 1948. We were both raised by loving parents, but neither of us was raised in the church. In 1953, after the birth of our second child, I remembered the promise I made to God when I was in England. Mary and I were both baptized and joined the Wayland Methodist Church. We attended regularly as a family and served and participated in all the church programs and activities. In the late sixties, still struggling with the horrors of war, I began doubting my faith. Instead of ignoring my faith, however, this time I went searching for it.

In 1970, as our church made plans to host a weekend program to share our faith with others, Mary and I reluctantly agreed to see what was involved. We spent the next twenty-five years going to and sometimes coordinating weekend meetings to share the good news of Jesus Christ and His power to heal emotional wounds. I began speaking in churches of my healing experiences. I shared my faith with others, including those at local prisons.

At one weekend program a married couple asked me, "Why did God allow you to live and others to die?"

The question startled me. I hadn't really brought myself to think about it much. I paused and replied, "I don't know that God allowed me to live and others to die. This I do know: He has helped me to deal with the repercussions from the war."

The couple smiled and said, "Thank you. That is very comforting."

The local minister came up to me after the couple walked away. He had overheard the conversation. "Don," he said, "I couldn't have answered that question any better myself. They lost their son during the Vietnam War."

Along with church activities I've done my best to serve God and country in my professional and civic life. I spent eight years as chaplain of the Rural Mail Carrier's Association. I was greatly blessed in helping build houses with Habitat for Humanity and served in veterans' clubs and other secular organizations that do charitable work.

Even though I have committed my life to God, I still have struggles with depression and anxiety. In 1994 I returned to Europe for the fiftieth anniversary of D-Day. I was able to tour Normandy and search for graves of some of my buddies, but while at Normandy American Cemetery in France, I was unable to find the grave of Hank Proppe. As I knelt at another grave, I looked up at Mary and asked her, "Am I a good man?" This was four years before the release of the movie *Saving Private Ryan,* which ends with Ryan asking his wife the same basic question. I suspect it is a natural reaction of many soldiers as they visit the graves of their comrades in arms. Having been in war causes these returned soldiers to question their goodness as a human being.

The process of healing is an ongoing one. It was only recently that I was able to release the bitterness in my heart over the death of the replacement soldier who slowly died when I was ordered not to go out under fire and get him. My bitterness was directed toward those who chose not to serve the nation by declaring conscientious objector status for religious reasons. Some of them could have joined as medics, of whom we never had enough.

The memories will always be with me, but the bitterness is finally gone after all these years.

The Lord is still giving me the pleasure of serving Him. John Wesley is quoted as saying, "We are called to do all the good we can, everywhere we can, and all the time we can." While eighty-seven years of life have weakened my body and mind, I can continue to serve. With God's help, you and I can change the world no matter what we've done.

Donald J. Rich
101st Airborne Division
327th Glider Infantry Regiment
Company G

FROM THE AUTHOR:

I've known Don since I was a small boy. He was a good friend of my dad. Don, always with a smile on his face, has always impressed me as a man who is confident in who he is. I was surprised to hear of his struggles with post-traumatic stress disorder.

I got the idea of writing this book following the death of my father's brother, Col. Charles Brooks, USA. Uncle Charles, who served in WWII and Korea, had a wealth of stories stored in his memory, but unfortunately he died in 1997, shortly after starting to talk to me about them. Don and I started working on this book in 1999.

For the first several years, Don provided basic information about his experiences with the Screaming Eagles. Then we ran into a wall when for some time little information came forth. His memories were all right, but he just didn't open up. Then, in March of 2003, when the Iraq War started, something about how that war unfolded triggered Don's memory. I think it was related to the similarities between how the US Army sped across Iraq without great amounts of opposition and how that paralleled the Screaming Eagles' advance across Germany after the Ruhr Pocket collapsed. A wealth of information began to flow freely with amazing accuracy as I checked and double-checked records against Don's memories.

For the writing of *Glider Infantryman* I interviewed many Screaming Eagles veterans. The help they have provided has been incredible. My life will forever be affected by the true heroism of these ordinary men. Much has been written and said about the struggle of veterans of Vietnam and recently Iraq and Afghanistan. The issues associated with those who experience combat is well documented in more recent wars. The young men of the Screaming Eagles were profoundly affected as well. All of them seem to handle their experiences differently, but the emotional and physical impact is still there, that I can tell. There is no way anyone could live through what Don and his comrades lived through without an immense emotional toll. Still, Don's faith in Jesus Christ penetrates through the dark cloud of having seen—and done—unimaginable things as an ordinary person.

My hope is that you will experience the emotion of *Glider Infantryman* as lived by Don. The writing is designed to be educational and in a way enjoyable for all who read, regardless of what one's opinions are about participating in war. Don speaks regularly to teenagers at local schools about the challenges of being a soldier in the 101st Airborne, and this book will continue his legacy for future generations.

Comments about Bastogne

Many questions have been asked over the years about why the Germans were not able to take Bastogne quickly when they had vastly numerically superior forces and firepower operating in the area. The Screaming Eagles and the other American units at Bastogne were incredibly outnumbered and outgunned. The reason for success in this battle can be attributed partly to training. The 101st was trained to operate behind enemy lines against superior forces. The division's mission fit perfectly with what it was trained to do.

The enemy was a formidable fighting force; however, the Germans had many of the same problems we had. They had been beaten up in France and the Netherlands. Their supplies were low, and many of their units were not at full strength.

Lt. Gen. Heinrich von Lüttwitz, commanding general of the German XXXXVII Panzer Corps, had a reputation for being especially kind to his troops. The general tended to move with regiments and squads rather than whole divisions.[1] Apparently he held back to see how the battle developed. Lüttwitz didn't like seeing his men getting killed by the ferocious Screaming Eagles. This may explain why attacks were repeatedly broken off and then tried in other locations. The general must have figured there were easier ways of getting to Bastogne than through Marvie. To the Germans it appeared that US forces were leaving the area before the attack began.

Lt. Gen. Fritz Bayerlein, commanding general of the Panzer Lehr Division, was known to be an aggressive commander, often described as being like a feisty dog. Bayerlein did not like Lüttwitz at all, and the two failed to work together as they should have. Bayerlein wanted to be the one to take

Bastogne, so he plunged ahead with his troops too quickly, without first properly assessing the battlefield. Several times he took bad advice from Belgian civilians. Early on in the Bastogne campaign, a Belgian man told Bayerlein that an American general had passed through east of Bastogne at midnight with a force of fifty tanks and forty other armored vehicles. In fact, a small force did pass through, but it was composed of a few tanks, half-tracks, and trucks at best.[2] As a result, Bayerlein, concerned about a major US counterattack, held back, giving the 101st time to set up better defenses.

Maj. Gen. Heinz Kolcott, commanding general of the 26th Volksgrenadier Division, was a shy and intelligent man. An optimist, he expected to win the battle for Bastogne. Kolcott was almost killed early in the Bastogne campaign when his command center was hit by a lucky shot from American artillery. Everyone else in the command center was killed, but Kolcott was outside when the shell hit and was thrown into a brick wall, which disoriented him. Later, when Kolcott saw US engineers leaving Marvie and heading north and a larger force heading south, he mistakenly thought the US defense of Bastogne was disintegrating. What he actually saw was the 327th moving into Marvie to set up the perimeter and relieving the engineers. Instead of running into light resistance, his unsuspecting troops ran right into Don and G Company, who were quite experienced at being challenged by superior German forces with tank support. In a major blunder by the Germans at Marvie, Kolcott was never informed that his tanks had broken through US lines behind Hill 500. His division was also starting to receive pressure from Patton's forces to the south. When the German tanks closed in on Bastogne, Kolcott had just received word that his superior, General Hasso von Manteuffel, was coming on Christmas to lead an assault on Bastogne personally. Consequently, Kolcott broke off the engagement to get his forces ready for Manteuffel. Kolcott never received information regarding the success of his troops' breakthrough.[3]

Finally, the manner in which General McAuliffe used the artillery at his disposal confused the Germans. Running low on artillery shells, the Germans fired artillery conservatively. McAuliffe, on the other hand, would concentrate fire aggressively into a small area, causing the enemy to believe the Americans had an ample supply of ammunition, even though they did not.[4] All these factors, in addition to the apparent attitudes of the German commanders toward each other, attributed to the German failure at Bastogne.

About Captain Evans

The men I interviewed had vigorous reactions toward Captain Evans. About half highly respected the man, and the other half had a strong disdain towards him. I would surmise this reaction is not atypical of common soldiers' opinions of an officer, especially if one adds to the equation the life-and-death situations the soldiers found themselves in.

Evans's shortcomings are mentioned in the book, so the focus here will be on a defense of the captain. As a schoolboy, Don had demonstrated a degree of defiance toward authority, although he was not mischievous. Evans's desire for impeccable military order may have been an area of conflict between Don and the captain.

Evans's blocking of a promotion for Don also fits into a common problem the Screaming Eagles were confronted with. Casualty rates were so high that command desired some experienced and very good soldiers not be promoted so they could help the replacements learn to be good soldiers under fire. Evans seemed to have respect for Don's ability, as demonstrated by his having Don lead squads even without the stripes on his shoulder. In 1946 at an officer training school, Evans specified, "Because of heavy casualties among small unit leaders, there should be at least three men qualified and trained for each rating."[5] Some of the interviewed veterans of G Company also cited a tendency for Evans to give Southern-born soldiers priority for promotion.

In an interview, Manuel Hildalgo specifically indicated that the captain was no-nonsense and wanted everything in proper military order. Denis Parsons said the same, and added that Evans showed compassion toward Lawrence Gentile when his twin brother Dominic was killed.

The chaos of the first Marvie battle, in which the captain was wounded, might be explained by the fact that command did not properly inform Evans that the enemy was in the immediate vicinity. Reports from within the company indicate that Evans believed the enemy was forty miles away. Being grossly outnumbered also contributed to chaos. Officers and everyday soldiers alike were in a desperate situation.

Kevin Brooks

Notes

37664459

1. Time Out London, *The Great Dictator,* www.timeout.com/film/reviews/70506/the_great_dictator.html, and *Yankee Doodle Dandy,* www.timeout.com/film/reviews/78392/yankee-doodle-dandy.html.

2. WorldWar-2.net, "A WW-2 Timeline: Pacific Naval War!" www.worldwar-2.net/timelines/asia-and-the-pacific/pacific-naval-war/pacific-naval-war-index-1942.htm; and "A WW-2 Timeline: War in the Desert!" www.worldwar-2.net/timelines/war-in-the-desert/war-in-the-desert-index-1942.htm.

3. WorldWar-2.net, "A WW-2 Timeline: Pacific Naval War!"

4. History on the Net.com, "World War Two—Japanese Internment Camps in the USA," www.historyonthenet.com/WW2/japan_internment_camps.htm.

Soldiering Basics

1. Robert H. Evans, Headquarters Company G, 327 G. I., APO 472, US Army, 2, Historical Records Section, Departmental Records Branch, Adjutant General's Office, Department of the Army, National Archives, Washington, D.C.

England

1. Federal Bureau of Investigation, "Famous Cases and Criminals: George John Dasch and the Nazi Saboteurs," accessed September 25, 2010, www.fbi.gov/about-us/history/famous-cases/nazi-saboteurs.

2. Robert H. Evans, Headquarters Company G, 327 G. I., APO 472, US Army, 2, Historical Records Section, Departmental Records Branch, Adjutant General's Office, Department of the Army, National Archives, Washington, D.C.

3. Norway-Heritage, "Hands across the Sea," accessed September 25, 2010, www.norwayheritage.com/p_ship.asp?sh=samas.

4. Evans, Headquarters Company G, 2.

5. Audrey Borzymowski, telephone interview with the author, Milwaukee, Wis., August 5, 2010.

6. Erma Parsons, interview with the author, San Rafael, Calif., June 17, 2010; Lloyd Gross, telephone interview with the author, Sartell, Minn., July 21, 2010.

7. Borzymowski, telephone interview.

8. Leonard Rapport and Arthur Northwood Jr., *Rendezvous with Destiny: A History of the 101st Airborne Division,* 60–61.

9. Gross, telephone interview, July 21, 2010.

10. Rapport and Northwood, *Rendezvous with Destiny,* 62.

11. Ibid., 66.

12. James L. McDonough and Richard S. Gardner, *Sky Riders: History of the 327/401 Glider Infantry,* 43.

13. Evans, Headquarters Company G, 3.

14. Manuel Hidalgo, telephone interview with the author, Beckley, W.V., August 2008.

15. Thomas Hidalgo, telephone interview with the author, Springfield, Mass., September 2010.

Welcome to France

1. Robert H. Evans, Headquarters Company G, 327 G. I., APO 472, US Army, 3, Historical Records Section, Departmental Records Branch, Adjutant General's Office, Department of the Army, National Archives, Washington, D.C.

2. Robert H. Evans, History of "G" Company, 327 Glider Infantry, 3, Historical Records Section, Departmental Records Branch, Adjutant General's Office, Department of the Army, National Archives, Washington, D.C.

3. Ibid.; John P. Cummer, "Modeling the Landing Craft Infantry (LCI)," http://steelnavy.com/LCICummer.htm.

4. George E. "Pete" Buckley, "Normandy: A Glider Pilot's Story," www.71stsos.com/normandygeobuckley.html.

5. Evans, History of "G" Company, 3.

6. Lloyd Gross, telephone interview with the author, Sartell, Minn., July 21, 2010.

7. Anonymous, Headquarters Company G, 327 G. I., APO 472, US Army, 3, Historical Records Section, Departmental Records Branch, Adjutant General's Office, Department of the Army, National Archives, Washington, D.C.

8. Gross, telephone interview, July 21, 2010; Evans, Headquarters Company G, 2.

9. Craig Whitely, telephone interview with the author, Tonawanda, N.Y., September 2010.

10. Leonard Rapport and Arthur Northwood Jr., *Rendezvous with Destiny: A History of the 101st Airborne Division,* 110–15.

Carentan

1. James L. McDonough and Richard S. Gardner, *Sky Riders: History of the 327/401 Glider Infantry,* 39.

2. Leonard Rapport and Arthur Northwood Jr., *Rendezvous with Destiny: A History of the 101st Airborne Division,* 221.

3. Robert H. Evans, History of "G" Company, 327 Glider Infantry, 3, Historical Records Section, Departmental Records Branch, Adjutant General's Office, Department of the Army, National Archives, Washington, D.C.

4. McDonough and Gardner, *Sky Riders,* 39.

5. Ibid., 44–45.

6. David Church, telephone interview with the author, February 2011; Evans, History of "G" Company, 3.

Market Garden

1. Leonard Rapport and Arthur Northwood Jr., *Rendezvous with Destiny: A History of the 101st Airborne Division,* 249.

2. Anonymous, Headquarters Company G, 327 G. I., APO 472, US Army, 2, Historical Records Section, Departmental Records Branch, Adjutant General's Office, Department of the Army, National Archives, Washington, D.C.

3. Robert H. Evans, Headquarters Company G, 327 G. I., APO 472, US Army, 3, Historical Records Section, Departmental Records Branch, Adjutant General's Office, Department of the Army, National Archives, Washington, D.C.

4. Piet M. Pulles, *Screaming Eagles of WWII: 327–401 GIR,* 1–60; Josh Nichols, telephone interview with the author, Nashville, Tenn., September 2010.

5. Rapport and Northwood, *Rendezvous with Destiny,* 800.

6. John Sherman, telephone interview with the author, Bend, Ore., July 2010.

7. Ibid.

8. Don is refering to the 969th Field Artillery Battalion, with which he came into closer contact near Bastogne. See the chapter "On the Offensive," p. 000.

9. Rapport and Northwood, *Rendezvous with Destiny,* 253–55.

10. Ibid.

11. Ibid.

12. Ibid., 264.

13. World War II History Info, "Operation Market-Garden," www.worldwar2history.info/Market-Garden/; Poland in Exile, "Operation Market Garden," www.polandinexile.com/marketgarden.htm.

14. Rapport and Northwood, *Rendezvous with Destiny,* 264.

15. Ibid.

16. Robert H. Evans, "The Operations of Company G, 327th Glider Infantry Regiment (101st Airborne Divison) in Holland, 18 September–15 October, 1944 (Ardennes Campaign) (Personal Experience of a Company Commander)," Report, Advanced Infantry Officers Course, Infantry School, Fort Benning, Ga., 1946–47, 6.

17. Ibid., 6–7.

18. James L. McDonough and Richard S. Gardner, *Sky Riders: History of the 327/401 Glider Infantry,* 61–63.

19. Evans, "Operations of Company G," 8; McDonough and Gardner, *Sky Riders,* 63.

20. Ibid.; Anonymous, Headquarters Company G; John G. Westover, 327 RGT at Zon, US Army, 1, Historical Records Section, Departmental Records Branch, Adjutant General's Office, Department of the Army, National Archives, Washington, D.C.

21. John Sherman, telephone interview with the author, Bend, Ore., July 2009.

22. Westover, 327 RGT at Zon, 1.

23. Anonymous, Headquarters Company G; Westover, 327 RGT at Zon, 1.

24. Evans, "Operations of Company G," 10.

25. McDonough and Gardner, *Sky Riders,* 66.

26. Ibid., 64, 65.

27. Rapport and Northwood, *Rendezvous with Destiny,* 273–75.

28. McDonough and Gardner, *Sky Riders,* 63–65.

29. Ibid., 67–68.

30. Evans, "Operations of Company G," 11–12.

31. The account of the Son Forest battle is a compilation of interviews with John Sherman and Don Rich and records from Westover, 327 at Zon, 2–5.

32. George E. Koskimaki, *Hell's Highway: Chronicle of the 101st Airborne Division in the Holland Campaign, September–November, 1944,* 130

33. Westover, 327 at Zon, 6, 7–8; McDonough and Gardner, *Sky Riders,* 69–70.

34. Ibid., 70–71.

35. Evans, "Operations of Company G," 15–16.

36. Sherman, telephone interview, July 2010.

37. Evans, "Operations of Company G," 16.

38. Peter Antill, Military History Encyclopedia on the Web, "Operation Market Garden, 17–27 September 1944," 16 September 2001, www.historyofwar.org/articles/battles_arnhem .html.

39. McDonough and Gardner, *Sky Riders,* 68–69.

40. Ibid., 69.

41. Koskimaki, *Hell's Highway,* 157–58.; Rapport and Northwood, *Rendezvous with Destiny,* 336.

42. McDonough and Gardner, *Sky Riders,* 71–72.

43. Craig Whitely, telephone interview with the author, Tonawanda, N.Y., September 2010.

44. McDonough and Gardner, *Sky Riders,* 72–77.

45. Evans, "Operations of Company G," 18.

46. Sherman, telephone interview, July 2009.

47. Evans, Headquarters Company G, 5.

48. McDonough and Gardner, *Sky Riders,* 77.

49. Sherman, telephone interview, July 2009.

50. Koskimaki, *Hell's Highway,* 289; Erwin Janssen, telephone interview with the author, Veghel, Netherlands, July 2008.

51. Evans, Headquarters Company G, 5.

52. Evans, "Operations of Company G," 19–20.

53. Thomas Niland Jr., letter to the author, Tonawanda, N.Y.

54. Ibid.

55. Evans, "Operations of Company G," 21.

56. Eddy Bauer, *The Marshall Cavendish Illustrated Encyclopedia of World War II: Based on the Original Text by Lieutenant Colonel Eddy Bauer,* vol. 15, *To the Siegfried Line,* 1973–88.

57. Antill, "Operation Market Garden, 17–27 September 1944," www.historyofwar.org/ articles/battles_arnhem.html.

Stuck on the Island

1. Robert H. Evans, "The Operations of Company G, 327th Glider Infantry Regiment (101st Airborne Divison) in Holland, 18 September–15 October, 1944 (Ardennes Campaign) (Personal Experience of a Company Commander)," Report, Advanced Infantry Officers Course, Infantry School, Fort Benning, Ga., 1946–47, 21.

2. Ibid., 22.

3. James L. McDonough and Richard S. Gardner, *Sky Riders: History of the 327/401 Glider Infantry,* 79–82.

4. Leonard Rapport and Arthur Northwood Jr., *Rendezvous with Destiny: A History of the 101st Airborne Division,* 388–92.

5. Evans, "Operations of Company G," 22–23.

6. Ibid., 23–24.

7. Ibid.

8. Ibid.

9. Charles W. Root, The Battle of Opheusden, 1, 327th Glider Infantry, Historical Records Section, Departmental Records Branch, Adjutant General's Office, Department of the Army, National Archives, Washington, D.C.

10. Rapport and Northwood, *Rendezvous with Destiny,* 390.

11. Evans, "Operations of Company G," 25–26.

12. Rapport and Northwood, *Rendezvous with Destiny,* 393.

13. Roy L. Inman, History of the Battle of Opheusden, Headquarters 2d Battalion, 327th Glider Infantry, APO 472, U.S. Army, 1, Historical Records Section, Departmental Records Branch, Adjutant General's Office, Department of the Army, National Archives, Washington, D.C.

14. John Sherman, telephone interview with the author, Bend, Ore., July 2009.

15. Robert H. Lemmon Jr., "E" Company Fights, Company "E" 327 Glider Infantry, APO 472, US Army, 24 October 1944, 1, Historical Records Section, Departmental Records Branch, Adjutant General's Office, Department of the Army, National Archives, Washington, D.C.

16. McDonough and Gardner, *Sky Riders,* 84–85; Robert H. Lemmon, Battle of Opheusden, Company "E," 327th Glider Infantry, APO 472, US Army, 2, Historical Records Section, Departmental Records Branch, Adjutant General's Office, Department of the Army, National Archives, Washington, D.C.

17. Evans, "Operations of Company G," 26–28.

18. Lloyd Gross, telephone interview with the author, Sartell, Minn., September 2010.

19. Sherman, telephone interview, July 2009; McDonough and Gardner, *Sky Riders,* 84, 85.

20. Sherman, telephone interview, July 2009; Denis Parsons, telephone interview with the author, San Rafael, Calif., 2007; Robert H. Evans, Headquarters Company G, 327 G. I., APO 472, US Army, 6, Historical Records Section, Departmental Records Branch, Adjutant General's Office, Department of the Army, National Archives, Washington, D.C.

21. Craig Whitely, telephone interview with the author, Tonawanda, N.Y., September 2010; Paul Panic, telephone interview with the author, January 2011.

22. Years later, Don would find out that Jay actually broke his back in the accident.

23. Inman, History of the Battle of Opheusden, 2.

24. Evans, "Operations of Company G," 28–29.

25. Ibid., 29.

26. Ibid., 30.

27. Ibid., 31.

28. Root, Battle of Opheusden, 2.

29. Robert H. Evans, History of "G" Company, 327 Glider Infantry, 2, Historical Records Section, Departmental Records Branch, Adjutant General's Office, Department of the Army, National Archives, Washington, D.C.

30. Thomas Niland Jr. letter to the author, Tonawanda, N.Y.

31. Evans, Headquarters Company G, 7.

32. Sherman, telephone interview, July 2009.

33. Evans, Headquarters Company G, 7.

34. Ibid.

Back into Battle

1. George E. Koskimaki, *The Battered Bastards of Bastogne: The 101st Airborne in the Battle of the Bulge, December 19, 1944–January 17, 1945,* 10.

2. Leonard Rapport and Arthur Northwood Jr., *Rendezvous with Destiny: A History of the 101st Airborne Division,* 422.

3. Robert H. Evans, "The Operations of Company G, 327th Glider Infantry Regiment (101st Airborne Divison) in Holland, 18 September–15 October, 1944 (Ardennes Campaign) (Personal Experience of a Company Commander)," Report, Advanced Infantry Officers

Course, Infantry School, Fort Benning, Ga., 1946–47, 5; James L. McDonough and Richard S. Gardner, *Sky Riders: History of the 327/401 Glider Infantry,* 90.

4. George E. Koskimaki, *Hell's Highway: Chronicle of the 101st Airborne Division in the Holland Campaign, September–November, 1944,* 434.

5. Koskimaki, *Battered Bastards of Bastogne,* 20; Rapport and Northwood, *Rendezvous with Destiny,* 430, 431.

6. Rapport and Northwood, *Rendezvous with Destiny,* 434.

7. Robert H. Evans, Headquarters Company G, 327 G. I., APO 472, US Army, 8, Historical Records Section, Departmental Records Branch, Adjutant General's Office, Department of the Army, National Archives, Washington, D.C.; Koskimaki, *Battered Bastards of Bastogne,* 40.

8. McDonough and Gardner, *Sky Riders,* 92–93; Evans, Headquarters Company G, 8.

9. Rapport and Northwood, *Rendezvous with Destiny,* 438.

10. Ibid., 440, 443.

11. Ibid., 445.

12. Ibid., 459–60, 495.

13. Ibid., 459–60.

14. McDonough and Gardner, *Sky Riders,* 93.

15. Ibid.

16. Ibid., 95.

17. Craig Whitely, telephone interview with the author, Tonawanda, N.Y., September 2010.

18. Koskimaki, *Battered Bastards of Bastogne,* 157.

19. Ibid., 160.

20. Rapport and Northwood, *Rendezvous with Destiny,* 459–95.

21. McDonough and Gardner, *Sky Riders,* 95.

22. Robert B. Galbreaith, "Operations of the 2d Battalion, 327th Glider Infantry Regiment (101st Airborne Division), in the Defense of Bastogne, Belgium, 19–26 December, 1944 (Ardennes Campaign) (Personal Experience of a Battalion Commander)," Report, Advanced Infantry Officers Course, Infantry School, Fort Benning, Ga., 1947–48, 12.

23. John Sherman, telephone interview with the author, Bend, Ore., July 2009.

24. Galbreaith, "Operations of the 2d Battalion," 12.

25. Koskimaki, *Battered Bastards of Bastogne,* 160.

26. Sherman, telephone interview, July 2009.

27. Rapport and Northwood, *Rendezvous with Destiny,* 497; Koskimaki, *Battered Bastards of Bastogne,* 160.

28. Sherman, telephone interview, July 2009; McDonough and Gardner, *Sky Riders,* 97.

29. McDonough and Gardner, *Sky Riders,* 97.

30. Rapport and Northwood, *Rendezvous with Destiny,* 501.

31. Sherman, telephone interview, July 2009.

32. Ibid.; Rapport and Northwood, *Rendezvous with Destiny,* 501.

33. Galbreaith, "Operations of the 2d Battalion," 13; Rapport and Northwood, *Rendezvous with Destiny,* 500.

34. McDonough and Gardner, *Sky Riders,* 96.

35. Rapport and Northwood, *Rendezvous with Destiny,* 501–2.

36. Ibid., 501.

37. Sherman, telephone interview, July 2009.

38. McDonough and Gardner, *Sky Riders,* 97.

39. James F. Adams, "The Operations of Company F, 327th Glider Infantry Regiment (101st Airborne Division) in the Defense of Bastogne, Belgium, 19–26 December 1944 (Ardennes

Campaign) (Personal Experience of a Company Commander)," Report, Advanced Infantry Officers Course, Infantry School, Fort Benning, Ga., 1946, 16.

Fighting the Enemy and the Elements

1. Robert B. Galbreaith, "Operations of the 2d Battalion, 327th Glider Infantry Regiment (101st Airborne Division), in the Defense of Bastogne, Belgium, 20–26 December 1944, (Ardennes Campaign) (Personal Experience of a Battalion Commander)," Report, Advanced Infantry Officers Course, Infantry School, Fort Benning, Ga., 1947–48, 11, 14–15.

2. Ibid.

3. Ibid., 16.

4. Ibid., 18.

5. David Church, telephone interview with the author, January 2011; John Sherman, telephone interview with the author, January 2011.

6. Ibid., 17–18.

7. James L. McDonough and Richard S. Gardner, *Sky Riders: History of the 327/401 Glider Infantry,* 93.

8. James F. Adams, "The Operations of Company F, 327th Glider Infantry Regiment (101st Airborne Division), in the Defense of Bastogne, Belgium, 19–26 December 1944 (Ardennes Campaign) (Personal Experience of a Company Commander)," Report, Advanced Infantry Officers Course, Infantry School, Fort Benning, Ga., 1946, 18–20.

9. Personal note from Harper at Pratt Museum, Fort Campbell, KY.

10. Ibid., 99.

11. Ibid., 99–100.

12. Adams, "Operations of Company F," 19–26. December 1944, 20–21.

13. Ibid., 21.

14. McDonough and Gardner, *Sky Riders,* 102.

15. Ibid., 103.

16. Leonard Rapport and Arthur Northwood Jr., *Rendezvous with Destiny: A History of the 101st Airborne Division,* 514.

17. George E. Koskimaki, *The Battered Bastards of Bastogne: The 101st Airborne in the Battle of the Bulge, December 19, 1944–January 17, 1945,* 267; Rapport and Northwood, *Rendezvous with Destiny,* 515.

18. Rapport and Northwood, *Rendezvous with Destiny,* 517–18.

19. Ibid., 517.

20. Ibid.

21. Koskimaki, *Battered Bastards of Bastogne,* 268.

22. Adams, "Operations of Company F," 23–24; McDonough and Gardner, *Sky Riders,* 104.

23. William Abernathy, Keepsake S-2 Journal Covering Period 18 Dec. 1944 to 31 Dec. 1944, entry for Dec. 23, Historical Records Section, Departmental Records Branch, Adjutant General's Office, Department of the Army, National Archives, Washington, D.C.; Adams, "Operations of Company F," 24, 25; McDonough and Gardner, *Sky Riders,* 104; Lloyd Gross, telephone interview with the author, Sartell, Minn., September, 2010.

24. McDonough and Gardner, *Sky Riders,* 104; Adams, "Operations of Company F," 26; Koskimaki, *Battered Bastards of Bastogne,* 268.

25. Rapport and Northwood, *Rendezvous with Destiny,* 525; Craig Whitely, telephone interview with the author, Tonawanda, N.Y., September 2010.

26. Rapport and Northwood, *Rendezvous with Destiny,* 522; Whitely, telephone interview.

27. McDonough and Gardner, *Sky Riders,* 104, 105; Koskimaki, *Battered Bastards of Bastogne,* 264–65.

28. John Sherman, telephone interview with the author, Bend, Ore., July 2009.

29. Galbreaith, "Operations of the 2d Battalion," 21–22.

30. Rapport and Northwood, *Rendezvous with Destiny,* 520; Adams, Operations of Company F; Robert H. Evans, Headquarters Company G, 327 G. I., APO 472, US Army, 9, Historical Records Section, Departmental Records Branch, Adjutant General's Office, Department of the Army, National Archives, Washington, D.C.

31. Rapport and Northwood, *Rendezvous with Destiny,* 525.

32. Ibid., 526; S-3 Periodic Reports for December 1944, 327 Glider Infantry, 4, Historical Records Section, Departmental Records Branch, Adjutant General's Office, Department of the Army, National Archives, Washington, D.C.

33. Sherman, telephone interview, July 2009.

34. Rapport and Northwood, *Rendezvous with Destiny,* 526.

35. Galbreaith, "Operations of the 2d Battalion," 27.

36. Adams, "Operations of Company F," 30.

37. McDonough and Gardner, *Sky Riders,* 107–9

38. Ibid., 107–12

39. Adams, "Operations of Company F," 28.

40. Rapport and Northwood, *Rendezvous with Destiny,* 544–45.

41. Adams, "Operations of Company F," 32; Abernathy, Keepsake S-2 Journal, 26 Dec. 1944, 1800, to 27 Dec. 1944, 1800.

42. Rapport and Northwood, *Rendezvous with Destiny,* 560; Adams, "Operations of Company F," 32.

43. Abernathy, Keepsake S-2 Journal, 18 Dec. 1944 to 31 Dec. 1944, 12; McDonough and Gardner, *Sky Riders,* 115.

44. Rapport and Northwood, *Rendezvous with Destiny,* 564.

45. Ibid., 600; Abernathy, Keepsake S-2 Journal, 18 Dec. 1944 to 31 Dec. 1944, 12.

46. Rapport and Northwood, *Rendezvous with Destiny,* 603; Abernathy, Keepsake S-2 Journal, 18 Dec. 1944 to 31 Dec 1944, 15.

On the Offensive

1. Joseph Harper, After Action Report, Belgium and France, December 1944, 7, Historical Records Section, Departmental Records Branch, Adjutant General's Office, Department of the Army, National Archives, Washington, D.C.

2. Leonard Rapport and Arthur Northwood Jr., *Rendezvous with Destiny: A History of the 101st Airborne Division,* 595.

3. S-1 Journal, 327th Glider Infantry for the Month of December [1944], 5, Historical Records Section, Departmental Records Branch, Adjutant General's Office, Department of the Army, National Archives, Washington, D.C.; Rapport and Northwood, *Rendezvous with Destiny,* 608.

4. Rapport and Northwood, *Rendezvous with Destiny,* 594–95.

5. Ibid., 609; Robert H. Evans, Headquarters Company G, 327 G. I., APO 472, US Army, 10, Historical Records Section, Departmental Records Branch, Adjutant General's Office, Department of the Army, National Archives, Washington, D.C.

6. Rapport and Northwood, *Rendezvous with Destiny,* 631.

7. Ibid., 624–25.

8. Ibid.

9. George E. Koskimaki, *The Battered Bastards of Bastogne: The 101st Airborne in the Battle of the Bulge, December 19, 1944–January 17, 1945,* 416.

10. Rapport and Northwood, *Rendezvous with Destiny,* 625.

11. Ibid.; Koskimaki, *Battered Bastards of Bastogne,* 425–26.
12. Rapport and Northwood, *Rendezvous with Destiny,* 627–29.
13. Ibid., 629.
14. James L. McDonough and Richard S. Gardner, *Sky Riders: History of the 327/401 Glider Infantry,* 117.
15. Koskimaki, *Battered Bastards of Bastogne,* 435.
16. Rapport and Northwood, *Rendezvous with Destiny,* 631.
17. Ibid., 634.
18. Ibid., 633, 636–37.
19. Ibid., 636–40.
20. Ibid., 640–43.
21. McDonough and Gardner, *Sky Riders,* 117.
22. Rapport and Northwood, *Rendezvous with Destiny,* 647–49.
23. McDonough and Gardner, *Sky Riders,* 117.
24. Ibid., 117–18; Rapport and Northwood, *Rendezvous with Destiny,* 649; Lloyd Gross, telephone interview with the author, Sartell, Minn., September 9, 2010.
25. Rapport and Northwood, *Rendezvous with Destiny,* 649–50.
26. Craig Whitely, telephone interview with the author, Tonawanda, N.Y., September 2010; Rapport and Northwood, *Rendezvous with Destiny,* 650; Evans, Headquarters Company G, 10.
27. Rapport and Northwood, *Rendezvous with Destiny,* 653; McDonough and Gardner, *Sky Riders,* 118; Koskimaki, *Battered Bastards of Bastogne,* 493.
28. Koskimaki, *Battered Bastards of Bastogne,* 493.
29. Rapport and Northwood, *Rendezvous with Destiny,* 655.
30. Ibid., 657–59.
31. Ibid., 663.
32. Ibid., 662–65.
33. Ibid., 665.

Alsace

1. Robert H. Evans, Headquarters Company G, 327 G. I., APO 472, US Army, 10, Historical Records Section, Departmental Records Branch, Adjutant General's Office, Department of the Army, National Archives, Washington, D.C.; Leonard Rapport and Arthur Northwood Jr., *Rendezvous with Destiny: A History of the 101st Airborne Division,* 665.
2. Rapport and Northwood, *Rendezvous with Destiny,* 666–69.
3. Ibid., 668; Evans, Headquarters Company G, 10.
4. Evans, Headquarters Company G, 10.
5. Rapport and Northwood, *Rendezvous with Destiny,* 669.
6. Ibid.
7. Ibid., 671–72.
8. Ibid., 674.
9. Ibid., 671, 673.
10. Ibid., 674–81.
11. James L. McDonough and Richard S. Gardner, *Sky Riders: History of the 327/401 Glider Infantry,* 128; Rapport and Northwood, *Rendezvous with Destiny,* 673.
12. Rapport and Northwood, *Rendezvous with Destiny,* 683.
13. Ibid., 673–74.
14. Ibid., 684.
15. McDonough and Gardner, *Sky Riders,* 128.

16. Ibid.; Rapport and Northwood, *Rendezvous with Destiny,* 685–86.
17. Evans, Headquarters Company G, 10.
18. McDonough and Gardner, *Sky Riders,* 128; Evans, Headquarters Company G, 11.
19. Rapport and Northwood, *Rendezvous with Destiny,* 694–95.
20. Ibid., 697–99.
21. Ibid., 699–700, 703.
22. Ibid., 702.

Germany

1. Leonard Rapport and Arthur Northwood Jr., *Rendezvous with Destiny: A History of the 101st Airborne Division,* 704.
2. Ibid., 703–4.
3. Ibid.; Robert H. Evans, Headquarters Company G, 327 G. I., APO 472, US Army, 11, Historical Records Section, Departmental Records Branch, Adjutant General's Office, Department of the Army, National Archives, Washington, D.C.
4. Rapport and Northwood, *Rendezvous with Destiny,* 706.
5. Ibid., 707.
6. Ibid., 708–11.
7. Ibid.
8. Ibid., 715–16.
9. Ibid., 717.
10. Ibid., 718.
11. James L. McDonough and Richard S. Gardner, *Sky Riders: History of the 327/401 Glider Infantry,* 130–32.
12. Rapport and Northwood, *Rendezvous with Destiny,* 722–23.
13. Ibid., 724.
14. Evans, Headquarters Company G, 11.
15. Rapport and Northwood, *Rendezvous with Destiny,* 724–25.
16. Ibid., 725.
17. Ibid.
18. Ibid., 729.
19. Ibid., 732.
20. EyeWitness to History.com, Voices of the 20th Century, "Radio Report on the Surrender of Germany, May 8, 1945," www.eyewitnesstohistory.com/vosurrender.htm; Joseph H. Harper, letter to the author, December 1978.
21. Evans, Headquarters Company G, 11.
22. Harper to the author, December 1978, 1–2.
23. Ibid., 2.
24. Ibid., 2–3.
25. Ibid., 6.
26. Ibid., 5.
27. Ibid.
28. John Sherman, e-mail interview with the author, Bend, Ore., October 8, 2010.
29. Ibid.
30. Evans, Headquarters Company G, 11; John Sherman, telephone interview with the author, Bend, Ore., July 2008.
31. Rapport and Northwood, *Rendezvous with Destiny,* 756.
32. Sherman, e-mail interview, Oct. 8, 2010.

Long Journey

1. Robert H. Evans, Headquarters Company G, 327 G. I., APO 472, US Army, 11, Historical Records Section, Departmental Records Branch, Adjutant General's Office, Department of the Army, National Archives, Washington, D.C.

Afterword

1. Leonard Rapport and Arthur Northwood Jr., *Rendezvous with Destiny: A History of the 101st Airborne Division,* 567.

2. Ibid., 567, 572.

3. Ibid., 580, 582, 583–84.

4. Ibid., 583.

5. Robert H. Evans, "The Operations of Company G, 327th Glider Infantry Regiment (101st Airborne Divison) in Holland, 18 September–15 October 1944 (Ardennes Campaign) (Personal Experience of a Company Commander)," Report, Advanced Infantry Officers Course, Infantry School, Fort Benning, Ga., 1946–47.

Sources

Abernathy, William. Keepsake S-2 Journal Covering Period 18 Dec. 1944 to 31 Dec. 1944. Historical Records Section, Departmental Records Branch, Adjutant General's Office, Department of the Army, National Archives, Washington, D.C.

Adams, James F. "The Operations of Company F, 327th Glider Infantry Regiment (101st Airborne Division) in the Defense of Bastogne, Belgium, 19–26 December 1944 (Ardennes Campaign) (Personal Experience of a Company Commander)." Report, Advanced Infantry Officers Course, Infantry School, Fort Benning, Ga., 1946.

Anonymous. Headquarters Company G, 327 G. I., APO 472, US Army. Historical Records Section, Departmental Records Branch, Adjutant General's Office, Department of the Army, National Archives, Washington, D.C.

Bando, Mark. *101st Airborne: the Screaming Eagles in World War II.* Saint Paul, Minn.: Zenith, 2007.

———. Trigger Time: 101st Airborne WW2. Summer 2008. www.101airborneww2.com.

Bauer, Eddy. *The Marshall Cavendish Illustrated Encyclopedia of World War II: Based on the Original Text by Lieutenant Colonel Eddy Bauer.* 25 vols. New York: Marshall Cavendish, 1972.

Burgett, Donald R. *Currahee!* Boston: Houghton Mifflin, 1967.

The Epic of the 101st Airborne: A Pictorial Biography of the United States 101st Airborne Division. [United States]: Weider History Group, 2006.

Evans, Robert H. Headquarters Company G, 327 G. I., APO 472, US Army. Historical Records Section, Departmental Records Branch, Adjutant General's Office, Department of the Army, National Archives, Washington, D.C.

———. History of "G" Company, 327 Glider Infantry. Historical Records Section, Departmental Records Branch, Adjutant General's Office, Department of the Army, National Archives, Washington, D.C.

———. "The Operations of Company G, 327th Glider Infantry Regiment (101st Airborne Division) in Holland, 18 September–15 October 1944 (Ardennes Campaign) (Personal Experience of a Company Commander)." Report, Advanced Infantry Officers Course, Infantry School, Fort Benning, Ga., 1946–47.

Galbreaith, Robert B. "The Operations of the 2d Battalion, 327th Glider Infantry Regiment (101st Airborne Division) in the Defense of Bastogne, Belgium, 19–26 December 1944 (Ardennes Campaign) (Personal Experience of a Battalion Commander)." Report, Advanced Infantry Officers Course, Infantry School, Fort Benning, Ga., 1947–48.

Harper, Joseph. After Action Report, Belgium and France, December 1944. Historical Records Section, Departmental Records Branch, Adjutant General's Office, Department of the Army, National Archives, Washington, D.C.

———. Personal note held in collection of Pratt Museum, Fort Campbell, KY.

Inman, Roy L. History of the Battle of Opheusden, Headquarters 2d Battalion, 327th Glider Infantry, APO 472, U.S. Army. Historical Records Section, Departmental Records Branch, Adjutant General's Office, Department of the Army, National Archives, Washington, D.C.

Koskimaki, George E. *The Battered Bastards of Bastogne: the 101st Airborne in the Battle of the Bulge, December 19, 1944–January 17, 1945*. New York: Presidio/Ballantine, 2007.

———. *Hell's Highway: Chronicle of the 101st Airborne Division in the Holland Campaign, September–November, 1944*. Sweetwater, Tenn.: G. & E. Koskimaki, 1989.

Lemmon, Robert H., Jr. Battle of Opheusden, Company "E" 327th Glider Infantry, APO 472, US Army. Historical Records Section, Departmental Records Branch, Adjutant General's Office, Department of the Army, National Archives, Washington, D.C.

———. "E" Company Fights, Company "E," 327 Glider Infantry, APO 472, US Army, 24 October 1944. Historical Records Section, Departmental Records Branch, Adjutant General's Office, Department of the Army, National Archives, Washington, D.C.

McDonough, James L., and Richard S. Gardner. *Sky Riders: History of the 327/401 Glider Infantry*. Nashville, Tenn.: Battery, 1980.

Pulles, Piet M. *Screaming Eagles of WWII: 327–401 GIR*. Eindhoven (Son), Netherlands: Elespe, 1994.

Rapport, Leonard, and Arthur Northwood Jr. *Rendezvous with Destiny: A History of the 101st Airborne Division*. Nashville, Tenn.: Battery, 2000.

Root, Charles W. Headquarters Company, 327th Glider Infantry, APO 472, The Battle of Opheusden. Historical Records Section, Departmental Records Branch, Adjutant General's Office, Department of the Army, National Archives, Washington, D.C.

S-1 Journal, 327th Glider Infantry for the Month of December [1944]. Historical Records Section, Departmental Records Branch, Adjutant General's Office, Department of the Army, National Archives, Washington, D.C.

S-3 Periodic Reports for December 1944, 327 Glider Infantry. Historical Records Section, Departmental Records Branch, Adjutant General's Office, Department of the Army, National Archives, Washington, D.C.

Utah Beach to Cherbourg (6 June–27 June 1944). American Forces in Action Vol. 13. Washington, DC: US Army Center of Military History, 1990.

Westover, John G. 327 RGT at Zon, US Army. Historical Records Section, Departmental Records Branch, Adjutant General's Office, Department of the Army, National Archives, Washington, D.C.

World War II. Alexandria, Va.: Time-Life, 1997.

Index